MW01502539

I would like to dedicate this novel to my Lord and Savior Jesus Christ, for never giving up on me, for carrying me throughout my life's journey, for never leaving me, nor forsaking me; and for allowing me to remain steadfast in my faith.

To my mother, who is the strongest person I have ever known, and is the reason I am the man I am today; and with whom I love more than anything in this world next to Jesus.

To my wonderful children, who have helped me to stay focused on what's most important. Thank you for always keeping a smile on my face and in my heart. I love YOU!

To my sister Denise, you have been the wind beneath my wings and a huge support throughout my life. Thank you!

I'd like to thank my best friend, Nat, for going above and beyond for our friendship and for being there for me the way only a true brother would. And I would also like to extend my love and condolences on your mother's passing in April of 2015.

I'd also like to thank my cousin T.O. for being there for me when I was growing up and always looking out for me.

Also I'd l like to thank my friend and publicist Mr. Ronald Hale for his support, help, and ideas throughout the creation of this novel.

Finally, I would like to thank everyone who has read or purchased a copy of this book. Your support and generosity is greatly appreciated.

To
Sundy Cruz

God Bless You
And Your Family.
Take Care of Jorge

Thank You
Ty Jenkins

The **LIES**
Within
My **TRUTH**

The LIES Within My TRUTH

Ty Jenkins

First published in 2016 by SITE Publishing
Richmond, VA
www.sitepublishingtoday.com
1-888-561-9038 [Ext. 101]

ISBN: 978-0-9796241-4-8
Library of Congress Control
Cataloging-in-Publication Data available upon request.

Text design by: SITE Publishing
Book Format: SITE Publishing
Cover Design: SITE Publishing
Cover Image: Ty Jenkins

Authors Contact Information
Ty Jenkins
1-310-855-2148
lieswithinmytruth@gmail.com

prelude

It was late, the cold night air nipping at my nose. We'd just received a tip that one of our perps was hiding out in the spot we were approaching. There were about 5 in my crew. Guns drawn, we crept silently to the door. I bashed the door in.

"Freeze!!!"

Our target started to run, but in the face of five gun barrels, thought different.

Going out chasing fugitives gave me such an adrenaline rush! I loved what I did! By midnight, we finished booking everyone and decided to head over to the nearest bar to grab a few drinks. I had something to celebrate. Tomorrow was my anniversary and because my wife and me were trying to make a fresh start in our relationship, I wanted to make it really special.

We finished up our drinks and I said my good-byes to the guys.

"Great work out there tonight, fellas."

"Damn right! Now go home and bang your wife's back out and give her those gifts," one of my boys yelled at me as I left the bar. I was in a good mood and for the first time in a long time, I was looking forward to seeing my wife and wishing her a happy anniversary. I turned on some old school R&B which was my favorite. Teddy P and Luther took me all the way home.

Stephanie had left my dinner in the microwave like she always did because I worked so late at night. I sat down in the kitchen and ate my dinner. Then, I checked on the kids, kissed them and told them I loved them, my nightly routine.

When I got to our bedroom, Stephanie was lying the bed asleep, with her phone on her chest. She always fell asleep with the phone on her chest because she likes to play games on it before she goes to bed. I walked over, like I always do, picked up her phone and plugged it into the charger in the wall. But, when I plugged the phone in, it lit up and an icon appeared that said Skype.

I picked the phone back up and started scrolling. She didn't know that I knew the passcode to her phone but she used the same password for everything so I figured it out. I found a conversation with a guy from Jamaica. He was saying things like, "I miss you, baby. When are you coming back to see me? We had a good time. You should've listened to your girlfriend. We should've gone further than we did."

Her response, "I've got a situation with my son's father. I really can't have sex right now. I think you know how much I want you."

I'm looking at this phone and then looking at her sleeping peacefully in the bed. What the hell? I'm your husband, not your baby daddy! I feel myself starting to lose my mind. I kept looking at the messages in the phone and as far I could tell, her and this dude never had sex but there was a lot of kissing and touching involved. He seemed to want more but she kept pulling away. From the dates on the phone, they've been staying in contact with each other since she left Jamaica, telling each other how much they miss each other. She was telling this dude that I don't give her any attention and that when she sees him again, they are going to go all the way.

I noticed that she kept referencing her girlfriend in her messages to him so I decided to pull up the text string between them.

Girlfriend: You just need to divorce Cody. Forget him. You need to be with this dude. He was sexy.

Stephanie: Yea, but Cody sexy.

Girlfriend: Yea, but he sexy with an accent from the islands.

Stephanie: You don't think he just running game on me to try and get into the U.S.?

Girlfriend: Who cares? You'll be walking around with that!

Stephanie: I don't know.

Girlfriend: I got another friend I want you to meet. If Cody can cheat, you can cheat. Do what you do.

Stephanie: I been thinking about that…maybe…I really don't know.

Her girlfriend was saying a lot to try and influence her and I was getting more pissed off with every message I read. I felt like I was going to explode.

I'd always taken pride in my wife being a lady and never stooping to my level on things like this. I told her that she was raised differently than me. This kind of lifestyle ain't for her. As a woman, you mess around with a man, he's inside you, and there are feelings involved. But, I can be with 10 women, wipe my penis off and it's like no one has ever been there. I told her to never forget that and reminded her over the years.

I sat in the corner of our bedroom looking at my wife sleeping peacefully in the bed. My emotions were so out of control, I wanted to jump on the bed and kill her. I walked outside the room and started to have an anxiety attack. I know that I had not been the model husband to her, but I sincerely was trying to turn things around. What was it about me that seemed to destroy every great thing in my life? How could I have driven this sweet, respectable woman into doing something like this?

I ran my hands across my baldhead, trying to calm my emotions. How did I get here?

chapter 1
the early years

"White boy!" the older boy yelled at me, laughing as I finally escaped his grasp and ran toward my house. Eyes closed, I just kept running, hoping that he and his friends wouldn't catch me before I reached the safe haven of my home.

Actually, my home wasn't really that safe. I lived at home with my mom and my four aunts. Our neighborhood wasn't the roughest neighborhood in New York, but we were surrounding by 7 different projects. I guess you could say we were the nucleus of the projects. All of my family was pretty much born and raised in the projects where someone was getting shot or stabbed every week.

Younger and smaller than most of my cousins with the lightest skin, I was always picked on for being different. Getting beat up was a regular routine with me. The fact that I never knew my father only gave the other kids more ammunition to assault me. When my little sister was born a few years ago, I thought my new stepfather might change things and actually give me a father to look up to. Turns out that Papa Lou was just a little more than sperm donor, popping in and out of our lives just to give my mom money to support us. We didn't live extravagantly. My mom worked at the hospital as a floor supervisor and her wages were enough to make sure our birthdays and Christmas were special, but on normal days - days like today, we wore generic brand shoes and clothes – yet another reason to get picked on. Name brand anything was foreign in our house. We didn't have Fruit Loops for breakfast; instead our family ate Toasted O's out of the bag. This was my normal. Used to being picked on, fear was my constant state of mind.

Heaving and out of breath, I ran into our three story row home and was immediately greeted by one of my older cousins.

"So, I hear you letting a little kid at your school bully you?"

He stood in front of the stairs, blocking my path to my room.

"T.O., let me by," I whined.

He didn't budge.

"I heard he took your lunch money today."

I stood there, silent.

"Didn't he?!" T.O. said, raising his voice.

I just stood there, embarrassed, yet scared at the same time.

T.O. grabbed me by the collar and jacked me up against the wall.

"Didn't he?!"

"Yes, yes, T.O.," I said with tears streaming down my face.

T.O. threw me on the floor in front of the stairs.

"You're such a little punk," he said looking at me disgusted, "That kid is smaller than you, and your punk ass is just letting him play you."

I sat there in a heap on the floor with tear stained cheeks.

A couple more of my cousins walked in the door.

"What's his problem?" Danny asked.

"T's punk ass is letting a little kid in his class smaller than him bully him and take his lunch money," T.O. volunteered.

Ready to rail into me, Danny started in on me fist first. I started to curl into a tighter ball on the floor to prepare for the blow. But, T.O. stopped him.

"Nah," he said, "leave him alone. He's had enough from us today. Plus, he's probably hungry since he let the little punk take his lunch money."

Feeling relieved, I let out a little sigh. T.O. was tough, but I'm glad he was looking out for me.

I got up slowly and got ready to up the stairs to my room.

T.O. grabbed me by the collar.

"It's time you manned up, cousin," he said, "I don't want to hear that you gave up your lunch money to this punk tomorrow. As a matter of fact, you better stand up to this little kid and show him what you're really made of. Otherwise, you'll have to answer to all of us when you get home."

Trying to wriggle out of my cousin's strong grip, "I don't know what you want me to do T.O. That kid is really mean."

He let me go and took a step back to join our two other cousins in the room.

"Well, then I guess you need to be meaner. You have two choices – man up and face this kid or face all of us when you get home tomorrow."

I tossed and turned all night, thinking about what was waiting for me the next day. Why did they always have to pick on me? What was so different about me? I wish they would just leave me alone. I just wanted to live a normal life, whatever that was. Going to school each day, I would see some kids that got dropped off by their father. I envied that. I often wondered what it would be like to have a father in my life. Someone to teach me things like how to ride a bike and deal with a bully. Jasper was the kid that had been bothering me lately. Truth is, I don't remember a time in my life when someone wasn't pushing me around or telling me what to do. It had become a way of life for me, and I was too afraid to push back. What my cousins didn't know was that Jasper had been taking my lunch money for two months now. He'd initially backed me in a corner and promised to beat me up if I didn't give it to him, so I've been trying to keep the peace and he hasn't bullied me much since, as long as I give him what he wants. It hasn't been that bad really. Mama usually has a snack for me when I come home from school, so I usually try to go straight home mainly because I'm starving by then. I don't know how T.O. found out about Jasper. All I know was now I was screwed. I didn't know how to fight this kid. And I was scared out of my mind.

I woke up, palms sweaty, heart racing. day was the day. I had to stand up to Jasper or my cousins would whip my behind, and they were way scarier than he was.

Mama fed me breakfast before heading off to the hospital, Toasted O's. I ate, trying to gather the strength to face my fear. My stomach was tied up into a billion knots. I almost got sick before running to the bus stop.

"You ok?" my Aunt Nae-Nae asked before I ran out the door, hunched over.

Taking a deep breath, I reassured my aunt.

"Yea, I'm ok."

Hoping to have time to myself as I walked to the bus stop, I was quickly disappointed. My cousin T.O. caught up with me, a big smile on his face.

"Are you ready for today, cuz?" he said, hand on my back.

My heart was racing at the thought of what might happen today.

I looked at him weakly, fear showing in my eyes.

T.O. grabbed me by the shoulders and looked me in the eyes.

"Today Ty, you finally become a man. No more running around here like you scared of everything. You're my cousin, and no man in this family should be bossed by some little kid smaller than him. Today, you get your lunch money back and stand up to this kid or you answer to me."

He patted me on the back with confidence and reassurance as we got on the bus.

I sat in the corner, silent. I couldn't afford to talk to anyone right now. There was too much going on inside of my head. I knew a fight was ahead of me because Jasper always got his money from me before class started.

As I walked through the halls, I took a deep breath.

"I can do this...I can do this."

I walked into my classroom a few minutes early. Maybe he would just leave me alone. Maybe there was an easy way out of this.

As I took out my textbook, I heard someone whisper my name.

"Hey Jenkins."

I turned around to see Jasper sitting in the desk behind me. I should have known there was no way of escaping him. We were in the same class. He didn't normally sit behind me, but he'd slid into the desk behind me this morning, obviously to get what he thought was coming to him. I looked him up and down and understood why my cousins were giving me grief about standing up to him.

He was about a head shorter than me. Scrawny too. I wasn't the biggest kid in my class, but I had some physical advantage over him both in size and height. But, what he did have was goons. Small as he was, he always came around with a posse, which is what made him even more intimidating. He wasn't alone.

"Yes," I answered.

"You know what I want," he said, his hand outstretched.

I turned around and looked at him, mustering all of the courage I had. "No."

Jasper looked at me, incredulous. He didn't have his posse around him now. Class was about to start and I knew he couldn't create but so much of a scene. But, I wasn't stupid. I knew there was a fight on the other side of this.

"No?" he said to make sure he heard me correctly.

"That's right. No. You can't have my lunch money."

He leaned in almost as if he were going to attack me, then stopped short, realizing that he could get expelled.

I immediately shirked back.

"You are going to regret this," he said as he got up from the desk and walked to the other side of the classroom to his rightful seat.

I smiled a bit to myself, proud of the small accomplishment I'd just had.

This was the first time I'd actually stood up to anyone, at the risk of being beat up. My heart was still pounding because I knew this wasn't over.

Throughout class, I glanced across the room at Jasper a couple of times, as he pounded fists at me, indicating that he planned to force me back into subjugation. My confidence from earlier quickly left me.

When lunchtime came, I was relieved to finally go to the cafeteria and eat lunch for the first time in months. I'd been starving.

I sat at the lunch table with a couple of my friends, Sean and Redd.

"So, you eating lunch today?" Redd asked surprised.

"Yea," I replied quickly, heart still racing.

Knowing my current bully situation, Sean decided to weigh in as we ate our chicken nuggets and fries.

"So, you finally decided to stand up to Jasper, huh?"

Head, down, I continued to scarf down my lunch.

"You did stand up to him, right?" Redd asked.

"Well, kind of..." I said taking a break between bites.

"What does that mean?" Redd asked.

"I just told him no."

"You just told him no?" Redd mimicked.

"Yes," I said, drinking my chocolate milk. It tasted so good. I hadn't had chocolate milk in months.

"And how exactly did that work out for you?" Sean asked.

Before I had a chance to answer him, Jasper came over to our lunch table, giving them both the answers they were looking for.

"Enjoying your lunch?" he asked sarcastically.

This time, he didn't come alone. He had his crew with him.

"You and me," he said. "After school."

No more words. With that, he and his crew were gone.

I sat there, paralyzed.

I already knew it would come to this, but now that it was real, I was having a hard time keeping down my lunch.

"Ty," Redd said, trying to get my attention, "you okay?"

I felt flushed.

"No, Redd, I'm not okay. I don't know how to fight. I'm scared."

"Then why didn't you just give him your lunch money like you always do," Sean said.

I took a deep breath to try and stop my heart from beating out of my chest.

"Because my older cousins found out yesterday that I've been getting bullied by a kid smaller than me. T.O. told me that if I didn't stand up to Jasper, they would kick my butt when I got home. So, basically, it's Jasper or them. Either way, I'm screwed."

Redd leaned back and crossed his arms.

"Yep, you pretty much are. Jasper is a pretty scrawny dude. But, it's his crew you gotta worry about."

Sean looked over to the other side of the cafeteria as Jasper and his crew stood there, mean mugging me.

"Man, they are ready to give you a beat down. You got a plan?"

I shook my head.

"I guess I just gotta do it. I mean, I really don't have no choice."

6

I was never more eager to stay in school than today. The kids around me were getting their backpacks ready to leave class as the teacher wrapped up class. I just hoped class could last just a little bit longer. Beads of sweat rolled down my temples as I watched the second hand on the wall clock tick one last time before the bell rang.

RING....!!!

I sat in my desk, paralyzed. I couldn't remember the last time I felt so scared. I was not a fighter. I didn't want to do this. I must have lingered in my desk too long because Ms. Johnson came over to me.

"Ty, I'm glad you enjoyed class, but it's time to go, honey. Get on before you miss your bus now."

I slowly rose to my feet at the prompting of Ms. Johnson.

Sean and Redd joined me in the hall.

"I just want to let you know that I'm your friend, and I got your back, Ty. But, I ain't taking no punches for you."

I always loved Redd's enthusiastic support.

"Thanks, just what a brother needs," I said sarcastically.

"Well, I guess it's time that I face my fate."

I walked out the door getting ready for my first real fight.

I had no idea how this was going to play out. I'd never thrown a punch in my life. I mostly always got beat up and picked on, but never had I thrown a punch.

When I rounded the buses, I saw him. Jasper was waiting there with his crew, just across the street from the school. This is where a lot of fights often happened after school because it was off school property and the school typically didn't break it up.

Heart racing, I took a big gulp and started walking toward them. The first time is always the hardest, right?

Sean and Redd gave me a little pat on the back as I got ready to face off my enemies.

As I walked toward them, all I could hear was the loud, obnoxious sound of my pounding heartbeat. And, I could almost hear the drops of sweat as the trickled off my temples. The last time I was this scared was the time Mama caught me stealing a $5 out of her purse.

"I'm surprised you actually showed," Jasper said with a smirk, looking me up and down.

I returned the favor and gained a little bit of confidence as I did. He was about 4 feet tall and maybe 65 pounds soaking wet. I mean, I know we were just little kids, but he was definitely small for his age. Unfortunately, he had enough mean in him to make up for it.

"I didn't say I wouldn't."

"Are you done sizing me up?" Jasper responded, clearly aware that I was sizing up my competition.

"Yea, I'm good," I said looking around, thinking Redd and Sean were still right behind me. Quickly I noticed that they'd backed up to join the small crowd of kids that had formed around us, eager to watch a fight.

I wiped my forehead, soaking wet from my sweat.

"Enough talking," Jasper said, "it's time you learned some respect."

As he advanced, ready to throw his first punch, my instincts immediately told me to back up.

"Where you running to? Take your whipping like a man."

Jasper threw the first punch, because I was too scared to do anything.

A stomach punch, knocking the wind went right out of me. I couldn't breathe. I faintly heard the kids around me yelling and cheering.

"Get up, Ty," I heard Redd say.

As I got ready to get up and attempt to throw what I thought was my first punch, I felt another jab hit me on the side of my face. I don't even know what direction it came from, but it stung. Still feeling the pain from the first punch, I immediately curled up into the fetal position as I felt a series of feet kicking and beating on me.

It felt like it lasted forever. All I wanted was for it to end. My body ached.

The last words I heard were Jasper's.

"Punk."

Then I heard footsteps run away. I stayed curled up in a ball, afraid to inspect the damage that had been done to my body in my first official beat down.

"Is he dead?" I heard Sean say.

"No fool. Can you see him breathing?" Redd mocked.

Bending down and shaking my feeble shoulders, Redd checked on my broken body.

"Ty, Ty, are you okay?"

My body was still curled up. Was I going into shock? Could I move? I had to try. I started to stretch my legs out so that I could stand in the upright position.

Ouch! My whole body hurt.

"Ty, your lip is bleeding," Sean pointed out.

I must have gotten that from that second big sucker punch. I could taste the blood seeping into my mouth.

I leaned over gingerly and picked up my backpack.

"You really took a beating," Redd said, "why didn't you fight back?"

Stretching to try and ease the ache in my bones, I shrugged my shoulders. Even that hurt.

"I really meant . He just came at me so fast. I didn't know what to do. The first thing that came to my mind was to just stay down and try to protect myself, so that is what I did. A lot of good that did, though," I said as I nursed my wounds.

"   We missed the bus," Sean said as we looked across the street at the empty bus lot.

"I guess we can walk," Redd said.

We didn't live that far from the school, so we figured we could all get home in about a 20-minute walk.

As we walked, very slowly, Sean and Redd kept grilling me about the fight.

"So, do you think Jasper will keep messing with you now? I mean you kind of stood up to him. But, you really just showed him that you could take a good beating."

I shook my head…my loyal friends.

"I don't know, Sean," I said as I limped up the road, "I'm not really worried that much about Jasper right now. I just don't want T.O. to get mad at me.

He told me to stand up to Jasper and I guess I kinda did."

"Well, at least now you know you can take a good punch," Sean said.

We walked the rest of the way home silently. Sean and Redd could tell I was in pain from the jabs and kicks I'd sustained and they gave me the space I needed to lick my literal wounds.

When we arrived home, we all went our separate ways. Sean and Redd lived just a few houses down from me.

"See ya later, Ty. I hope you feel better."

Glad to reach the steps of home, I got ready to go up the steps but didn't realize that my cousin T.O. was sitting right there on the stoop blocking my way.

"T.O., let me by," I said.

Leaning in, T.O. observed my busted lip.

"What's that?" he said pointing to my wound.

I rolled my eyes.

"T.O., you know exactly what it is. You told me I had to fight Jasper today, so I did."

"You did, huh?" he asked, eyebrows rose.

"Yeah, now let me by."

Leaning back on the stoop, belligerently, T.O. continued to block my entry into the house.

"That's not what I heard."

I was starting to get frustrated. My body hurt even more after walking the last 20 minutes to get home. I just wanted to lie down, maybe even take a hot bath.

"What did you hear T.O.? Can't you see the evidence right here that I was in a fight today?" I said pointing to my lip.

He leaned forward, inspecting my busted lip.

"Yes, it's obvious that you were in some kind of fight, but from what I hear, you got your butt handed to you."

"What do you want T.O.? You told me stand up to Jasper? I did that. But, that didn't mean I was going to win a fight with him."

"I don't care that you lost. You get in a fight and sometimes you lose. That happens. What I care about is that you didn't even put up a fight."

"What are you talking about?"

"I'm talking about you curling up in a little ball like a little punk while these kids beat you up."

"What was I supposed to do, T.O.?" I yelled, tears now streaming from my eyes.

10

Angry, T.O. stood up on the stoop.

"Fight!" he said pounding his fists, "do you remember what I told you yesterday?"

"What? No, T.O. I did what you told me. You guys can't beat me up. I already got beat up once today."

"If you'd actually stood up to this kid and tried to fight him, I'd let you off the hook, but you gotta learn, Ty. I can't have my little cousin out there looking like a punk. You already took one beating today. It's time to get ready for another one."

"Yo," T.O. yelled inside the house and 3 more of my larger cousins emerged.

"Ty, one thing I know you can do is take a beating. Sooner or later, you're gonna get tired of getting your tail whipped. When that happens, your little butt will learn how to fight and stand up for yourself and stop being scared of everything. But, apparently, today ain't the day."

All four of my cousins ganged up on me and gave me the beating of a lifetime. I thought I knew pain after my first beat down. Now, I could barely move. Every inch of my body hurt. As I hobbled into the house, I was thankful that my mom was still working at the hospital because I wouldn't want her to see me like this. I went straight to the bathroom and took a hot bath to nurse my wounds. I had bruises all over my body. Every move hurt, even when I blinked.

I never wanted to feel pain like this. Maybe my cousin was right. Maybe I was too soft. But, I was just a little kid. How much was I supposed to know about fighting? I laid in bed that night wondering why do things like this always happen to me? What did I ever do to deserve the hand I'd been dealt? Truth is, my beat down today pales in comparison to some of the things I'd experienced just a couple years ago.

Flashback 2 years… I was about 8 years old, playing stickball with my buddies Sean and Redd. My cousins were sitting outside our apartment just chilling while we played.

"Psst...hey, Ty," I heard from the top steps.

I looked up from my game and saw my cousin Danny standing at the door of his apartment, motioning me to come over.

Exasperated, I walked over with hunched shoulders. We all knew Danny was a bit off, but mostly because of all the WET he was taking. WET in the streets was known as angel dust/PCP, the hard stuff.

"What do you want Danny?" I asked, clearly annoyed, "I'm playing with my friends."

"This won't take long, Ty. Can you come in the house for a minute?"

I hesitated for a minute, because I was certain this was about to be a big waste of time, and I was winning the game before his dumb butt called me. I turned back to my friends to let them know I'd be a minute.

"Hey guys, I'll be right back. I just need to run into the house for a minute."

I walked into the apartment with Danny, hoping this would be quick. He never really wanted anything.

He motioned me in the house. None of my aunts were there and the rest of my cousins were just outside hanging out.

"Ok, what do you want Danny?"

Danny stood in front of me, a disheveled mess as usual. Clothes mismatched and hair barely combed. He stood there, a bit spastic. Any other kid would probably be freaked out by his behavior, but I'd grown used to it. He was just high.

"Come here, Ty. I need to tell you something."

I was standing only a couple feet away from him.

"Danny, I'm right here. What do you need to say?"

"Shh," he said, acting paranoid, "I don't want nobody to hear."

I looked around at the empty house.

"There's nobody here!" I yelled at him.

Frustrated that I did not come closer to him, he came closer to me. Too close – I backed up.

He came closer, leaned in and whispered in my ear.

"I want to do something for you," he said, a devious smile forming on his face, "I think you're really going to like it."

I tried to back away because his behavior was more strange than usual and he wreaked. I don't think he'd taken a bath in a few days.

"Danny," I said trying to move away, but he grabbed me.

"Let me show you what I'm gonna do," he said and then he started to reach for the zipper on my pants.

I was so shocked by his behavior that he almost got into my pants, but I came to my senses, used all the strength I had in my little kid body and snatched away from him and ran out the door.

I came out the house, a horrified look on my face.

T.O. noticed immediately that something was up.

"What's wrong little man?" he asked.

I turned and saw Danny standing at the front door looking like he needed to be locked in an asylum.

"Danny tried to molest me," I said plainly.

T.O. grabbed me. make sure he heard the words I said correctly.

"He what?!"

Tears had started to flow now because it sounded even worse coming out of my mouth. I started to really realize what had almost happened.

"D-Danny tried to touch my privates," I said.

"I can't believe it," T.O. mouthed, looking at our crazy cousin still standing in the doorway.

"Stay right here," he ordered me before heading into the house with the rest of my cousins in tow.

I sat there on the stoop, a bit in shock.

Sean and Redd came up to meet me.

"What's wrong, Ty? You don't want to play anymore?" Redd asked.

I wasn't in the mood to play right now. I wanted to know why Danny would try to do something like that to me. I know he wasn't right, but he knew better. Why would he do that to me?

"No guys, I don't think I want to play anymore."

"What did your cousin want?" Sean asked.

"Nothing," I lied, "as usual. I'll see you guys tomorrow."

As Sean and Redd left T.O. emerged back from the house.

"Come here, Ty," he said, "We took care of him, okay? He won't mess with you anymore. Don't you ever go anywhere with him again, you hear me? Did he actually touch you?"

13

I shook my head.

"No, I got away before he could."

T.O. breathed a sigh of relief.

"Good."

I sat outside on for a while just wondering why my own family would do something like this to me.

A few months later, I'd learned to stay clear of Danny. The seasons had changed and we'd just gotten our first big snow. Happy to get a rare snow day, I rounded up my buddies, Sean and Redd, to build a snowman. We'd been at it for a little while now, and our snowman was starting to look pretty good, but he needed arms.

"Over there," Redd pointed, further into the street.

I saw two small sticks in the street that would make perfect arms for our snowman.

"Got it," I said, running over to pick up the sticks.

It all happened so fast. All I remember was leaning over to pick up the sticks and everything after that was a blur. A car had come out of nowhere and hit me. As I laid face down in the snow, my short life started to pass before my eyes. I thought about the incident that had happened with Danny just a few months ago. Now, I was pretty sure I was going to die and I was yet to experience what it was like to be joyful, to have fun, to be a kid. Why did things like this keep happening to me?

God, I know that we don't talk often, but I need your help. I try so hard to be a good kid. I love my mom and don't talk back to her. I listen and do what I'm told. I make good grades in school. I try so hard to be good, but bad things just keep happening to me. Why God? What am I doing wrong? Please just tell me what to do, and I'll do it. I don't want to die.

I opened my eyes and felt a little disoriented. I couldn't move much, but right away I sensed that my whole body ached and I couldn't move my leg. I blinked so that my eyes could adjust more to my surroundings.

"He's awake."

Mom? I tried to talk but words would not come out.

I could see more clearly now.

My mother was sitting down on a chair in front of me. Where was I? I wasn't home. I knew that.

Still unable to find my voice, I gave my mother a puzzled look, seeking an explanation of what had happened to me.

She leaned in and stroked my cheek.

"Don't try to talk baby, okay?"

I nodded in obedience.

"Sweetheart, you were hit by a car. You scared all of us pretty good, but you're going to be fine. Thank the lord! You did suffer a few cuts so you did have to get some stitches and your leg is broken."

I reached up and felt the tubes going in and out of my nose and tried to take them out.

"No sweetie," my mom said, moving my hand away, "that is giving you oxygen so don't take that out. Hopefully, it won't be in long. You just let me know if you're in pain. Your leg was broken pretty bad so you had to go into surgery. That's why you're probably feeling a little groggy right now. Can you remember anything about what happened to you?"

I tried talking again and this time a small voice came out.

"I don't remember anything, mommy. I was trying to build a snowman outside with Redd and Sean. He needed arms and we spotted 2 sticks for his arms. I ran to get them and that's all I remember."

"Okay, baby," she said patting my arm, "we'll get to the bottom of this. The fool that hit you kept going but I believe the Lord will pay him back for his wrong in time if the police are not able to track him down. You just rest baby."

And so I did. I was in the hospital for a few more days after that. It turns out that I broke my left femur and tibia so I had to wear a full leg cast. The next few weeks were difficult. I had to adjust to being on crutches, taking special baths and I couldn't go to school or out to play. Mom couldn't take any more time to stay home with me because we were falling behind in our bills already so she usually asked one of my aunts to stay with me during the day if they weren't working or hired a babysitter.

I still searched for answers to why these things kept happening to me. I remember saying a prayer when I was in the hospital, which is the first time I really remember praying in my young life. I wanted something to change and really hoped God listened to little kids like me. I was hoping to get some kind of break in life, especially since I was allowed to live and not die. That had to mean something.

The next 6 weeks continued to be tough. Having broken bones was no joke, but tomorrow I had a doctor's appointment to get my cast off and I was hoping life could go back to normal and I could go out and play with my friends again.

The doctor examined my leg after he'd sawed off the cast, which was pretty cool. I looked at my leg compared to my other leg and it looked really weird. It was ashy and shriveled looking. My leg looked sick.

"It looks pretty good," the doctor said.

"Really?" I said reaching down to touch my weird leg, "what's wrong with it? Why does it look like that?"

The doctor and my mother both laughed at my comments, as my concern was clearly real.

"Ty, your leg has been wrapped up in a cast for 12 weeks. That's why it looks like that. But, the good news is the bone has healed so your leg is not broken anymore. Take your time getting back into regular activity. Nothing too active yet, okay?"

I nodded.

"And once you've bathed and cleaned it up, that leg will start to look better."

"Will it still look that skinny?" I said making a face.

The doctor laughed again.

"For a little while. You need to give that leg some time to build up and get as strong as your other leg again. Remember, you haven't used it in a while.

So, give it a few weeks and it should look a little better. Any more questions?"

I shook my head no, and for the first time, I was able to walk out of the doctor's office on my own two feet, even though one of them was a bit weird.

As we got in the car to ride back home, my mom told me how proud she was of me.

"What did I do?" I asked.

"Ty, I know it hasn't been easy going through all of this. It wasn't your fault that a car hit you and I hate to see you going through all of this pain. So, I wanted to do something to make you feel better. Do you know what this weekend is?"

I leaned my head back in the car, thinking. What was this weekend? Oh! I leaned forward in my seat, excited.

"It's my birthday!"

"That's right, baby. And, you deserve to have a great birthday after all that has happened so we're going to throw you a big party at the house."

I beamed. Thank you, God, for answering my prayers. Finally, something good was happening for me.

I lay in bed that night, excited for the first time in a long time. The doctor had finally taken my cast off so I didn't have to go around in those awful crutches anymore. It felt so good to be walking on my own two feet. And, now mom was going to throw me a birthday party. Life was good.

I woke up that Saturday morning excited about more than turning a year older.

I was excited about things taking a turn for the good in my life, and it was all starting today. I swung out of the bed and smelled bacon in the air.

I followed my nose down the stairs into the kitchen where my mom was cooking breakfast. This was a treat. Mom worked so hard and money was so tight, a home cooked breakfast was a rarity.

"Good morning, my birthday boy," she said with a smile on her face as she leaned down to give me a kiss on the cheek, "go ahead and grab a seat at the table. Your breakfast is almost ready."

I followed my mother's instructions and sat down at the kitchen table, beaming. I looked around and did not see my sister.

"Mom, where's Diana?"

"Oh, she's with your aunts doing some shopping for your party later today," she said affectionately rubbing my shoulders before she placed my breakfast in front of me.

Pancakes, bacon, eggs and toast – best breakfast ever!

Mom could see the excitement in my face.

"Happy Birthday, baby. Enjoy your breakfast."

Today was going to be a great day. I was so excited for the party, but for now, I was going to enjoy this great breakfast Mom has prepared. No Toasted O's for me today!

Sugar Hill Gang was blaring on the radio,

"To the bang bang boogie, say up jump the boogie…"

My Mom and aunts were dancing in the kitchen and playing cards. My uncle and grandfather were upstairs hanging out watching some sports, my cousins, my friends, and me were playing hide and seek. We'd just filled our bellies on my mom's great cooking which included everything from hot dogs and hamburgers to grilled chicken and pork chops. Mom had really gone out of her way to make this birthday special for me. And it was! She even made me a cake, with my name on it and everything.

"10-9-8-7…" Sean was counting as we all ran through the house trying to find a hiding place.

"In here," my cousin Stan whispered to me.

"4-3…"

"Now!" Stan almost yelled. Stan, T.O., and I piled into the closet and waited as we heard Sean looking through the house for his targets.

"Ready or not, here I come!" he said.

We all stood still and silent in the closet, hoping that our hiding spot would not be compromised. But, as we were hiding in the closet, something weird happened. It felt like something or someone was standing over us, a weird presence. At one point, I think I even felt breathing on my shoulder. I couldn't take it anymore. I came storming out of the closet.

Sean had just walked into my room.

"Gotcha," he said tagging me.

Stan and T.O. emerged from the closet, disappointed.

"Dang Ty, why you run out? Sean would have never found us," Stan complained.

I ignored my cousins and ran into the kitchen where my mom and aunts were sitting at the kitchen table playing spades.

"Mom, mom," I said frantically, tugging on her shirt.

"What's wrong, Ty?" she said, never taking her eyes off the game.

"Mom, there's a monster in my closet."

Everyone at the table started laughing hysterically.

"You better get on outta here boy before you mess up my hand. You know there are no such things as monsters."

"But, mom…"

"That's enough, Ty. Now, get all those toys up in your room and put them back in your closet where they belong. I mean it."

I walked away head down. Maybe Mom was right. Monsters weren't real. They were just in the movies and on TV. Maybe I just imagined something was in the closet since we were crammed in the dark.

"Where'd you run off to?" Stan asked when I got back to my room.

"I just had to ask my mom something real quick."

"What are we gonna play now?" Stan asked.

"I don't know, but my mom wants me to pick up all of these toys and put them back in the closet. We can figure out what we want to play after we do that."

The trio went to work picking up my toys off the floor and chucking them into the closet. We'd been playing for a while so there were a lot of toys on the floor. As I was getting ready to toss the last of the toys into the closet, a huge man with a stocking on his face came flying out of the closet.

Afraid, I took off running down the hall. Everywhere I went; there he was chasing me. He made a beeline through our bathroom, breaking the mirror in the process. We eventually made it to the kitchen and my mom and aunts started yelling, trying to get the attention of the men upstairs.

I ran toward my mom and my aunts for protection as this maniac flew through my kitchen. My cousins made their way into the room and one of them was able to grab a hold of the thief's sleeve. As he tried to work his way out my cousin's grasp his eyes remained fixed on me. Dark and mysterious, I felt as if his eyes pierced my soul through that stocking cap. The entire time he struggled with my cousin, his gaze never left me. He eventually broke my cousin's grasp and escaped out of the kitchen backdoor.

By this time, the rest of my cousins and my uncle had made their way downstairs, but by then it was too late, he was gone. My mom had called the cops and they searched the neighborhood but he was never found. My perfect day had ended in a nightmare.

That guy haunted my dreams for years. Those scary, piercing eyes followed me everywhere. I looked around every corner when I went outside with my friends; afraid that he would come for me to finish whatever he came to my house to start. The one-day I thought things were going my way, things still ended in disaster! I struggled to understand why these things kept happening to my family and me.

Now, I struggled with overcoming the humiliation of getting beat to a pulp in front of all my peers at school, only to come home and get an old fashioned whipping from my cousins. This was the last time I was ever going to be humiliated like that. I made a vow to work on building my courage and start standing up for myself a little bit more. Maybe if I learned to stand up for myself more and stop being so scared, bad things would stop happening to me. Maybe I had to take the first step to really change things. No more beat downs like that.

My new courageous attempts actually started with girls. I'd always gotten attention from girls, but I've always been too shy and scared of them to act on anything. I liked girls and thought they were cute, but didn't know the first thing about what to do with them. And, actually the thought of it scared me a little bit. I saw my cousins with girls all the time and they often smiled and flirted with me. T.O. kept messing with me, telling me that I needed to talk to girls more.

"Ty, we gotta get you a girlfriend or something. It looks like the ladies love you."

Truth is, I really liked the ladies, too. But, the unknown was always too scary for me. But, as I started working on building my courage to stand up to guys and talk to girls, my confidence grew. I realized the attention I was getting from the girls was a good thing. And, I liked it. The girls liked this little light skinned kid. They didn't shun me as different, as I'd always been used to from the fellas. They actually thought I was cute. And, so I started talking to girls more and realized they weren't so bad.

One evening, I was home working on my schoolwork. It was a weeknight and mom was working at the hospital so she'd brought in a babysitter for my sister and me. Tawana was a little older than me, a freshman in high school and I liked it when she babysat because she always let me stay up later than my mom would. She was nice, and she was kind of pretty, too. I was just getting to the point of really noticing girls, mainly because they'd really started noticing me. Tawana was tall, brown skinned with short hair. She was well developed for her age, with full breasts and a nice booty.

I was at the kitchen table working on my homework and she was in the living room picking up my sister's toys off the floor. I looked up and couldn't help but admire her nice, round booty. Unfortunately, I wasn't that slick. My quick glance turned into a little bit of a stare.

Before I knew, it, I was caught.

"You like what you see?" Tawana asked me, bending over more to give me an even better view.

Excited for the opportunity, I continued to stare.

She saw me staring at her and took advantage of the audience. She walked over to the radio in the kitchen and turned it on. Prince and the Revolution were singing, "When Doves Cry."

"Ohh, I love this song," she said and started swaying her hips seductively, all the while staring at me.

I couldn't look away.

She walked over to me. I was sitting on the couch.

Shyness kicked in immediately. My cheeks flushed, embarrassed. She wasn't supposed to have caught me looking at her like that. This felt awkward. Tawana came to my house to babysit my sister and me all the time.

She stared at me until I felt so uncomfortable that I had to look away.

She grabbed my face gently and turned it back towards her.

"You know, you really are a cutie," she said.

I immediately looked down again. I was so uncomfortable.

"Why are you so shy?" she asked.

"I don't know," I replied, head still facing down.

Her voice then got low and sultry.

"Ty, have you even been with a girl?" she said.

Not fully understanding exactly what she was referring to, I replied naively.

"I see girls at school all the time."

Tipping my head back up to face me.

"I know you see girls, but have you ever been with a girl," she said, hinting at what she meant by slowly unbuttoning her shirt revealing part of her full breasts.

My cheeks flushed and I felt embarrassed. I liked what I saw and my body immediately responded to her visual display. I covered myself.

Sensing my embarrassment and the fact that her tactics to arouse me were working, she grabbed my hands and removed them from my lap.

"You don't have to do that," she said, "this is perfectly natural." And, she proceeded to place her hand on my private parts.

I started to squirm. I didn't know what was happening. I didn't know what I should do.

"Tawana, I…." I started.

"Shhh…" she said placing her fingers to my lips to silence me. "It's okay. I know just what to do. I'm going to help you become a man tonight." Then, she proceeded to unbutton my jeans.

I looked at her worried, because I knew what was happening down there and I was afraid to let her see it. I was still trying to understand what this even meant. As scared as I was, I didn't stop her. Part of me wanted to, but another part of me was curious, wanted to see how this would play out.

After she'd placed her hands on my privates, she turned her attention back to me directly.

"Have you ever kissed a girl before?"

Still paralyzed from what was happening right now, I just shook my head no.

Hand still on my privates, she used her other hand to bring me closer to her and she proceeded to place her tongue in my mouth. It felt really weird at first.

She pulled away for a minute.

"Relax," she said, squeezing me.

I did, and she started to kiss me again. I tried to follow her lead and do what she was doing, and realized that this actually felt kinda good. After kissing me, she pulled away and looked down at my unzipped jeans.

"Take off your pants," she ordered.

"Right here?" I asked, concerned about being naked in the open.

"Yes, right here," she said.

Scared but more curious about what she would do next, I followed her instructions. I took off my jeans and stood there in front of her in my white underwear.

"Take those off too," she ordered.

I followed her instructions, and stood there in our living room, fully exposed and aroused. Strangely, I felt less embarrassed and more excited about what was about to happen next.

Tawana sensed my excitement as she grabbed hold of me.

I didn't stop her. I was starting to like this.

"Sit down right here," she said pointing to the couch.

I sat my bare bottom on the couch. But, nothing could have prepared me for what she was going to do next.

She got down on her knees in front of me and proceeded to put her mouth on me.

My first instinct was to pull away because I didn't know what she was doing, but then it started to feel good. It felt so good that I started to feel some things happening down there that I'd never felt before. All of a sudden, I felt out of control for a moment, but the sensation felt so good.

Was I having sex? I don't think I'm a virgin anymore!

Walking to the bus stop the next day, I had a different strut in my step. I was a man! TO immediately noticed my big smile as I was waiting on Redd and Sean to catch up with me.

"What's that big, goofy smile all about, Ty?"

I just stood there, beaming.

T.O. shook me to get my attention.

"What you smiling so hard about, boy?" he demanded.

"I'm a man now."

T.O. started laughing, and I took offense.

"What's so funny T.O.? I mean it."

"I'm sorry, Ty. Not too long ago, we had to whip your tail because you let a kid in your class smaller than you bully you and then lay a whipping' on you after school. Forgive me if I don't believe your newfound claim that you are now a man."

I frowned at the painful memory of that day.

"I'm not talking about that."

Then, my smile returned, hinting at my cousin what I really mean.

"I'm talking about something else."

T.O. looked at me more closely, then leaned in and lowered his voice.

"You mean, you got some," he said.

I smiled and nodded my head excitedly.

T.O. shook his head.

"No way," he said. "You're just a young, little buck. There's no way you know what you doing."

"I didn't have to. She did," I volunteered.

"You mean you got with an older chick," T.O. asked, even more surprised.

"Yep," I said confidently.

Just then, Redd and Sean caught up with us ready to go to the bus stop.

"Hey Ty, let's go. The bus is almost here," Redd said.

"Hold up, little man. I'm rapping with my cousin for a minute," T.O. said.

"Ty, why don't you let me take you to school this morning? I want to hear more about this."

Anxious to hang out with my older cousin, I agreed.

"I'll catch up with you guys at school," I told Sean and Redd.

Sean and Redd ran to the bus stop just in time to catch the bus while I walked with T.O. to his car.

"Okay little cuz, tell me about this older girl you just got with," he said, eager to learn about my new experience.

Excited to get some positive attention from my cousin, I settled into the car and started to tell him about what happened with Tawana last night. I told him about how she told me to take my pants off and what she did to me after that.

T.O. smiled, eyes focused on the road as he was driving me to school.

"You liked that, didn't you?" he said.

I nodded, smiling widely.

"Did it feel good?" he said.

"It felt really good," I said.

"Wow, Ty, you are starting to become a little man."

I kept smiling.

"See T.O., I told you. I had sex."

T.O. started laughing, shaking his head. By this time, we'd arrived at my school and T.O. stopped the car and put it into park and turned his attention to me directly.

"Ty, you did not have sex, buddy," he said, still snickering.

I did not see any humor in this.

"Yes, I did, T.O. I took my clothes off and she did things to my thang."

"Yes, she did and I'm glad you're getting a little experience and enjoyed it. But, you didn't actually have sex. You did a little bit of what we call foreplay, specifically a blowjob. What did you say this girl's name was?"

"Tawana, She's the babysitter mom calls when she has to work late."

"Tawana…Tawana," T.O. kept reciting out loud as if he was trying to recall something.

"Oh yeah, I know that girl. She is fast as hell. Now that I think of it, I don't know too many fellas that haven't hit that. She's a little freak and gets around. Be careful with her if you do anything else. Make sure you protect your little man with a Jimmy."

"A Jimmy?" I asked, looking puzzled.

"A condom, Ty, a condom," T.O. said, shaking his head at my naïveté.

"Ok." I said, taking a mental note of that.

"But, buddy you did not have sex last night? Trust me, when you do have sex, you'll know it. Okay?"

"Okay." I said, and then got out of the car.

I decided to keep my little experience to myself until I learned more about the real thing. Last night was fun, but I wanted to see how it compared to the real thing and I'm glad that T.O. saved me from being embarrassed and bragging to my friends before I knew what had actually happened. I was determined to learn more about this sex thing and see how much I really liked it. From hearing my cousins talk about it, I think I was going to like it. If it was anything like last night, I think I might like this sex thing.

chapter 2
the hustle

It turns out my suspicions about sex were right. It was great. Less than a year later, I got my first chance to have sex – the real thing. Older girls were really into me, which gave me a chance to experiment and learn a lot. By the time I was 13, sex and girls were a part of my lifestyle. And, as my confidence and popularity grew with the girls, I also gained more confidence and stature at school. My cousin, T.O., gave me enough tough love at home to help me learn how to stand up for myself so that I did not have many more instances like I did with Jasper. I learned how to stand up for myself and didn't back down when challenged.

Things were looking up. I wasn't looked at as the wimp anymore. And, I liked it. But, things weren't perfect. Mom still worked hard, and making ends meet had become even harder because she wasn't at the hospital anymore. It's crazy because while I was getting more confident and popular among the girls in school, things fell apart a little bit on the home front.

The tri-level home that we lived in with my aunts and cousins burned down. My neighbors in the building next door had caused a fire while barbecuing on the roof, which burned both their home and ours down. So, we had to move to an apartment, which in New York on my mom's salary with 2 kids meant small, tight spaces. Around the same time, my grandfather was diagnosed with colon cancer and was admitted into the same hospital that my mom worked at. Granddaddy never got any better and died in that hospital. This was the one and only true man I had ever had in my life. It devastated mom and she couldn't bring herself to continue working at the hospital anymore, so she started working as a teacher for a local daycare. The upside was that she didn't have to work evenings anymore; the downside was that she took a huge pay cut from what she was making at the hospital. But, for her, it was worth it not to have to work where her daddy died.

Things were tight, which meant more hand me downs, generic sneakers and Toasted O's for breakfast. It didn't matter that I got attention from the girls for my looks when I was at school, when I still got clowned for my cheap sneakers and hand me down clothes. I got angry thinking about how hard my mom worked and how little we had. There had to be a better way.

On my way home from school one day, I ran into a guy I'd seen around plenty of times before. He caught me admiring the nice pair of Nike's he was wearing.

"Hey kid, you like these?" he said sticking his foot out for me to get a better look.

My eyes lit up.

"Yeah man! Those are the new Jordan's right?"

"Damn right," he said confidently. Then he looked down at my raggedy pair of shoes, "you know I can help you get a pair just like these if you're interested."

I looked down at my shoes and then back at his again.

"Yeah right," I said.

"Come here kid," he said pulling me into a corner out of plain sight.

"What's your name?" he said.

"Ty," I said.

"My name's Curtis."

"What's up, Curtis?" I said shaking his outstretched hand.

"Ty, I know your cousins and I've seen how popular you are with the girls. But, we've got to do something about this get up," he said looking me up and down.

I shuffled, head down, embarrassed.

"It's all that we can afford."

"Ty, look at me."

I stopped shuffling my feet and looked up at Mr. Curtis.

"You can always control what you can afford. Never let anyone tell you any different."

I stood there as he reached into his backpack and pulled out several packs of white powder.

"Do you know what this is?" he asked.

I shook my head yes.

"I think there might be some opportunity for us to help each other out. You see, I need someone to make drops for me and you need to make some extra money. You run these packs to my distributors, pick up the money and bring it back to me and I'm going to pay you."

I stood there with my mouth wide open.

"You going to pay me just to drop this off and pick up your money?"

"Yep," Curtis said sitting back, arms crossed.

"That's it?" I said, a little skeptical.

"That's it, little man. Now, I know you need the money, so do we have a deal?"

I thought about all of times I had to ask my aunt for something to eat when we'd been short and them complaining about me asking for stuff. I looked down at my shoes and clothes and knew exactly what I had to do.

"Yes," I said, "what do you need me to do?"

Curtis put his arm around me.

"Well, for starters, let's get you a new pair of sneakers, and we'll talk about getting you started tomorrow."

Curtis took me to the department store and bought me a brand new pair of Nike's. I was ecstatic! I was so excited that I took off my raggedy pair and threw them away immediately. I wanted to know what it felt like to wear a new pair of shoes. It felt good!

As I got out of the car, Curtis gave me instructions on meeting up with him the next day so that I could start my new job.

"I think you're gonna do great kid! Enjoy the shoes," he said.

"Thanks Curtis!" I said.

I ran into the house excited about my new shoes and the chance to earn money to upgrade even more of my wardrobe and maybe even our lifestyle.

Mom was cooking dinner when I walked into the apartment.

"Hey Ty," she said, "Go get washed up and ready for dinner. Do you have homework?"

Walking into the living room, I shed my backpack right away.

"A little," I said, walking back toward the kitchen to give my mom a kiss.

"Well, dinner is almost ready. Go get washed up and start on your homework right after dinner, alright?"

"Yes, ma'am," I said and started walking toward the bathroom to wash up.

"Ty," I heard my mom yell as I walked away.

"Ma'am?"

"Where did you get those shoes?"

I stopped in my tracks. I was so excited about getting these new shoes, I didn't think about how I was going to tell mom about them. I had to think of something fast.

"What?"

By this time, mom had turned away from the dinner she was cooking to face me directly.

"Those shoes on your feet, son," she said, "where did you get them because I know I did not buy them for you?"

"Ummm…"

"Well, Ty, don't make me whip it out of you!"

"When I was leaving school today, I saw them in the classroom. A kid had left them behind, and I couldn't help myself mom. I never had shoes this nice."

"You didn't steal them?"

"No, mom, I promise I didn't steal it. Someone just left it behind in class."

She looked at me closely to inspect for any fallacies.

"Okay," she said, "but if that kid comes back to class and reports them missing, you'd better turn them in, you hear me

"Yes ma'am."

"Okay, now go wash up."

I walked into the bathroom and followed my mom's instructions. Whew! That was a close one. I was so excited about my new kicks that I didn't even think about mom asking about them.

Dinner was particularly good that night. I don't think it was anything special about what mom cooked as much as it was my excitement about doing something to change our situation. I was so tired of people looking down on us and I still didn't understand why mom took a job making so much less than she used to make. It didn't make sense to me. I always felt that we could do better than we were doing but mom always told me that I didn't understand, so I stayed in my place.

But, now it was different. Now, I had a chance to make a difference. If what Curtis said was true, I'd have a chance to change the future of our family and get us out of the gutter. And, that made me happy.

The next day I started working for Curtis and he did make good on his promise.

He told me that all I needed to do was drop the crack off and pick up money from his dealers and that is what I did, and he paid me for that. Little by little, I started to make some money and worked on upgrading my look. I got real good at coming up with lies to tell my mom about the new income stream I'd created. The latest was that I'd picked up a paper route and she seemed to buy that one so I stuck with it.

As I got used to delivering, people started approaching me for crack. An opportunist, I started taking a few packs from each bag Curtis gave me to deliver so that I could sell my own. It wasn't long before Curtis caught on to what I was doing. He called me on it while I was delivering his money to him one day.

"What's up, Ty?" he said, giving me a fist bump.

I handed him his money, and he reached in his pocket and gave me my cut.

"Little man, you've been doing your thang! You've become a real asset on my payroll and my dealers seem to like you so I definitely want to keep you around. How you like this gig?"

I shook my head with a smile. It was nice to have extra money and to be able to get some attention for wearing something besides hand-me-downs.

"I like it, Curtis."

He put his arm around me.

"Good. I think you're doing a great job. But, I did want to ask you something?"

"What's that, Curtis?"

"When you bring me back the money from the runs, I'm noticing that I'm always short a few bags. Do you know what's up with that? Is there a dealer I need to hit up on this?"

"Oh no, Curtis, I've been taking a few bags out from the supply you give me. People started asking me for it, so I wanted to have a few to sell myself."

"Oh ok. Why didn't you just ask me, little man?"

I shrugged my shoulders.

"I don't know. I had the supply with me already and people were asking so I just sold it to them."

"Am I not paying you enough little man?" Curtis asked as he lit up a joint.

"Oh no, Curtis, you pay me real good. People were just asking and if I could make more, I wanted to do it."

"Like I said, Ty, if you wanted to make more money, all you had to do was ask."

I looked at him as he puffed away at his joint.

"Do you want to make more money?"

"Yes," I said.

"Are you ready to do more than just make runs? Do you think you can handle it?"

"Yes, I can handle it. I'm already doing it."

Surprised a little by my confidence, Curtis cracked a smile.

"Well, why don't we put that to the test?"

He reached into his bag to retrieve his drug stash.

He pulled out a 50-pack of crack.

"I want you to sell all of these for $20 bucks a piece," he said, "when you're done, bring me $850 and keep the rest for your cut."

I was good at math so I knew that meant $150 for me, which was a fortune for what he was asking me to do.

"Yea, okay," I said, excited about the opportunity.

"Welcome to the business, little man – officially," he said reached out his hand to shake mine.

I shook his hand and took off with his precious package in my backpack.

Because I'd been doing runs for Curtis for a little while now, I'd started to get to know the market pretty well and had developed a few customers of my own. When I came out with a larger supply, I was able to sell more aggressively and moved through my supply quickly.

Unfortunately, my cousins started to learn about what I was doing in the streets and approached me about it.

I was out on the stoop just hanging out with my boys Redd and Sean one afternoon after school.

"Ty," T.O. yelled from his car as he rolled up in our neighborhood.

"Hey T.O.," I said.

"Come here little man," he said, "I need to rap with you for a minute."

I walked over to his window.

"What's up T.O.?"

"Word on the street is that you are moving crack," he said, "is that true?"

I looked down and started shuffling my feet. I was hoping he wouldn't find out what I was doing. It was easy money but I also knew it was wrong.

"Ty," he prompted.

"Yes," I finally admitted.

"What did I tell you about that crap? Didn't I tell you to stay away from it?" he said, clearly angry.

"I'm not doing any of it," I said pleading my case, "I'm only selling it to make a little extra money so I could get me some sneakers. Please don't tell mom."

T.O. shook his head.

"I'm not going to tell your mom, Ty, but you need to be careful. I don't want you out there doing that stuff. Who are you working for?"

I hesitated.

"Ty," T.O. repeated again, getting agitated this time.

"You know him, I think," I said, "his name is Curtis."

"Curtis?" he said, surprised by my answer, "that little fake hustler got you running game?"

I just nodded my head.

"Okay," he said and started driving away.

"T.O.," I yelled after him.

T.O. stopped his car and stared at me.

"What Ty?"

"It's not his fault," I said.

He took a slight pause.

"Yea, it never is," and with that he was gone.

I just stood there for a moment. I had no time to warn Curtis. T.O. was much faster on his wheels that I'd ever be on foot. T.O. was a proficient fighter and always defended me and helped keep me tough. I saw the anger in his eyes so it was definitely going down. I just hoped he knew what he was in for. I didn't know Curtis' fighting skills but he has an entourage and they all had guns.

A couple of days passed before I heard anything about what happened. But, I'd heeded T.O's advice and stayed away. I still had the $1,000 in my backpack from the packs I'd sold. I was supposed to bring Curtis the $1,000 back but I was too scared to go back that way after T.O's warning.

I was sitting outside my apartment trying to discretely count my new-found money when Redd stopped by.

"What's up, man?" I said, quickly zipping my backpack.

"Did you hear?" he said.

"Hear what?"

"About that guy Curtis?"

Knowing full well who Curtis was, I played dumb.

"Curtis?"

"Yeah," Redd went on, "I think he knows some of your cousins, but he's a pretty well-known dealer around here."

I shrugged my shoulders.

"What about him?"

"Word on the street is T.O. and some of your other cousins ambushed

34

him the other day. They beat him up pretty bad. I think he might even be in the hospital."

I shook my head.

"Damn."

"I know," Redd said, "remind me to never get on your cousins' bad side. He must have done something to really piss them off."

Knowing exactly what he'd done, I continued to play dumb with my friend.

"Yeah, he really must have."

It was almost dusk.

"I'd better head home," Redd said, "my mom will beat my tail if I'm out after dark."

We said our good-byes and I headed into the house as well. Mom was in the kitchen cooking dinner and I headed to my bedroom to finish up my homework.

As I sat on my bed, my mind started to wander. What was I going to do with this $1,000 in my backpack? It was a lot of money. But, it wasn't going to last forever. And, now that T.O. had pretty much busted my hustle with Curtis, that deal was dead. I needed to find another way to make money. Mom was cooking pancakes for dinner again! We deserved better and it was up to me to find a way.

At 13, I realized that I was in a new place in my life. I'd allowed bitterness to set in and started to develop a bit of a chip on my shoulder. I was pretty much tired of being treated like second-class citizens by my family and other people in the neighborhood. The comments that people made, some subtle and some not so subtle never seemed to bother my mom, but they infuriated me. I never understood why people thought they were better than us. I wanted a change desperately. I think my mom sensed my uneasiness so she enrolled me in martial arts classes. And this was a good thing because I found release in these classes. In addition to this, my cousin T.O. started to take time out to teach me how to street fight. After my debacle a couple years back with Jasper, he decided that he needed to teach me how to fend for myself. But, that was after a couple of beat downs and he started to see my confidence level rising, especially with the girls.

After being enrolled in my martial arts training for a while and working with T.O., I finally got an opportunity for retribution for my humiliation with Jasper a couple years back.

Every week T.O. took me to his project, where he lived, and taught me how to box. As we were wrapping up training one day, he asked me about Jasper.

"Fly Ty, what ever happened to that little kid that whipped your butt a couple years ago?"

I thought for a minute. Unfortunately, beat downs were pretty regular for me back then.

"Oh, you mean Jasper?"

"Yea, yea, the little kid. He was a lot smaller than you, right?"

Embarrassed, I lowered my head.

"Yes."

"Is he still in your class?"

I was in middle school now, so I didn't cross paths with Jasper that much anymore. We were in the same school but he'd backed down considerably since elementary school. I wasn't really sure why.

"We go to the same school, but we don't have all of the same classes."

"He still mess with you?"

"Not anymore."

Punching his fists together, my cousin looked at me deviously.

"Time for a little payback."

"Payback?" I said a little confused.

"Yea man. This kid beat your tail when you were in elementary school, and all you did was crawl up in a ball and barely fight back. It's time for you to show him what you're made of now. I know you can take him now. Has he grown anymore? Is he still small?"

I'd been training both in martial arts and with T.O. and my confidence in my ability to fight had certainly grown, but I had not had a chance to put it to the test. The fight with Jasper was a long time ago and he hadn't bothered me in a while. I wasn't sure if I was up for picking a fight.

"Yea, he's still small," I said, "but T.O., I don't know if I need to go picking a fight with Jasper. He has not bothered me since back then. Why should I go and start something?"

T.O. grabbed me by the collar.

"Were you doing anything to make him bully you, take your lunch money and then beat you up back then?"

I thought about what T.O. said. He had a point. I never deserved the way Jasper treated me. He just knew that I was scared of everything and he fed on my fear.

"Back then, you were scared of anything that moved. Show him you're not scared of him anymore."

T.O. let my collar go, and he saw the anger return to my face as I reminisced about what Jasper had done to me. I let all of the emotions of how people had treated my mom and me flood back and all of a sudden I was ready to unleash.

I pounded my fists.

"I'm not scared."

I went to school the next day with a renewed confidence. I needed to practice my newfound fighting skills and T.O. was right; what better opportunity than to approach my former bully who'd humiliated me in elementary school.

Jasper and I had not interacted much since going to middle school but I still saw him around so I knew how to track him down. Classes had wrapped up for the day and I was getting some things out of my locker when my buddies Redd and Sean approached me.

"Ready to go?" Sean said.

"In a minute," I said as I closed my locker and quickly spotted my target, "I've got something to take care of first."

Redd followed my eyes and immediately sensed what was about to go down.

"Ty, man, what are you about to do?"

"Payback," I said pounding my fists and I started in toward Jasper before my friends even had a chance to try and hold me back.

Jasper was standing in front of his locker, his usual goons hanging around him. Sensing my presence, he stopped what he was doing and looked me up and down and snickered.

"What the hell do you want? You didn't get enough of an beat down the last time you approached me?"

"That was a long time ago, Jasper. Things are different now."

Jasper slammed his locker shut and faced me head on. He was a good 2 inches shorter than me.

"Oh really now?" he challenged.

"I'm not scared of you anymore."

"Prove it."

"Me and you. In the yard past the school. 10 minutes."

And with that, I left, Redd and Sean in tow.

As I was walking away, I decided to throw a little salt in the wound to further antagonize my opponent.

"And if you don't show, I understand. Then, I'll really know you're just a coward."

Jasper started in towards me as I walked out of the school, but his boys held him back.

"Da—mn!" Sean said as we headed toward the yard, "you told told him! But, Ty, can you really fight him?"

I brushed off my friend.

"I'm gonna wipe the floor with his behind."

"You sure," Redd chimed in, "you flaked the last time this happened."

Redd and Sean knew I'd been taking marital arts classes every afternoon but they had no idea that I'd been training with T.O.

"Yea, I don't know how much that martial arts crap is going to work on these guys," Sean said.

I stopped in my tracks to set my boys straight.

"First of all, that was a long time ago. I'm different now. I can take these guys. But, it would be nice if you guys could back me up sometime and do more than duck and weave."

"I'm a lover, not a fighter. I can let anyone mess up this pretty face," Sean said, stroking his waves.

"Fool, I could get my tail beat today and still get more loving than you," I said.

Redd busted a gut.

"True dat."

While we were clowning in the yard, we saw Jasper roll up with his crew, Jasper looking mad as hell. His angry face just got me more fired up. I couldn't wait to mess up that face.

"Surprised I showed?" he asked.

I shook my head.

"Not really. I didn't say you were a punk, but we will soon find out. Are you going to fight me yourself or do you need your boys to do the job for you?" Throwing off his backpack, Jasper got into a fighting stance, waving off his entourage.

"I don't need these fools to beat your tail."

I cracked a laugh.

"Little? You do realize I'm bigger than you, right?"

"Your mother---"and Jasper leaned in on me with his fist.

I ducked and punched him square in the mouth, drawing first blood.

By now, a small crowd had started gathering around us as kids from school learned that a fight was going on.

Jasper looked at me, shocked that I'd hit him, and even worse, that I'd made him bleed.

"Oh, that looks like it hurts," I teased, "you ready to run home to mommy now?"

Jasper came in again, but I was ready for him again.

I hit him with a combination uppercut that T.O. had taught me and weaved in some martial arts kicks I'd learned in class.

By the time I was done with Jasper, he was on the ground heaving, begging me to stop.

"Ty, please," he pleaded.

"Oh so you're begging now. Looks like the tables have finally turned. You'll think twice before you mess with me again, I bet."

I picked up my backpack and walked off with Redd and Sean.

"Ty! How did you learn how to fight like that? You whipped his butt!" Sean said excitedly.

"Yeah, can you teach me to fight like that? I mean, you already in good with the girls but I bet now they gonna be drooling over you even more," Redd said.

I smiled as we walked down the road. I was hesitant to do this when T.O. had suggested it at first, now I understood why he told me to do it. I needed to gain respect, and now I had it.

"Who taught you to fight like that for real, Ty?" Redd asked.

"T.O."

"T.O.?" Sean asked, "well, he can fight."

"Yeah, and he's been taking me to the boxing ring almost every day and training me. He didn't want to see me get beat up like I used to. So, yea, I can fight now."

"Well, damn brotha, you did your thing," he said as he fist pumped me.

We went our separate ways and I headed to our apartment complex where I saw T.O. hanging out with some of my other cousins outside.

"How'd it go?" he asked.

I just smiled.

"That good huh?" he said.

"I whipped his butt!"

T.O. bumped fists with me with approval.

"That's what I'm talking about," he said. Then he leaned in, lowering his voice.

"You think the girls are chasing you now. Just wait – and get ready to tap – that – back out."

I laughed bashfully.

Even though I was sexually active, mostly with girls much older than me, it still made me blush to talk about it with my cousin.

T.O. put his arm around me.

"I'm proud of you, cuz. You went out there and handled your business. Those kids won't see you as a punk no more."

"Nope," I said proudly before turning the conversation to something a little more serious.

I'd debated back and forth in my mind whether or not I wanted to approach him about the fight with Curtis, but T.O. and I had grown closer lately.

I'd always looked up to him, but now even more so. I needed to hear from him what happened and see what connections he might have to get me back in the game. I wanted to make more money.

"T.O.?"

"Yea, little man," T.O. said, smiling. He was in a good mood after my victory. Now was a good time to approach him about this.

"I need to ask you something."

"Shoot," he said.

"What happened between you and Curtis?"

The smile on his face quickly dissipated.

"You heard?"

"Redd and Sean told me that you beat him up pretty bad."

"Ty, that guy's bad news. You should have never got mixed up with him."

"T.O., I swear I didn't know anything about him. He asked me after school one day if I wanted to make some easy money. He said all I needed to do was some runs for him."

T.O. grabbed me by the collar.

"When I talked to you the other day, you admitted to doing a lot more than runs, Ty. Don't lie to me."

"I'm not lying T.O., I swear," I pleaded, "I started out making runs and then I started getting requests for packs so I started taking from the stash and selling some on the side. That's when Curtis told me that I could sell some packs for him and make more money. It wasn't him T.O., it was me."

T.O. released me, exasperated.

"Still little man, I don't want you mixed up in that. You're too smart for that crap."

We both stood there silent for a minute. I wasn't sure exactly where to take the conversation. I understood what T.O. was saying, but I needed to make the money. My family needed me.

"You weren't sniffing any of that crap, were you Ty?"

"No, no T.O. I just sold it, I swear."

Satisfied, T.O. backed down a bit.

"But, T.O…"

"But, what Ty?"

"I kind of need the money, T.O.," I said.

"Get a paper route like normal kids," T.O. said, "Damn!"

I felt bad. Bringing up this issue had completely changed his mood. I liked it better when he was happy.

"T.O., you know I can't make that kind of money with a paper route. Besides, it's not like you haven't done it. I've seen you."

T.O. was in my face.

"You just don't get it, do you? I don't want you to end up like me. You can be so much better than me, Ty? Don't look at me as an example."

What T.O. didn't realize was that he was all I looked at. I didn't have a father in my life, and T.O. was more like a big brother than a cousin. He always looked out for me, kept me tough when I needed to be. He was the only example I saw in the neighborhood, good or bad.

"T.O., you don't get it, either? I don't have a dad. You are an example. I look up to you. And, right now, I need to help out my mom. We don't have a lot of money. I just want things to be better than they are."

By now, tears had started to flow and I didn't realize it.

T.O. turned around and saw the emotion in my face.

"I guess I didn't realize things were that bad with you guys."

"Mom would never admit to it. She thinks it's okay, but look at me T.O. Look at my clothes. For once, I'd like to know what it would be like to eat Fruit

Loops instead of Toasted O's but that's not in the budget. I just want us to live a normal life like the other kids. I want to fix this. I can fix this."

"By selling drugs?"

I took a pause and lowered my head, because this was not a solution I was proud of but I'd gotten a taste of what it could do and it was hard to walk away.

"It's not what I want to do forever, but I do think it can help us out right now. Mom can never know, of course. But, if you don't want to help me, I'm just going to tell you, I'll find someone else to work for."

T.O. took a deep breath before making his next statement. I saw the frustration all over his face.

"No, don't do that. I know some guys that I can introduce you to, guys that are more decent than Curtis. But, I'm not happy about this, Ty. I really don't want you in this game. You gotta promise me that this is temporary until you save enough money to help out your mom. You get in, you get out, get it?"

Surprised that T.O. actually agreed to help me, I nodded.

"Yea, I got it."

"Good," he said, "go in the house to your mom. I'll make some calls and let you know what to do."

I started walking up the steps to the apartment building.

"Thanks T.O."

Lighting a joint before walking back toward his car.

"You can thank me when you promise me you've stopped all this mess. It's not a good life, Ty."

And, that was the start of my career as a dealer. It was that easy. Reluctantly, T.O. hooked me up with some dealers in the area that he felt comfortable with me working with. I'm sure he made some threats that if they crossed me, they'd have to answer to him, but luckily, I could defend myself pretty good these days as well, thanks to him. I pocketed the money that I was supposed to take back to Curtis.

I learned the game quickly and started to learn the best way to turn a profit. I went to school every day and sold rocks in between time. It was an effective business. Observing the other dealers I picked up on how to increase my profit margin. I started buying the coke myself in its pure form and cooked it myself at home and then took it to the street to sell rocks. At my young age, I learned the value of investing to make more money. I'd spend as much as $1,500 to buy the coke and once I cooked it and sold it, I made $3,000. Not a bad profit for a little kid! Because I was a little kid, I spent the money as I made it, buying pizza for my friends, buying gifts girls and buying nice suits and swag for my dates when I went out.

One thing you couldn't tell from looking at me was how much money I was actually making because I wore the same raggedly sweat suit and T-shirt when I went out to the street and sold.

"Look at Ty. He's such a bum," a lot of people would say.

I wasn't offended by these comments because those same people bought rocks from me. I dressed the way I did by design. I did not want to be in the streets in my best. No one needed to know my business or what I was doing. They just needed to know that if they needed rocks, see Fly Ty (that's what they called me). I'd gained respect from other dealers in the area. I had my area that I sold in, but if I was in another neighborhood, I never got any resistance from the dealers there. They all knew me as Little Ty and supported the little game I was running. I think part of it had to do with the word my cousin T.O. spread when he got me set up. Either way, I had a pretty nice set up.

Now, when I had a date with a nice girl, I did not dress like a bum. I dressed like a kid that expected to get some that night – and I did. I had my nice sneakers, Fendi suits and gold chains that I threw on just for these special occasions. And, these occasions were becoming more frequent as I started dating more women. Because women gave sex so freely to me, it became my impression that this was what relationships were all about. I'd never really seen any strong examples of male/female relationships in my household. The one relationship I observed with my mom was with my stepfather but he never really has a presence in our lives. My aunts had boyfriends but all of their relationships in my eyes were fleeting so I naturally never really understood what a healthy relationship consisted of. So, based on my own experience, I came to the conclusion that the only substance of a male/female relationship was sex. And, I tested that theory over and over and over again. So much so, that it wasn't long before I was introduced to early fatherhood.

Because of who my cousin T.O. was, I was in good with and hung around with all of the older guys in the neighborhood. I got to do things and go places at 13 and 14 that most guys don't get to do until they're in their early twenties; I attracted older women. Jackie caught my attention right away. Coke bottle body, long brown hair and beautiful eyes. She locked eyes with me at one of my boy's house parties one evening.

"Hey cutie," she said stroking my face, "what's your name?"

"Ty," I said flashing her my best smile.

"I've been hearing about you."

"Good things, I hope."

"Well, I hear that you are popular with the ladies."

"Well, I'm talking to you, so that must mean something. Can I get you a drink? What do you want?"

"Rum and coke," she said.

I went over to the kitchen and got a rum and coke for her.

"What's your name?" I asked as I handed her my version of the drink.

"Jackie," she said leaning forward giving me a good view of her boobs.

I didn't resist the invitation to look, she had a nice rack.

"So, Jackie, what kind of things have you been hearing about me from these chicks you talk about?"

Jackie swished her drink around a little bit, giving me a flirtatious grin.

"Just that you have some skills – for a kid."

I laughed sarcastically.

"You think I'm a kid?"

I knew I was a kid, but the attention that I was getting from the women along with my growing status in the streets was starting to give me a bit of swagger. I did not consider myself in the same league with kids my age. I considered myself a man.

"Well, you're like 14 or 15 right?" she asked.

"14" I clarified, "but, your friends are right. I'm not your average 14-year-old."

She sipped her drink, and then took a bigger gulp.

Leaning in closer she said, "Why don't you show me?"

Although shocked I said, "All I needed was an invitation. You got a place where we can chill?"

"Yea, we can to the Winds Motel. We don't need ID for that."

I already knew about the Winds Motel, but if she knew about it then I knew it was really about to go down.

I let my boys know I was leaving and then followed this brick house outside where we hopped into a cab to the motel.

Jackie showed me some things that night. I wasn't exactly the most experienced yet, but I was starting to get this sex thing down. At least I knew the difference between foreplay and the real thing now. But, Jackie, she did it all. Foreplay included everything from a blowjob to experimenting with positions. Jackie was 17 but she clearly had been around the block. That night was unforgettable and I definitely planned on using some of the things she taught me as I continued to build my sexual portfolio.

chapter 3
new responsibilities

About 5 months went by and I didn't expect to ever see Jackie again. I was in the streets after school doing my thing when I saw her, but she looked very different than the last time I'd seen her. Her coke bottle figure was replaced with a big pregnant belly.

"Yo Ty," Sean said, "isn't that the girl from the party a few months ago? That brick house you left with?"

I just looked as she walked over to us. Was that really her?

"Not a brick house anymore," another one of the guys weighed in.

"Hey Ty," she said.

"Hey..." I struggled to remember her name.

"Jackie," she finished my sentence.

"Jackie," I said, "yea, I knew that. How you doing?"

Jackie was not ready for any small talk.

"Fat and pregnant, or haven't you noticed?"

"I think we all noticed. So, how did you find me?"

"I asked around."

"Okay, so what do you want? I know it's not sex, looking at your current condition."

"No, but we did have sex. And, as you can see I'm pregnant, so we have some things to discuss."

I looked at her surprised.

"Oh, so you're saying it's mine?"

Jackie rolled her eyes.

"Yes, Ty, it's yours."

My boys started clowning in the background.

"Yo, Ty, you about to be a daddy?"

"Shut up," I said before facing Jackie, this time more serious, "so, you for real, this is my baby?"

"Yea, it's yours," she said as she took my hand and placed it on her round belly.

I felt the baby move. It was almost like there was an alien moving inside of her. Fascinated and freaked out a little at the same time, I drew my hand away.

"So, what do we do now?"

She shrugged her shoulders.

"I don't really know. This is my first time in a situation like this. I just thought you should know and was hoping that you would help me take care of it."

"Jackie, if this is my baby, I definitely want to take care of it. I never knew my father. That will never happen with my child."

Jackie leaned over and gave me a hug.

"Thank you. I'll be in touch."

"Okay."

I went home that night after my hustle with a heavy weight on my shoulders. At 14, I was about to be a father. Unfortunately, I did not know what being a good father involved because I'd never seen an example of that in my own life. What I did know was that my child would never have to grow up without me. I'll be damned if that would ever happen.

As much as I hated to do this, I needed to tell my mom. If I was going to father this child properly, I was going to need her help. I was too young to figure this out all by myself. Mom was sitting in the living room after dinner, and I slowly crept into the room, a little afraid to approach her. But, mother's intuition, she sensed me in the room before I was even in plain view.

"What's wrong Ty?"

"Hey mom," I said.

"Don't you, 'hey mom,' me. I saw you creeping around that corner. What do you want?"

"I need to tell you something."

Mom looked me in the eye, trying to read me.

"From your body language, it must not be good news. Did you get a girl pregnant or something?"

I stood there still and silent. How did she guess that quickly? I couldn't hide anything from her. It's no wonder she didn't know about my street hustle. But, I worked my hardest to keep that concealed from her. It would kill her if she knew I was dealing drugs.

I lifted my head and nodded.

"Dammit, Ty, I didn't even think you were having sex at this age. But, even so, don't you know to keep that thing wrapped up? You're too young to be dealing with something like this."

"I know, mom. I'm sorry."

I hated disappointing my mother.

"Who is the girl? Do we need to call her parents?"

"I don't know much about her parents. She's older than me. Her name is Jackie."

"How much older, Ty?"

"She's 17."

"Ty!"

I just stood there silently.

"Okay, we'll figure this out. I guess we've got some time. Do you know how far along she is?"

"Pretty far. She just told me today and she had a big belly."

Mom went into thinking mode.

"Okay, she's probably at least 6 months then. Alright, go on to bed. I need some time to process this. But, I do appreciate you being honest with me and letting me know about this so that I didn't have to find out from someone else. But there's a part of me that wants to beat the crap out you... What were you thinking Ty?"

I walked toward the hall to my bedroom.

"Ty," my mother called.

"Yes, mom."

"We all make mistakes, baby. Just know that no matter what, I'll always love you."

That made me smile.

"I love you, too, mom."

"But it doesn't mean that I don't wanna whoop your butt."

I know Mom was disappointed to learn that I was becoming a father at such a young age, yet it freed me to have everything out on the table with her. It was better for me to tell her now than to have Jackie show up at the house with my kid. Fact was, I really needed her. I was only 14 and didn't have the first clue as to how to take care of a kid, but I'll be damned if I would abandon this baby.

A couple of months went by and Jackie had the baby, a little boy. We named him Marcus. I took to fatherhood a lot easier than I thought. There's nothing that can quite describe the love you feel for your own child, even when you're just a child yourself. I remember looking at him right after he was born and making a vow to always be there for him.

And, I was, I took care of my son, probably more so than his mother. I vowed to have an active role in his life, and mom and me kept him at our house more than Jackie had him at hers. She was too busy going out drinking and smoking with her friends.

One afternoon, I had Marcus home with me, and was playing with him in the living room with my little sister, Diana. The doorbell rang and mom went to the door.

A messenger stood there, looking pretty official. I felt the blood in my veins almost going cold, thinking that someone had found out about me dealing.

"Is Ty Jenkins home?" he asked.

"Ty is my son. Can I help you?" my mother defended.

The messenger handed over a paper that looked like a court document.

"You've been served," and then he was gone.

I picked my son up and walked to my mom as she shut the door.

"Mom, what does that mean? What is that?" I asked pointing to the piece of paper in her hand.

She looked carefully over the court ordered subpoena.

"It says," she chose her words carefully as she tried to digest them herself, "that Jackie and her parents are taking you to court for child support."

"She what?" I exploded, startling my son and causing him to cry.

"Look what you did," my mom said taking the baby from my arms.

"Mom," I said, "she can't do this. This child has been with us since he has been born. We've taken care of him more than she has. I have not neglected my son."

My mom had moved into the kitchen to warm up a bottle for Marcus.

"Even so," she said, "she has that right. We just need to show up in court and prove that you have been a good parent to this child. At least – as good as a 14 year-old boy can be."

Furious did not even begin to channel my emotions.

I got on the phone with Jackie immediately.

"Hello."

"Just what the hell do you think you're doing?"

"Who is this?" Jackie asked.

"You know damn well who this is. And you know that I'm the only one taking care of our son."

"Oh," Jackie said nonchalantly, "Ty, I see you got the subpoena from the court."

"What are you doing?"

"I'm just getting what's mine. You may come and pick him up and play with him. But, Ty, a kid is not free. He needs clothes and milk and diapers."

"And, I've helped you buy all that for him. I've never failed to provide for my son."

"Well, it isn't enough."

"What else do you need?" I said getting more agitated the longer I was on the phone with her, "Why didn't you just come to me instead of taking me to court?"

"Because I know the court will make you pay."

I couldn't continue to have a conversation with this girl or I was going to cuss her out and my mom was right there. Instead, I just chose to take the high road and end the conversation.

"Whatever Jackie, if you want to go court, then we'll go to court. But, I can tell you this – you're not going to win." And, then I hung up the phone.

There was no way she was going to portray me as an unfit father. I may be young, but I handled my business.

Our case went to family court because it was over child support. I'd never been in a courtroom before, and I honestly never had any desire to come back again.

My mom and I walked into this expansive room with high ceilings and the smell of old mahogany. The judge had not yet arrived in the courtroom, but his place was perched in the center of the room, elevated above everyone else. The bailiff stood to the right of the judge platform.

Jackie and her family sat on the plaintiff side while we sat on the defendant side, like we were damn criminals. The bailiff announced the judge and I stood with my mom and our court appointed attorney as a man in a long, flowing black robe walked in and took his place.

I already felt small, standing behind the small wood table with my mom, ready to be judged. The judge asked to hear Jackie's case first. She lied and claimed that she needed support to care for the child and that I had not been supporting him financially.

I'd been told by my mom and our attorney to be silent and let them handle communication with the judge and so I was, although it was very difficult with Jackie up there telling lies on me. The judge could see how uncomfortable I was, so he asked for my direct testimony after hearing from my mom and our attorney.

"Young man, would you care to tell me what you have done for this child since he was born?"

Not expecting a chance to speak during this appearance, I looked over to my mom and attorney for approval before speaking.

They both nodded their approval for me to speak.

"Well, Mr. Judge," I said, "I have been there for this child since the day he was born; and I'd never want my own child to go through life not knowing his father. My mom and I have been taking care of him since he was born."

"I'm not making a ruling on this case until a blood test is administered verifying the paternity of this child. We will reconvene once results of this test are received."

He banged his gavel and we were done for the day.

I walked out of the room that day a little confused. Why would the judge order a blood test? Marcus was my son.

About six weeks later, after I'd completed my blood test as the judge had instructed, my mom and I were told to come back to court so that the judge could give his ruling on the case. My mind was all over the place. I honestly did not know what to expect. I was angry with Jackie for demanding child support for our son when I know that I've been nothing but a good father to our child.

My mom and I walked back into the cold, intimidating courtroom. Our lawyer was seated behind the mahogany desk on one side of the courtroom. We walked over to join him.

My mom whispered something I could not hear to our lawyer and then the judge entered the courtroom. Everyone stood to acknowledge him and then we took a seat.

The judge looked at Jackie and then at me, a wave of disappointment on his face. I was thinking it was because we were both so young.

"This is a case of child support from this young man, Mr. Jenkins. During our last meeting, I ordered a blood test to confirm the paternity of the child in question. Do we have the results of this test?"

The bailiff walked over to the judge and handed him a sealed envelope.

The judge paused for a moment, put on his glasses and opened the envelope.

He pored over its contents for a moment before announcing anything.

"Ty Jenkins," he said, "you are not the father of this child. This case is dismissed."

He banged his gavel and prepared to exit the courtroom, but before he was fully out of the room, I leapt across the table in an attempt to strangle Jackie.

"Trick," I yelled going after her before a few bailiffs grabbed me and detained me while she exited the courtroom.

The judge came over to me where bailiffs had forced me down in one of the court room pews.

To my surprise, he sat down beside me.

I was still fuming, breathing erratic. I tried to calm my breathing so that I could talk to the judge.

I looked up at him, pain in my eyes. Marcus had been my son. I loved that kid. I took care of him almost every day. Now, he wasn't even mine.

The judge placed a compassionate arm around my shoulder.

"I know you are a little emotional right now. From what I heard in your testimony, you took care of this child and became quite attached. Is that right?"

I nodded my head yes, tears forming in the corners of my eyes.

"Listen to me son," he said, "Consider this a blessing. You're a very young man, and damn near a baby yourself. Focus on your education and making a life for yourself. You dodged a bullet this time. Next time you might now be so lucky.

If you're out there having sex with girls, wrap it up. You hear me?"

I nodded yes.

He squeezed his arms around me a little tighter.

"You're going be alright," he said and then he got up, instructed the guards to let me go and exited to his chambers.

I went home with my mom that night, the words of the judge resonating in my ears. "You dodged a bullet this time." He was right. I was too young to be a father, but I was willing to step up and be a father to my child and Jackie had played me. It hurt really badly, because I really loved that kid. Now, I had to get used to life without him.

But, maybe the judge was right. Maybe I really did dodge a bullet this time. I needed to learn how to be more careful. I didn't need to be a childhood father.

chapter 4
faith tested

With my growing confidence in the streets, I found myself getting jaded and cocky. Cocky because I'd learned how to fight and defend myself in the streets and I held my own with the ladies. But, I was jaded because I never really understood why things kept happening to me, like the situation with Jackie. I found myself getting into a lot of trouble in school. If someone had the slightest thing to say to me, I was ready to fight. It had gotten so bad that my mom even called my stepfather in to talk to me which was rare because I really didn't see him that often.

I saw him pull up to the apartment complex after I'd come home from school one day.

"Hey little man," he said as he got out of his car.

"What's up, S.T.?" I said giving him a fist bump.

Even though he wasn't around that much, I liked S.T. He was cool when he was here.

"Your mom wanted me to talk to you?" he said,

I sat down next to him, kind of knowing where this conversation was going, but played dumb anyway.

"What about?"

He gave me a look that said, you know why boy, and I conceded.

"I know. I'm getting into too many fights in school," I said with my head down.

"What's going on with you, Ty? Are the kids still picking on you?"

I shook my head and poked out my chest like a proud peacock.

"No, that doesn't happen anymore. The kids are scared of me."

"So, why you beating them up?" he asked.

I quickly defended myself.

"If I beat someone up, it's because they deserve it, S.T."

S.T. just lowered his head, shaking it back and forth.

"Ty, you gotta stop getting in so many fights. You're getting in too much trouble at school, and it's stressing your mother out."

I sat there silently.

"You don't want to upset your mother, do you?" he asked.

I shook my head yes.

"Then, cool it with all this fighting, you hear?"

I nodded yes.

"Good," he said patting me on the head before getting up from the steps, "now let me see what your mother is up to."

I took to heart what S.T. said to me because I actually respected him. He was one of the few father figures I had in my life, even though he was barely around. I worked hard over the next couple of months to clean up my act and it was working. I wasn't getting into any trouble. Things were going pretty good.

But, one day a fight broke out in the middle of English class. The two guys that got into the fight were actually friends of mine but they had major beef with each other. One of them had talked just enough crap to send my boy over the edge and the first punch was thrown. The fight started getting crazy. Both of them were all over the floor, up against the chalkboard. It was hard not to suffer any collateral damage in this fight. Seeing how crazy it was getting, I tried to jump in to break up the fight. Ms. Lewis, the English teacher, had immediately run out to get help because she couldn't control the mob in the classroom.

In the meantime, I was still working to separate my two friends, unfortunately unsuccessfully, while a mob of other students surrounded me. It was chaos. As I kept tugging on my friends, trying to separate them and end this mess, I felt someone grab me from behind. Thinking it was another student trying to spin another fight off this one, I acted on impulse, punching the assailant in the face sending them right through the atrium window of the classroom.

What I didn't realize was that I'd just punched the assistant principal of the school. He'd come back in the room with Ms. Lewis to try and break up the fight. Unfortunately, you can't get away with punching the assistant principal without consequences, even if it was by mistake. I was suspended for a week, but even worse than that, the school took out a PINNS petition on me. A PINNS petition was essentially a petition that says the child needs more guidance than they can receive at home and has to be settled at family court. As a result, we had to go to an emergency hearing where I did not really get to say much. I was pretty much a sentence from the judge once he heard what happened. He sentenced me to go to a place called McQueen. It was a maximum-security group home and it was 3 hours from my home in upstate New York. Minus the bars, it was essentially a prison for kids.

We all had our own rooms but when we turned in and went to bed at night, the doors locked behind us. If we needed to get up in the middle of the night to go to the bathroom, we had to knock on the door and one of the staff members outside would open it to allow us outside. Even the windows were locked with a special lock that only the guards had access to.

The good thing about this place was I still got to go to school. I actually did okay here. I made good grades. I didn't have to worry about anyone messing with me. For the most part, everyone was nice. They also offered counseling and they taught trades, which was impressive since we were just young teenage boys.

Despite the circumstances, things were going okay for me. I was thriving here, though I did miss my family and my friends. Out of the blue, one day the head counselor, program director and psychologist called me into one of the main offices. This concerned me because these people usually only got involved when someone was in trouble.

I walked into the room cautiously, eyes darting curiously, from one person to the other.

"What did I do? I thought I was being good," I said sounding concerned.

The psychologist walked forward and put her hand on my back gently.

"Hi Ty, you've been doing great. You're not in trouble. Why don't you have a seat?" she said.

I hesitated for a moment; eyes still darting back and forth at all three people in the room. The program director motioned for me to take a seat on the couch next to him. I sat down.

"If I didn't do anything, why did you ask me to come here? What's wrong?" I knew something was wrong; I just didn't know what it was.

The head counselor was sitting in a chair across from me. She leaned forward and took my hands in hers kindly.

"Ty," she said, "we have some news about your mother."

Immediately, my mind went to the worst possible scenario. Oh my god! My mom is dead! I knew it was a bad idea to come here. She needed me and I abandoned her. I started to think of all of the things I hadn't told her. I worried that she didn't know how much I loved her. I felt ashamed for the grief that I'd caused her by getting into fights and having to come out here. This was my fault. I started crying uncontrollably.

The psychologist immediately embraced me, taking me in her arms to comfort me. They all gave me a moment to gather myself together before saying anything.

"She's dead, isn't she?" I cried, unable to stop the flow of tears.

"Oh my god, no," the head counselor said immediately dispelling my fears.

Then she picked up a box of tissues and handed them over to me.

I grabbed a few and started to wipe the tears from my face.

"She's not?' I asked, a small smile and sigh of relief forming. But, then I quickly snapped back to reality. Something was wrong, though. Why else would they bring me in here with all three of these guys? I wiped my eyes and straightened my spine.

"Then, why am I here? What's wrong?"

The psychologist placed her hand gently on my back.

"Your mom is going to have a serious surgery in a couple of days, and she wanted us to let you know beforehand so you could talk to her. She has cancer. She..."

I didn't hear anything else she said after the word cancer. There was no way. My mom couldn't have cancer. She was a good person. Things like this don't happen to people like her. Cancer killed people. The tears started streaming again. My imagination was getting the best of me and it was not in a good way.

"Ty," I finally heard the counselor saying.

I don't know how long he or any of the other people in the room had been speaking to me. I'd unconsciously blocked them out. I was in a state of shock. I needed to see my mom. I stared at everyone in somewhat of a daze.

"Ty, sweetheart, are you okay?" the psychologist asked me, still rubbing the small of my back.

I wiped my tears for the second time in the last 10 minutes.

"I need to talk to her," I said resolutely.

I needed to know if this was real. I prayed that I was in the middle of a bad dream and I'd wake up soon.

"Of course," the program director said, "like we said earlier, that's the reason we brought you in here, so that you can talk to her. Do you feel okay to talk to her right now, or do you need a little time?"

The sooner I spoke to her, maybe the sooner I'd wake up. This wasn't real. I was dreaming. I was sure of it.

"I'm okay. I'd like to talk to her now."

"Okay," the program director said. He took me over to the phone on the desk, motioned for me to sit and began to dial the number.

Part of me didn't even want her to answer. I wanted to talk to her but I was afraid of the conversation. I was afraid of losing her. She was the most important person in my life. The only person who'd loved me through all of my screw-ups in life. I doubted the motives and the love of a lot of people in my life, including family, but I'd never doubted my mother's love. She loved me through everything. I couldn't imagine life without her.

"Ms. Sandra, hello, this is Patrick, the program director over here at McQueen. We've just spoken with Ty. He's right here and he's ready to speak with you."

Patrick handed the phone over to me.

I hesitated for a moment. I needed answers, needed to speak to her, but for some reason, I was nervous.

Patrick walked toward the door. The counselor and psychologist had already left the room.

"I'll give you two some privacy," he whispered as he closed the door.

"Mom," I said into the receiver faintly.

"Hey baby," she said, her voice full of love. It had been a while since I'd heard my mother's voice. I just wanted to feel her arms around me right now.

"Is it true," I said, tears forming again in the creases of my eyes, "what they said?"

I could not bring myself to repeat what they'd said. I could not even form the words with my lips.

"Yes baby," she said, "I'm going to have surgery in a couple of days. The doctors are very positive that they will be able to remove all of it and I can be healthy again."

I blinked my eyes. I wanted to wake up. This wasn't a dream. It was real. My mom was sick – really sick.

"So, it's really true? You have c-c-c…"

"Cancer," my mom finished my sentence, "it's okay baby, and you can say it. It doesn't have power over me. It's in the Lord's hands and I believe he will heal me."

I couldn't speak. I was going through shock all over again. Then, the tears started rolling again. My mom couldn't have cancer. She just couldn't.

"Ty, baby, are you alright?"

I tried to get myself together. I needed to be strong – for mom.

"How long have you known?" I asked.

My mom paused for a little bit, telling me that she'd known longer than a few days.

"I've known for a few months now," she said.

"A few months?" I almost yelled into the phone, "Mom – why didn't you tell me before they sent me here?"

"Ty," she said, "I didn't want you to worry. With everything that has been happening lately, I was afraid you would react badly and just get into more trouble. I honestly thought you'd be here with me but it's okay, I hear that you've been doing good over there and I want you to continue to do good so you can come home. You don't need to be stressed out and worried about your old mother."

60

"But, mom, I'm worried now," said, growing more concerned about my mom by the minute, "I need to be there with you."

"Baby, you don't need to worry about me. I've been going through treatment for the last couple of months. And, now they just have to do surgery to remove the last of everything. I'm in the home stretch. I want you to focus on finishing your time there. I'll be fine. Your aunts will be here with me for my surgery on Thursday. I won't be alone."

I started looking around the room I was in, desiring an escape. My mom needed me.

"Wh-where is the c-cancer?" I said, asked, barely able to get the words out of my mouth.

"It's breast cancer," my mom answered directly.

I was silent for a moment. I didn't know how to process this.

"I need to be there with you, mommy," I said crying, "I've got to get out of here."

"Listen to me, Ty," she said sternly, "I don't want you to do anything crazy. I told you that I will be okay. I need you to stay out of trouble. You'll be home before you know it. In the meantime, I will have one of your aunts call you when I'm out of surgery, okay?"

"Okay," I said, sniffling.

"And, then as soon as I'm strong enough, I'll call you myself, alright baby? I love you so much."

Mom and I talked for a while longer, at least an hour from what I can remember. It was the most emotionally charged conversation of my life. When I got off the phone, the psychologist came in the room to check on me but I insisted that I was okay, so she allowed me to go back into the group home with the other kids.

But, she probably I probably should have talked to her. Not even 2 hours after getting off the phone with my mom, I got into a pretty big fight with one of the guys in the home. It was pretty intense. We pretty much rearranged the room we were in. The counselors broke us up and immediately sent me to my room. The funny thing is, I cannot even remember what started the fight. Right now, I just felt like a ticking time bomb ready to go off. I needed to get out of this place.

I needed to see my mom. She needed me. What if the surgery goes wrong and I never get a chance to see her? I couldn't bear it. I needed an escape.

I laid in my bed that night thinking about how I would get out this place. It would not be any easy task. This place was on pretty tight lock down, but it wasn't a jail. There were no bars or barbed wire. If I could just manage to find a way out of my room at night, I might have a shot.

The next day, I was very careful to survey my surroundings while walking around the campus. My observant eye began to notice every little detail of how this place was laid out. My plan was in place.

It was lights out. Doors were closed and locked, and the counselors had already made their first rounds. It was about 1am. I reached under my pillow and retrieved a small tool I'd found on campus that would help me to unlock the window.

I climbed up to the window and used the tool to unlock it. Before climbing out, I looked back and saw my roommate looking right at me.

"I swear Vernon, if you breathe a word about this to anybody, I will kill you," I said.

Vernon immediately backed down, placing his hands up in surrender.

"Naw Ty, I'm not telling anybody. I understand. You need to go see your mom. I'd do the same thing if I were you. Go ahead. If anyone asks, I didn't see anything. I was sleep."

I nodded at my roommate in approval of his plan and then proceeded to climb out of the window.

I looked around and didn't see anyone patrolling, so I made a run for it. I started down the mountain. I kept going and going. I'd always heard a train when I was walking around outside so this was my target. I came to a creek. I kept going, getting my clothes muddy and dirty in the process, but nothing was going to stop me. I was on a mission. I just kept going. Eventually, I reached the metro train station. I'm not sure how far I'd walked at this point but I knew it had been miles.

I was glad to have reached my target, but how was I going to get on the train. I had no money. I needed to get on that train. That was the only way I was going to get to my mom. Think Ty, Think!

I ran up to the attendant on the train.

"Please, please, mister, I need your help. A man is trying to hurt me. I need to get home to Yonkers. P-Please help me!"

The attendant started looking around the station for my assailant, immediately motioning for me to get on the train.

"Come on son, get on, quick," he said.

I got on the train, smiling inside, at my theatrical performance.

He motioned for me to take a seat on the train.

"You just take a seat here," he said.

By that time, the conductor had come to check on the situation.

"Is everything okay?" he asked.

The attendant explained my situation to him and they immediately called the police.

"It's going to be okay, little buddy. We just called the cops and we'll get you home to your parents in Yonkers. No one is going to hurt you," the conductor said.

I breathed a sigh of relief because I'd almost made it. But, Yonkers was not the destination I was seeking. I needed to go to White Plains where the hospital was. I knew this metro line passed through White Plains so I would need to sneak off the train at this stop without being noticed.

I knew that I had a little bit of a ride before we reached White Plains so I took a little breather. It had been a very long night and I was exhausted. I closed my eyes for a brief moment.

"White Plains!" I heard the conductor announce.

I opened my eyes and immediately surveyed my surroundings. The conductor was not in my section of the train and the attendant had moved to a different section as well. The train stopped and people started getting off. Luckily this was a popular stop so a lot of people were getting off the train. I ran and wedged myself in between the crowd and was able to get off the train undetected amongst the large crowd.

I got off the train, remembering this stop vividly when my mom and I used to take the train to the hospital when she used to work there. We used to take the bus to the hospital because it was about 4 miles from the train station, but I did not have that luxury tonight, so I began the 4-mile trek. Long as the walk might have seemed under normal circumstances, I was going off pure adrenaline. I needed to see my mom. As I walked the last block, I saw the hospital in the distance and breathed a sigh of relief.

I'd made it! Anxious to get to my mother, I picked up my pace to a quick jog until I reached the doors of the hospital. When I walked into the hospital entrance, I glanced at the clock and noticed that it was almost 10:00 in the morning. It had been a long night, but I wasn't even tired. I just needed to see my mom. That was all that mattered at this moment.

As I walked further into the hospital, I heard my name in the distance.

"Ty?"

I froze for a moment, afraid that someone had caught up to me to take me back to McQueen, or the cops had tracked me down from my train ride.

The voice rang out again.

"Ty!"

I recognized that voice. I turned around slowly. It was Ms. Nancy. She'd worked with my mom back when she used to work at this hospital. She ran over to me and started inspecting me immediately.

"Sweetheart," she said, caressing my dirty face, "how did you get here?"

She waved me off before I really had a chance to come up with a story.

"Never mind that. You are filthy. Let's get you cleaned up and out of these clothes."

She went through their stash and was able to find me a clean sweatshirt and sent me to the bathroom to clean up. As I was heading to the bathroom, she went to the nurse's station and picked up the phone.

"I'm going to call your family. The whole world is probably looking for you by now."

As she picked up the phone, I ran over to her from the bathroom door and pleaded.

"Pl-ease Ms. Nancy, don't call my family. They'll just send me back and I need to see my mom. She needs me, ple-ase."

Ms. Nancy hesitated, holding the phone in her hand. She could see how desperate I was and slowly put the phone down.

"Okay, go get cleaned up. But, I will at least need to call one of your aunts to let you know you're here."

Happy with her solution, I went to the bathroom to clean up. I started to clean the mud and dirt that had gotten all over me as I trekked through the creek to get to the train station. Last night was an adventure but I was totally okay if I never had to go through anything like that again. All I wanted was to see my mom's face. I couldn't take it anymore.

I came out of the bathroom and my Aunt Missy was standing there waiting on me.

"Ty," she said, "how in the world did you get here? The school didn't let you out, did they?"

I just stood there sheepishly.

"Ty?" my aunt's voice got a bit sterner.

"I talked to mom a couple of days ago. She told me that she had c-cancer. I couldn't just stay there while she went through surgery. Mom needs me. I had to be here," and the tears started again.

My aunt engulfed me in a huge embrace, wiping my tears.

"It's okay, baby," she said, "We'll figure everything out later. Your mom is in surgery right now. You can see her as soon as she gets out. In the meantime, you can wait out here with these ladies until she gets out. I don't want to bring you around your other aunts and the family because they are just going to start asking questions about how you got here. So, you just stay right here where you are for right now, okay?"

I nodded in agreement.

My aunt went over to Ms. Nancy and talked to her for a couple of minutes.

"I'll be right back here as soon as your mom is out of surgery and then you can see her, okay?"

"Okay."

I waited there with Ms. Nancy and the rest of the hospital staff for what seemed like an eternity. The clock on the wall taunted me with its slow ticks every minute. During that time, I started to let my imagination get the best of me. As exhausted as my body was from running all night, sleep was the last thing that was on my mind. My mind was active, awake, thinking about what my mom was going through with every tick of the clock. What if she didn't make it out of this?

How dangerous was this surgery? Would she still be the same afterwards? I was so scared. I just wanted to be there with her, holding her hand, telling her that I loved her.

My battle with sleep was lost after 2 hours of waiting.

"Ty," I heard as someone lightly tapped my shoulder.

I slowly opened my eyes and saw the silhouette of my Aunt Missy through blurred vision.

"Ty," she said, "your mother is out of surgery. You can go see her now."

I jumped up from my seat, anxiously. I'd never been more excited to see my mother ever in my life.

My aunt guided me through the hospital, to a private room where I saw my mother lying in a hospital bed sleeping.

"Go ahead," she said, "she's sleeping right now but you can sit with her."

I walked in and took a seat beside my mom. She looked so peaceful sleeping there.

My heart rate finally slowed. I'd been so anxious the last couple of days, and I felt a sense of peace just seeing her there, sleeping. I reached out and gently held her hand. I was home.

I'm not sure how much time passed by because once again, the fatigue from the last 24 hours set in and I'd laid my head by my mom's beside and fallen asleep.

"Ty," I heard my mother's voice. It was soft and weak.

I lifted my head from the bed and looked at her with a smile.

I'd never been so happy to see her staring back at me in my life.

But, her expression said something completely different.

"What are you doing here?"

"Mom, I had to be here. I needed to be here with you."

"How did you get here? Never mind. I'm not even sure if I wanna know. Did you talk to one of your aunts?"

"Yes," I nodded, "Aunt Missy is the one who let me in here. She didn't tell anybody else because she was afraid they'd make too much of a fuss about me being here."

My mom shifted in the bed a little bit, wincing in pain.

I reached out to her in concern and she steadied my hand, assuring me that she was fine.

"Your Aunt Missy is a smart woman. Your other aunts will just cause more drama and I'm sure the whole world is already looking for you because I'm

66

sure you did not leave the school with their permission, did you Ty?"

I lowered my head, afraid of disappointing my mom.

"No, "I answered.

"Don't worry, baby," she said, "I know you were just worried about me. We'll figure it out."

I stayed in the room with my mom all night. I had all that I really wanted, to be with her. The doctors had gotten the cancer and it looked like she was on the road to being cancer-free but she had a long road of recovery ahead of her. She had to stay in the hospital for a week and my mom and my aunt somehow worked it out so that I could stay right there with her where I wanted to be. I stayed there every night, and Ms. Nancy and the other ladies at the hospital made sure I was well taken care of.

Each day I could see my mom getting a little bit stronger, in a little less pain from surgery. When she went home, I helped her get settled back in and took care of her along with my aunts while she worked on getting her strength back. When she was strong enough, she called an emergency hearing with family court to address my situation with McQueen.

When we walked into the courtroom, my spine stiffened, afraid of what would happen. I did not want to go back to McQueen. My mom still needed me. She wasn't 100% and I was taking care of her.

There was a representative from McQueen in the court who gave a full statement of when I got the news about my mother and the scene of events that followed the news, including my fight and escape from the premises. The only feather in my cap is that I'd pretty much demonstrated good behavior prior to learning about my mother.

After the case was presented and my mother recommended that I be allowed to come home, the judge made his ruling.

"Facilities like McQueen are designed to help rehabilitate young men like Ty. However, I feel that we've made a mistake removing this child from his mother, the only person he really believes cares for him. I think he is better off with her and may be subject to getting into more trouble if we continue separate them. Therefore, I'm ruling that this child go home with his mother, permanently."

And, with the bang of the gavel, it was done. I could go home. I didn't have to go back to McQueen. I could continue to stay with my mother and take care of her. I turned around and hugged my mother, thankful for this second chance.

I went back home with my mom and really just chilled out for a while. I kept things low key in school and didn't get into trouble. I focused on looking after my mom and making sure she had a good, speedy recovery. I didn't want to do anything to add any grief to her life. She deserved more.

I got back to hustling, especially since my mom was out of work for a little while recovering from surgery. I knew we needed the money, so I fell back into my old routine pretty easily. My old routine also included messing with a steady stream of girls. My appetite for sex continued to grow the more I got it. It was almost becoming an addiction.

After my scare with Jackie, I tried to be careful, but my thirst was becoming more insatiable the more I experimented. At 14, I met Robin. Unlike most of the girls that I messed around with, she was younger around 13 and a virgin. But, she wanted me. So, we experimented together and I took her virginity.

About 7 months later, I had a repeat of almost the same scenario that happened with Jackie. Robin showed up at my apartment complex, with a round, pregnant belly.

"This is getting to be a thing for you," Redd said.

"Shut up," I said as I walked toward her.

My boys took off to give us some privacy. Despite being burned by Jackie a year ago, I knew the child Robin was carrying was my baby. She told me that she was a virgin when we got together and because I'd already had some experience with older women, I could tell. This was my baby.

She came to me and we just stood there in silence for a moment. I didn't need to ask her if the baby was mine.

"Why didn't you tell me?"

Robin just shook her head.

"I don't know. I was scared, I guess. I wasn't sure what to do. My mom doesn't even know yet."

I looked at her big, pregnant belly, and then back at her in complete shock.

"What??" I said, "Do you stay at the same house as your mom?"

She nodded.

"Then how in the hell does she not notice this?" I said pointing at her protruding belly.

She shook her head.

"I don't know, but she doesn't. Or, at least she hasn't said anything to me. So, what are we going to do?"

I scratched me head.

"Well, I'm going to help you take care of it. Do you know about how far along you are?"

"I'm about 8 months."

"Okay, I'm going to have to break this to my mom so she knows and we'll help you take care of the baby."

chapter 5
becoming a father

Telling my mom wasn't as hard the second time. What was hard was seeing the disappointment on her face. She'd hoped that I learned my lesson with Jackie and I hoped that, too. Unfortunately, that did not stop me from wanting to be with all of these girls, especially when they were throwing themselves at me the way they did. Far be it from me to turn away free coochie.

And, even though I knew Robin was going to have my kid, I still continued to indulge in my free sexual lifestyle. By the time my son was born, I was sleeping with about 5 different women, all older than me. I had an attraction to older women and they to me. Robin and I getting together was a bit out of the norm for me since she was about a year younger than me.

When Anthony was born, my mother insisted that we get a paternity test because of what had happened with Jackie just a year ago. I went along with it, although I knew this kid was mine. I could tell the first time I held him in my arms. He had my eyes and my nose. A few weeks after he was born, the test came back positive. He was mine. My mom was satisfied and disappointed at the same time. I think she was hoping I would catch a lucky break like I did with Jackie, but I knew this was only bound to happen once with the amount of sex I was having on a regular basis.

With new responsibilities on my plate, I continued to get a little deeper in the drug game. My desire to make money went beyond just trying to help my mom out and get some nice sneakers every now and then. I had a son that needed diapers, formula and clothes and I knew my mom would do whatever she could to help support him but he was my responsibility. I needed more, and so I kept selling rocks, and I must have been doing pretty well, too, because I got my first opportunity to go out of state to sell.

"Yo Ty," Jax, the dealer I'd been working for approached me after school one afternoon.

"Jax, what's up man?"

"I like what you been doing," he said as he lit a cigarette, "so I've got an opportunity for you to sell more rocks and make a little more cash. Interested?"

Interested? I had another mouth to feed now.

"Yes," I said without hesitation.

"Great," he said, "me and the boys are planning a trip out to PA. We're leaving this weekend. Do you think you can get an excuse to tell your mom to get out of town?"

"I'll think of something," I said, already thinking of a story to concoct for mom.

"Great," he said, "we leave tomorrow night. Be ready."

With a brand new baby, I wanted to make sure someone would be able to look after Robin and my son while I was gone for a couple of days, so I reached out to my boy Paulie. Paulie and I had been friends for several years now, and I knew he had my back when I needed him. He came by the apartment that night after I'd told my mom that I was going on a trip with T.O. to hang out for the weekend.

"What's up man?" he said.

"Nothing much," I said, "You hear I got a son now?"

"Yeah, I know. Is this one really yours?"

"Yea," I said, smiling, "he's mine. Mom made Robin get a paternity test."

"Can you blame her?" he asked.

"Nah, I guess not. After the situation with Jackie, you never can be too careful. Anyway, I wanted you to do me a favor."

"Anything man. What do you need?"

"Jax just asked me to go on a run with him over in PA this weekend. It's a chance for me to score a little more cash, and with a little one, you know I could use all the money I can get right now. Robin just came home with the baby about week ago. I just wanted to know if you can just look out for her and my son while I'm gone."

"Of course, man. I got you."

"Thanks," I said giving him a quick hug, "I just want to make sure she's ok because she's just getting used to having a baby at home and it can be a bit overwhelming, you know."

"Yea."

"I really appreciate it, man."

The PA trip was very lucrative. We were able to sell most of our stash and I was able to come home with a good amount of cash in my pocket, cash Robin and I needed for diapers and formula and all the things that babies needed.

I was looking forward to coming home to see my boy. Even though I was new to fatherhood and it was more responsibility than I was really ready for at my age, there was something special about it. I loved my son.

My buddy, Paulie, was a little bit older than me, around 18, and he had a place of his own. It was late when Jax and the crew got back in town so I had them drop me by Paulie's so I could check on things and see how my son was doing.

I walked into the building and heard the sound of a party.

"Yo Paulie," I said as I got ready to knock on the door, but the door the slowly creaked open on its own.

Public Enemy's "Don't Believe the Hype" was blaring over the stereo speakers in Paulie's tiny one-bedroom apartment. The small space with packed with people in every square inch, the couch, the balcony and the kitchen. The smell of marijuana was in the air, but that is not what caught my attention. What caught my attention was my newborn son on the floor of his filthy apartment, inches away from a crack pipe.

Fuming, I ran to pick up my son.

"Paulie," I yelled.

I looked around the apartment, out on the deck where his friends were drinking and smoking, toting my son in my arms.

"Paulie, you punk!" I yelled, "Get your butt out here now!"

I continued combing the apartment. Seeing how angry I was, and knowing my reputation for fighting in the neighborhood, everyone moved out of my way as I headed to the bedroom.

I slammed open the door, and as angry as I was, I don't think anything could have prepared me for what my eyes actually saw.

My friend Paulie was having sex with my girl, Robin. In shock, I held my breath for a moment, but the soft gargle of my newborn son caught both of their attention.

"Ty," Robin yelled, immediately covering her breasts with the bed sheet.

I stood there, staring, fire in my eyes.

"Get dressed and take our son. I've got some business to handle," I said, not taking my eyes of Paulie, my friend, the man I'd trusted to take care of my girl and my son. The man who chose instead to sleep my girl while my baby lay on a drug infested floor.

I was well past angry.

"Would you like to get dressed before I beat the crap out of you? I'll wait."

"Ty," Paulie begged, "I can explain."

"I'll give you 5 minutes to get yourself dressed so that I can beat your ass with a little bit of dignity. If you don't come out in 5 minutes, I'm coming for you."

Robin had gotten dressed by now, and I waved for her to come out of the room with my son.

We both stepped out and I closed the door.

Robin looked at me, tears in her eyes.

"Ty, I'm sorry, I…" she started.

I just held up my hand to silence her. I was tired of hearing excuses. I was over it.

"What the hell are you doing here anyway? Why aren't you home with our son? Instead, I come here and find him on the floor next to a crack pipe. What the hell, Robin?"

"He was sleep when I got here. I just needed somewhere to lay him. This place is small and one of my friends said she'd watch him while I…"

"While you had sex with Paulie," I finished her sentence.

Then, she just started crying. I had no sympathy for her since she had no loyalty for me.

Paulie walked slowly from the bedroom, a timid look on his face.

I pounded my fist.

"You ready to take your whipping like man?" I said.

Robin ran in between us, trying to keep the peace.

"Ty, you really don't have to do this," she cried.

"Get out of my way, Robin," I said as I pushed her out of the way and went right in for Paulie, with a swift uppercut to the jaw.

He was down.

"Get up," I said, "you earned this fight."

Paulie slowly got up and wiped the blood from his cut lip.

"Ty, we don't have to do this," he said.

I laughed a sarcastic chuckle.

"Oh Paulie, I think we do."

"Fine," he said conceding, "suit yourself."

He came in for a punch; I ducked and punched him in his stomach.

He doubled over on the floor, wind knocked out of him.

"Get up, punk," I said advancing toward him.

Paulie scrambled to his feet and I proceed to pummel him with combination after combination, learned from my cousin T.O. and the numerous street fights I'd now been in, fueled by pure rage. I only stopped when a couple of guys pulled me off of him.

"Ty man, that's enough. You got him," I heard them say.

I backed away and wiped my lip, the side of effect of one punch Paulie was able to land during our fight.

I looked over at Robin in disgust, grabbed my son and left the apartment, Robin running after me.

It wasn't even 2 weeks after this incident before I received a call at my house one evening after school. I'd just come home from selling rocks after school.

75

My mom was in the kitchen cooking dinner for my sister and me so I picked up the phone.

"Hello."

"You need to come get this kid."

"What?" I said confused, as I couldn't quite make out the voice.

"Ty, your son will not stop crying. He is driving me crazy. I don't want him anymore. You need to come and get him."

I didn't even argue with her. I did not want her anywhere near my son if she didn't want him.

"Fine," I said, "when can I come and get him?"

"Now," she said and hung up the phone.

Mom was putting dinner on the table by the time I got off the phone.

"Ty, who was that?"

"Robin," I said, sounding agitated, "Mom, we need to go get Anthony."

"Right now?" she asked.

"Robin just told me she don't want him no more. She wants me to come and get him."

Mom calmly set the silverware out on the table.

"Right now, you're going to sit down and eat dinner with your sister and me. When we've finished having dinner, we'll go over to Robin's house and talk to her and her mother about this. You both had this baby together and you need to learn how to work together in taking care of him. She can't just unload that child on you when she doesn't feel like dealing with him. That's not how parenthood works."

I didn't argue with my mother. I sat down and had dinner with her and Diana. When we finished eating, Mom got up, grabbed her jacket and the three of us walked over to Robin's house.

Robin answered the door when we got there.

"It's about time you got here. Take him," she said, shoving the baby into my arms.

She didn't realize that my mother and sister were right behind me.

"Robin, is your mother here?" Mom said, stepping forward and making her presence known.

"Yes ma'am," Robin said bashfully, "please come in."

"Why didn't you tell me your mom was there?" she whispered to me as we walked into her house.

"You didn't give me a chance," I said.

Robin's mother was sitting on the couch when we walked in.

"Mom," Robin said, "this is Ms. Jenkins, Ty's mother."

Robin's mom barely glanced from the television set to acknowledge our presence.

"Hey," she said.

My mother stepped forward.

"Ms. Waters," she said, "I don't mean to intrude. I just thought that we should talk. Your daughter just called my son tonight asking him to come and get the baby because she doesn't want him anymore."

Ms. Waters looked up from the TV for the first time.

"That's because she doesn't," she said.

"I understand that she might feel that way. She's young – very young. Neither of these kids have any business being parents, but the fact is, they are and they have a responsibility to care for this child."

"Well, what do you expect us to do?" Ms. Waters said, almost copping an attitude, "You're right, they are too young to take care of a kid. They are kids themselves, and I don't have the money to take care of a baby. I can barely take care of the kids I got. I don't want another mouth to feed. Heck, I didn't even know this child was pregnant until she was about to go into labor."

My mom looked at her incredulously. How in the world can you not know your daughter is pregnant? But, neither of us decided to go there. You have to pick your battles and that was not one we wanted to have with this woman.

"Okay, so you don't want to take care of this child. What do you want to do? Give up all parental rights?"

"You can do that?" Robin piped in, sounding almost excited at the thought.

"Yes, you can do that," my mom cut her eyes at my baby's mother, "but we will need to go to family court to settle this. Are you both sure this is something you want to do?"

"Set it up," Ms. Waters said averting her eyes back to the television set.

We left the house that night with all of my son's things, my mom just shaking her head as we walked back home.

A couple of weeks later, the four of us went to family court where Robin signed away all parental rights to our son. When she said she didn't want him anymore, she really meant it. She didn't want anything to do with our son. I gladly took on the responsibility of caring for my son, especially since she'd already proven to me that she couldn't be a great mother with the Paulie incident. But, it was still always hard for me to understand how a mother could just give up her child just like that, no matter how young and irresponsible she was.

With parental rights signed away, I thought that would be the last I ever heard of Robin. But, a couple months later, I got a call from my boy Redd.

"What's up Redd?"

"Man, you need to come get your girl," he said.

"My girl?" I said, the list of women I'd been with lately running through my head, "who are you talking about?"

"Robin," Redd, said, an obvious hint in his tone, "your baby mama."

I rolled my eyes. Robin was the last person I expected him to say. I thought I'd washed my hands of this girl.

"Why? What did she do now?"

"She's over here at this party on Elm, drunk off her butt. I think you need to come get her. You know she's just a kid anyway."

I took a deep breath. I really didn't feel like dealing with this chick anymore, yet for some strange reason, I felt a responsibility for her.

"Fine," I said, "I'll be there in 30."

I looked at the clock. It was late, after 11:00, and mom and Diana had already turned in for the night.

I dressed in my best Kani suit and sneakers, called one of my boys and hitched a ride over to Elm.

I showed up at the party and there she was; the sloppiest drunk I may have ever seen.

I watched her slink around to the music in the room, teasing the guys in the room and damn near taking her clothes off. The guys around seemed to be enjoying the show. I knew I needed to do something before these guys ran a train on her by the end of the night. And I knew them. They would do it.

Redd walked up to me beer in hand.

"See," he said, pointing toward her, "I wasn't lying."

"No," I said, "no, you weren't. Thanks for calling me, man. I'll take care of this."

I walked over to my strip-teasing ex-girlfriend.

"Robin, baby, come on, let's go home."

"Ty," she said, smiling and leaning on me, a rubbery frame, the buttons on her blouse exposing her chocolate breasts, "I'm glad you came. This party is off the chain. Dance with me."

She leaned in against me, sexily swaying her hips.

"You know you want it," she whispered in my ear, the smell of alcohol heavy on her breath.

I gazed down at her full breasts, validating the words she'd just said. Despite all that she'd done to me in the last couple of months, I still wanted her. I was still attracted to her, and standing here looking at her, blouse open in a sexy mini skirt, all I could think of was doing her.

I grabbed her by the arm.

"Come on Robin, we're getting out of here," and I started to lead her out of the room.

She didn't protest, just silently complied, although I had to guide her steps because her legs were like rubber. I looked at the clock and saw how late it was. Young as she was, you'd think her mom would be worried or waiting up for her, but I knew better than that. I'd met her mother.

"Look baby, it's late. Let me get you a room tonight so you can sleep it off. Then, you can go home in the morning."

She nodded as her body swayed back and forth, drunk of liquor.

I hailed a cab and took her to a nearby hotel. The plan was to just get her checked in and then go home.

But, she had different plans for me.

After getting checked in, I laid her in the bed, took her shoes off and she seemed to be dozing off nicely.

"Good," I whispered to myself, "now you can sleep this off and you should be fine in the morning."

After getting her settled in, I ran to the bathroom to freshen up before leaving, proud of myself for not taking advantage of my very drunk ex-girlfriend because I'd seriously thought otherwise when we were at that party.

When I came out of the bathroom, Robin was not in the bed. I looked up to find my ex-girlfriend, my baby's mama, buck naked in front of me.

"You like?" she said, her movements still unsteady.

I couldn't deny that I liked what I saw. It was what had gotten me in trouble the first time we'd had sex. Standing before me was just a girl of 14, but she had the body of a woman, luscious curves, full breasts and an butt that wouldn't quit. That night all my willpower went out of the door.

"Baby, you know daddy likes," I said as I started unbuttoning my shirt and secured the lock on the hotel room door.

I woke up early the next morning with my ex-girlfriend lying beside me. I really did not mean to sleep with her. But, who is going to resist a naked girl standing in a hotel room? Not me! I got up and dressed while she continued to sleep soundly. I snuck out of the room, undetected.

I caught a ride home. I had just enough time to get home and get dressed before school. I didn't have to worry about catching it from mom because I knew she'd already left for work by now and dropped my sister off on the way. Still, I opened the door slowly in preparation for the lean possibility that she was waiting up for me. I walked inside to an empty apartment and breathed a sigh of relief.

I couldn't help but reflect back on the events of last night. I'd never seen Robin like that before. I mean, I know she was only 14 and she'd thrown back a couple of beers when we'd been together and had gotten a little tipsy, but never anything like that. She'd completely surprised me. And, where was Paulie's punk butt? Wasn't he supposed to be her new boyfriend? Who lets their girl go out to a party and behave like that? I couldn't stand this fool. He'd completely violated my trust, running around with my girl like that. We were done! And, I thought

Robin and I were done, too, but last night told a different story. I mean, I know she was drunk but things were different between us then. She'd definitely gained some experience and I really liked all of the new little tricks she'd learned.

I'd also been around the block a few times, so when we made love last night, it was explosive. I could definitely see getting in that again.

I glanced at the clock and realized I was running late for school so I ran out the door.

Around lunch, I caught up with my boys Sean and Redd.

"So, did you get your girl taken care of last night?" Redd asked while we found a place to sit with our food.

I took a seat and looked at my friend with a devilish grin.

Redd and Sean both started laughing.

"Oh, so you took care of her?" Redd said, making gyrating motions with his pelvis.

I just shook my head.

"Redd, sit your crazy butt down," I said, "but yes, I did."

"What!" Redd said before giving me dap over my sexual conquest.

Sean finally piped in.

"So, does this mean ya'll are back together?"

"Naw, I didn't say all that," I replied.

Redd leaned in across the table and lowered his voice to a whisper.

"How was it? I mean she was pretty drunk."

I leaned back in my chair, reminiscing about the events of last night.

"Yeah, she was," then I leaned forward, "I don't know if it was the alcohol or what, but her skills were on point last night."

"Really? I would think the opposite since she was so drunk."

I shook my head.

"That's what I thought too, but man," I said, just shaking my head.

"So, what happened? I thought you were just taking her home," Redd said.

"That was the plan," I said shaking my head.

"What changed?" Redd asked.

"I decided to just get her a hotel room since it was so late. Now, I'm realizing that was probably my first mistake. She was damn near passed out when we got there, so I put her in the bed, and went to the bathroom to freshen up. I planned on leaving right afterward, but when I came out the bathroom, there she was, standing in front of the bed, buck naked."

"DAA-MN," Redd and Sean said in unison.

"Yeah, I know right. Was I just supposed to walk away from that? You guys have seen how this girl is built."

Sean nodded.

"Brick. House."

"So, that's what happened. She was still pretty much passed out when I woke up this morning, so I snuck out of the room, ran home and got showered and dressed and came to school."

"So, you sure you don't want to get back with her? She is your baby's mama," Sean said.

"She is," I said, "but I don't have to have a relationship with her just because we have a kid together. She gave up parental rights to him remember? And, besides that, I don't know if I can really get over what she and Paulie did to me. That crap hurt."

"Ty, I get that, but you were still messing with other girls," Redd pointed out.

"Yeah, but none of those girls were chicks she been running with for the last couple of years. I wouldn't do that. She don't even know the chicks I been messing with, and most of them are way older than her anyway."

Both of them decided to just leave it alone. We finished our lunch before the bell rang and we went back to class.

Several months later, things were good. Robin and I never spoke again. We can just chalk that one night up to one good night of sex between the two of us, and I was honestly okay with that. Word on the street was that she was still with Paulie. They deserved each other. In the meantime, I was enjoying watching my little man grow and hearing him say daddy for the first time and seeing him take his first steps. He became the main reason for my hustle every day. I wanted to provide for him and give him a better life than what I grew up with. And he would have that. He'd just turned a year old, and mom and I had a big party for him with a cake and everything. He played with the toys we bought him, but as young as he was, he still probably couldn't fully appreciate the privilege of having a party in his honor. It didn't matter. I just wanted to be able to give him everything he ever needed.

About a week after his birthday, I was on the streets getting my usual hustle on after school. My boy Jax came up to me.

"What's up, man?" I said, "is the product good?"

"Nah man," he said, "you're good. But, when is the last time you caught up with your girl?"

"My girl?" I was sleeping with several women, none of which I would dub my girl.

"Yeah, Robin. Don't you have a son with her?"

I shook my head. She was the last girl that was on my mind.

"Yes, but I don't know why people keep calling her my girl. We are not together."

"Well, she's at the park. You should go see her," he said with a smile on his face.

"Whatever man," I said and just kept on working.

A few minutes later, I saw Sean and Redd come around the corner.

"Yo Ty," Redd said, "I think you need to go to the park."

I just rolled my eyes.

"Let me guess," I said, "because Robin is there."

"How'd you know?" Sean said.

"Word is getting around," I said glancing at Jax standing a few feet away.

"Did you know that she had a baby?" Redd said.

I shrugged my shoulders.

"Good for her. Maybe she'll keep this one and actually be a real mother."

"Have you seen the baby?" Sean said.

"Negro, you just told me the chick had a baby. How the hell do I know what it looks like?"

I was getting pissed off now.

"Are you guys trying to tell me something? Spit it out!"

Both of my friends just stood there silent.

I needed to find out what the hell was going on and why everyone still wanted me to go see this girl and her new baby.

I walked over to Jax. He was standing on the corner smoking a cigarette.

"I need to go down to the park."

I chuckled under his breath.

"I know you do," was all he said.

I headed over to the park, Sean and Redd in tow.

When I got there, I saw Robin and Paulie together by the monkey bars. Robin had a baby carrier in front of her and Paulie was sitting next to her smoking a cigarette.

I took a deep breath before walking over. Paulie and I had not faced off since I found him and Robin together so I really wasn't sure what was going to happen here.

As I walked over, I saw Paulie stand up, immediately in defense mode.

I ignored him and looked straight at Robin.

"So, I hear you had a baby?"

"Yeah," she said, her voice low.

I looked at everyone's face around me. It was like everyone knew something I didn't.

I turned the baby carrier around, and inside was a newborn baby girl, bright yellow. Robin was dark skinned and Paulie was even darker than her. As I looked at this little girl in this carrier, it felt almost as if I was looking in a mirror. Then, I started to count back the months since Robin and I had sex in that hotel room. This was my child.

I reached down and picked the baby up from the carrier. Paulie started to move toward me.

I held my hand up.

"Don't even think about it," I said, "and if you ever come near my daughter again, I'll kill you punk."

Robin started to protest but then stopped herself. She knew better than to even try to come in between my kid and me.

The first place I took my little girl was to my grandmother. Grandma had a gift for being able to tell you if a kid belonged to you. She was like an old fashioned DNA test.

When I walked into my grandmother's house, toting my daughter, she validated my suspicions immediately.

"Oh Ty," she said, "your daughter is beautiful."

She took my little girl in her arms and started to dote on her.

Meanwhile, I started to think about how I was going to care for the 2 kids I had now, and I wasn't even 16 yet. I realized that I needed to slow down, but that was so much easier said than done. Fact was I liked my lifestyle. I loved the girls, and I liked the hustle. The girls loved me and gave to me freely whatever I asked. The hustle game was getting easier the longer I did it, and the more I learned, the more lucrative it became.

After visiting with my grandmother for a little while, I took my daughter home and explained to my mother that I'd gone out and fathered, yet another child. She wasn't too thrilled to become a grandmother for a second time, but she welcomed my daughter with open arms.

The hustle game started to become a more prominent part of my life. Because I was Fly Ty, the kid on the block and my cousins looked out for me, I really did not get any trouble from anyone. Hustling on the streets meant that I was hanging out with a lot of people older than me, which meant I got into clubs even though I was underage. They didn't sell me alcohol but I partied and had a good time just like the rest of them.

The one thing I didn't do was get personally involved in the drug game. Selling it, I saw firsthand what it did to people and I had no desire to participate.

One evening though, I was persuaded to try weed. I'd heard from a lot of my friends that weed was harmless, that it was from the earth and was actually good for you. We were at a party one night. I was dressed in my button down shirt, slacks and gold chains, a change from what I wore in the streets. In the streets, I didn't want the reputation for being a baller. People pretty much looked at me as a bum because I wore the same old clothes and dirty sneakers 3-4 days in a row. I liked this reputation because I didn't want anyone to know what I had and I knew that I posed no threat to the other dealers out there. The nice clothes I bought, I stashed in my closet for occasions like tonight when I went to a party with my friends and a fine girl on my arm. My date tonight more than fit that description. Amber was the most popular girl in high school a few years ago.

She was the IT girl in high school and she still was today. She was Dominican so she had long, thick flowing black hair, honey skin and a body like a coke bottle. Every time I showed up at a party with a different beautiful girl on my arm, usually several years older than me, my boys just shook their head. They didn't understand how I did it. After hanging out at the party for a little while, my boy Coop approached again about trying some weed.

"Hey Ty man," he said, "you gonna finally try some weed tonight?"

He'd been trying to get me to try this stuff for a long time now. I knew I wasn't going to mess with any crack or cocaine because I'd seen its side effect. But, I knew a lot of people who smoked weed and they seemed okay. I guess it wouldn't do me any harm to try it out.

"What the hell," I said.

I followed Coop into a smoky room in the back of the apartment we were in.

He ushered me inside and I followed him, cautiously.

I sat on the bed with a few other guys who were puffing heavily.

Coop handed me a tightly wrapped joint.

"Here Ty, suck on this," he said.

I took what looked like a small cigarette in my hand.

Aware that I wasn't sure how to proceed, Coop gave me directions on how to smoke.

"Just take a puff, Ty," he said, demonstrating with a joint he had in his hand.

It seemed easy enough.

So, I proceeded to follow his instructions, sucking on the joint, but something went wrong in the process because I immediately started choking.

"Inhale," Coop instructed, "inhale, Ty."

I couldn't breathe. I did not enjoy this at all, and the room reeked of it. I took a minute to observe all of the guys in the room who'd been smoking for some time now. All of them were clearly high off this substance, not a care in the world. If an intruder were to bust in right now with a gun, everyone would get shot. "From the earth, yeah right." I don't care what anyone says about weed, it's still a drug and when you smoke it, it affects you, and not in a good way.

I got up from the bed, once I finally caught my breath, and handed the joint back to my buddy Coop.

"That's it?" Coop asked, surprised that I'd given up so easily, "you not even going to try again?"

"Nope," I said as I headed for the door, "Coop, that crap ain't for me. I told you I would try and I did. Didn't like it."

I walked out the room and grabbed a beer with my girl. Drugs weren't my thing. I could sell them but I'd never get addicted to them. But, alcohol was different; it had become my poison. By the time I was 16, I was throwing back bourbon like it was nothing.

Partying was my scene and I felt myself growing up fast as I spent more and more time in the streets. As we got older, Redd and I got closer as friends. I knew that no matter what, he'd have my back. And, he even hustled with me for a little while. We developed a code in the streets while we were hustling. One of the first rules we developed was we didn't sell to pregnant women. You would think this would not be a problem but when these chicks got hooked on this stuff, they couldn't help themselves. It was not uncommon for a woman with a huge pregnant belly to come up and try to score drugs off you. We never sold to these women and if we saw anyone in the neighborhood doing it, they were in for an beat down from us. We didn't play that! We didn't sell to kids either. Growing up in this kind of environment, kids got hooked on drugs early. It was sad. We tried to protect these kids as much as we could, sending them home to their parents, if they had anyone at home.

We were different from a lot of our counterparts in the streets because we actually did care about people. Selling drugs was just a way to make money and that was it. Unlike a lot of people that got caught up in this game, I still went to school every day. I made pretty decent grades. I kept my hustle and my home life separate.

But, as I got older, I got cocky. My attitude changed. I think it is because my whole life, people, including certain family members treated me like the bottom of their shoe. I had one aunt in particular that never really seemed to like me. I never quite understood it. But, I remember one Christmas in particular when I was about 8 or 9. My mom had gone out of her way to get everyone really nice gifts. Everyone got something nice. My aunt did the same and was actually in a better position to afford it because she worked 2 jobs. She got everyone really nice gifts. Then, I opened mine and she'd gotten me a $0.50 bag of green army men. I was so upset. The following year, she got me nothing. I never quite understood why she didn't like me because I'd never done anything to her. I think my bitterness as I got older was, in part, due to experiences like this in my life.

By the 11th grade, the fact that I was out on the street hustling became more outwardly apparent. I was hanging out with model chicks practically every day and carried a couple thousand in my pocket all the time, and I'd adopted a new nickname, Cody. This evening, I was getting ready to go out with one of my model girlfriends. I had on my thick rope chains and one of my nice sweat suits. I came into the kitchen and my mom and aunt were sitting at the kitchen table rummaging through their purses with a couple of menus sitting on the table.

"What are you guys doing?" I asked.

"We're trying to decide what we can afford for dinner tonight," my mom said.

Now, I knew at this point that we were behind in our rent and that my mom needed a lot more than just food for dinner. So, I reached into my pocket and pulled out a big wad of cash and handed it to my mom.

"Here," I said, "Get something to eat. And, that should be enough to help with the rent too."

My mom looked at me and just stared at the wad of money in my hand. One of my cousins was lurking in the kitchen.

"That's drug money boy," he said trying to get me in trouble.

At this point, I really didn't care anymore. Who cares where the money came from? We needed it.

"So?" I said.

My mother quickly jumped up from the table and grabbed me by my collar.

As a young man, I was already a head taller than her, but that did not intimidate her one bit.

"Boy, if you are out in these streets selling drugs, so help me, I will beat the hell out of you, you hear me?"

Her eyes burned a hole into my skull, while her grip on my shirt tightened.

"Alright mom, yeah, I hear," I said shaking away from her grip.

She sat back down at the kitchen table and kept going through her purse.

"So, you not going to take this money?" I asked flashing the wad at her.

My mom stopped what she was doing briefly to look me in my eyes.

"If that money in your hands is dirty, drug money, no, I don't want no part in it," she said proudly.

My aunt, the one who never seemed to like me was sitting across the table from my mom.

"Give it to me," she said with a chuckle, "I'll put it to good use. I don't care where it came from."

I rolled my eyes and ignored her. I couldn't believe my mom was going to let her pride get in the way of this. Our rent was behind.

I tapped my mom on her back.

"I don't understand why you won't take this," I said waving the money in her face, "We need this money. I know we are behind in the rent."

My mom got up from the table and got back in my face.

"It's not your job to tell me what I need," she said pointing her finger in my face, "You are the child and I am the parent, okay? I said I want no part in that dirty money and I mean it. I don't want to see you in my face again with that."

"But…"

She held her hand up to my face.

"And don't you dare tell me you earned all that money with a paper route. You think I'm stupid?"

"Mom, how are you going to pay the rent?"

My mom held her head high and started quoting scripture.

"My God shall supply all my needs according to his riches and glory," she recited.

I started to interrupt, but she stopped me.

"I don't recall anywhere in the Bible where it says, Ty shall supply my needs," she said. Mom never really caught on to my new nickname. Her argument was always. I gave birth to you and named you Ty and that's what I'm going to call you.

"But, that is what I'm supposed to do," I said, chest puffed out, "I'm the man of this house."

"Oh, so you a man now?" my mom said sarcastically, "And a man takes care of his family? Does a man care for his family with dirty drug money?"

I knew my mom did not approve of what I was doing but I wasn't ashamed because it provided us with a better way to live, if she'd just put her stupid pride aside.

"A man does whatever he need to do to take care of his family. So, you not going to take this money?"

Mom tipped her head up in the air.

"Nope."

"Alright," I said tucking the money back in my pocket and I walked out of the kitchen.

That was the first time I could remember having an altercation like that with my mom. I loved and respected my mom but I just couldn't understand why she wouldn't take that money. How could she allow her pride to outweigh the fact that we might get kicked out of our apartment? I thought about sneaking behind her back to pay the rent, but I know how angry that would make her, so I thought otherwise.

I got ready to go out with my fly model honey that night and knew I'd wash these worries away later with a little Remi and Hennessey.

chapter 6
mini empire

Life became pretty fast paced over the next couple of years. Despite the fact that I was doing well in school, it was a deterrent from my hustle game. So, I dropped out of school and started dealing in a major way. The more money I made, the more addicted I became to the lifestyle and what it could provide me. I had friends who went to school and had what most people would tout as 'good jobs' but none of them made as much money I was making dealing.

Since dealing drugs became my new career, I needed to work with someone to build to the level I wanted. So, by the time I was 19, I picked up a partner. Slim was much older than me and had more life experience and street smarts to contribute to the business. And, he was not what his name implied. At 6'5, 270 pounds, he was anything but slim, but he had good business and street smarts. We often threw people off when we had to handle altercations because people were naturally intimidated by Slim because of his size but he couldn't fight at all. Half his size, I was the fighter so we made a great pair. Plus, I was sleeping with his younger sister.

We sold our product in all of the local neighborhoods and we were doing well, but I wanted to get an edge on the market to increase our profits. The only way to do this was to duplicate ourselves more and get more dealers working with us. Most dealers were getting paid $25 for every $100 of product they sold. We decided to think like businessmen and pay our dealers $40 for every $100 they sold. This would give them incentive to sell more and would also attract more quality dealers to our small enterprise. Slim was a little weary of this business model to start with because after giving $40 to our dealer, we would take $30 to re-up on product, and then split the remaining $15 down the middle. The $15 profit seemed like a small amount of money until you multiplied it by the amount of product sold by the dealers and the amount of dealers we had on the street, putting thousands of dollars in our pocket.

For example, with just one dealer working for you, it didn't make much sense, but with 10 dealers working for you making $1,000/day, Slim and I would be splitting $6,000. As we put our business spin on the drug game, it worked and we started making good money. For Slim, the money went more to his head. He was a bit of a show-off and wanted people to know he had money. He started buying expensive cars, wearing nicer suits and sported more gold chains. Me – I was content to keep working the streets in my old sweatpants and dirty sneakers. Slim was into appearances. I, on the other hand, didn't give a damn what people thought about me. My mama taught me better than that. I knew she wouldn't approve of my little business I had going on right now, but I never forgot where I came from or what she taught me growing up; and, one was to never judge a book by its cover.

So, things were going pretty well in the neighborhood when one day one of my regulars, Twitch approached me. Twitch was one of the local crack heads in the neighborhood and had earned his nickname for obvious reasons, the nervous twitches and ticks you typically saw with excessive drug users.

"Cody," he said scratching on his head, "You and Slim need to check something out."

"What's up, Twitch?"

"I've got some friends and family out in the West Virginia and Virginia area. There's a lot of money in that market. I think you guys should go check it out."

"Really?" I said, intrigued, "Ok."

Twitch went on his way and I contemplated whether or not we were ready to check out another market. Things were going good for us here in New

York – really good. But, a good businessman doesn't pass up a good opportunity.

I approached Slim about it while we picked up a quick dinner that night. We'd just finished reviewing our numbers for the last month.

"Slim, how do you feel about expansion?"

Slim looked up from his plate, eyebrows raised.

"Cody, do you think we are ready for expansion already?"

"Things are going really well here in New York. Maybe it wouldn't hurt to just check out any other opportunities that come our way. Twitch told me that he has some family out in the Virginia area and that there is a lot of money out there. What do you think about checking this out?"

Slim leaned back in his chair and thought for a moment.

"I guess it couldn't hurt. Do you want to head down there?"

"I think we should roll down there and check it out and see what's up. Twitch can roll with us since these are his peeps. We can check out the lay of the land and determine if it's worth putting something together there."

"Sounds like a plan."

Slim and I planned to head down to Virginia the next day to see if this market was everything Twitch said it was. We took Twitch with us and just a small amount of our supply, an ounce of coke, 3 ounces of crack and about a ½ pound of weed.

We got there and were immediately disappointed. Where was all of this money Twitch was talking about? We got no bites whatsoever. What a waste of a trip. With our entire first day being a bust, Slim and I decided to leave the next day. We did not want to waste one more hour in this place. Plus, I was already feeling paranoid about driving all the way from New York with a car full of drugs.

It was about 3 am and Slim was already in his hotel room but I was wide-awake. I just couldn't sleep, so I decided to clear my head by going out and taking a walk.

While I was out, a guy approached me.

"Hey, you got that?"

I turned around to him.

"What?"

"You got that? You got something on you?" he said.

My interest was piqued now.

"What do you need?"

"I want an 8-ball," he said anxiously.

"You want coke or crack?" I asked.

"What you got?" he shot back at me.

"You don't know what you want?" I shot back.

"I want crack. I want crack," he said immediately.

"Ok," I said, "how much you got on you?"

"$200," he said reaching into his pockets to pull out his cash.

"Ok," I said reaching into my stash breaking him off a piece, "Put your money away for now. I want you to take this. If you like it, I want you to let people know where you got it from, ok?"

He nodded and took the sample of crack I'd broken off for him.

Less than an hour later, he was back with 7 more people and Twitch all eager to get in on the action.

I asked all of them to put their money together and it added up to $1,100. I gave them the rest of my crack for their $1,100 price. Then, they told me that they knew some ladies that liked to smoke weed after they did their coke. They tracked down these ladies and I sold them my coke and my weed.

The next morning, Slim and I were checking out of our hotel to head back to New York.

We sat down and had breakfast before hitting the road.

"So Slim, you remember the stash we brought up here?"

"Yeah," he said never looking up from his eggs.

"Well, it's all gone"

Slim stopped eating and looked at me in a panic.

"Did we get robbed?"

"No fool!" I said, "I sold it all. Well, actually, I practically gave it away, but that's because I wanted to get a taste of the market and wanted to see how quick we could get something going here. I think Twitch was right. There's a good market here for us. I think we need to plan another trip and we're going to need a lot more stash."

Slim trusted my judgment and we headed back to New York that morning with a much more optimistic attitude toward our new opportunity.

We planned another trip to VA just a week and a half later, taking much more product with us this time – a pound of weed, 12 ounces of coke and 12 ounces of crack.

Once we got in town, I sat down with Twitch and started going over some numbers with him.

"Look Twitch," I said, "You introduced this opportunity to me and Slim and I appreciate that. So, you bring the business and we are going to give you a cut on whatever you bring to us. Sound like a plan?"

"Yes," Twitch said.

We were sitting down catching up outside my hotel room. I reached into my bag and took out a small notebook.

"Now, this market clearly is different than New York," I said grabbing a pen, "so I need you to give me an idea of what things go for around here. Now, a vial of crack in New York goes for about $10. What is the going rate here?"

"$25," Twitch said.

"$25?" I asked, "Really?"

"Yep."

I wrote my notes down in my notebook.

"How about coke? We sell it for about $25 in New York."

"Coke?" Twitch said thinking for a moment, "here Coke is a premium. It goes for $75."

I shook my head as I wrote down my notes. We were walking into a goldmine here. I liked it!

"How about a nickel bag of weed?"

"$10."

Excellent. We were going to clean house here. I sent Twitch on his way as I mapped out the business plan for our new venture here. With the difference in price, we would be doubling and tripling our profits here. And, because our product was a better product, we also packaged it a little smaller than what we did in New York, increasing our profit margin even more.

As we started digging into the market, driving back and forth from New York to Virginia, the money started flowing in pretty good, but it wasn't long before we noticed that our business was cycling through the same people. We weren't gaining much new business and we weren't sure why. Because Twitch was our new informant, we sat him down to figure out why we weren't growing anymore.

"Oh, the Jamaicans have all the apartment complexes pretty much locked up," he said.

"Okay," I said, "Twitch, I need you to go over there and get some of their product. I want to see what they're pushing."

I gave Twitch some money to go and purchase product from the Jamaicans at the apartment complexes. He brought it back and I had him and some of our associates sample it. There was no comparison to the product we were bringing to the market.

A couple days later, Slim and I were in a local Virginia restaurant grabbing some dinner.

We noticed a crew of about 5 or 6 guys come into the restaurant. They came right up to our table.

"Hey fellas," I said, putting my fork down, "what can we do for you?"

One guy stepped forward from the group, not cracking a smile, face stern.

"What are you doing here?" he said, with a clear Jamaican accent.

Okay, I knew what we were dealing with now. These guys felt like we were treading on their territory. Slim did not like confrontations because he couldn't fight, so he just sat there, silent. Me, on the other hand, I just stared at their leader, not intimidated at all by him and his crew. He broke the silence.

"Don't you come to our complex anymore," he said.

"Okay," I said calmly.

"You go back to where you came from," he said.

"Okay," I said again, "No problem."

Thinking that he'd gotten his point across to us, he left with his crew. After those guys left, Slim breathed a sigh of relief.

"Cody, those guys meant business. This is their territory. Maybe we should pull out."

I looked at my partner like he was crazy.

"Hell no," I said, "What we are going to do is go back home like they suggested. But, we're coming back with reinforcements."

Then, I finished up my dinner.

Slim and I did head back to New York and I immediately went to work putting together my crew. I got some of my friends from the neighborhood and my boy Redd and we formed a crew of about 8. And, these were not just my friends; these were the guys you called when you had a problem. The only cost of getting this crew was Slim and I had to share our new best-kept secret, the fact that there was money in this new market. But, we were already cleaning up so well, it was worth the investment to pay these guys. We had an asset to protect.

As we were packing up to head back to Virginia, Slim approached me with a proposition.

"Why don't you guys head on down?" he said, "I'm going to stay here. We've got some cash set aside and I need to open up this gym and pet store that I'd been planning."

I just looked at him. Slim was a good business partner with smart business sense but he was a coward. I knew that he really just didn't want to deal with confronting these Jamaican guys.

"So, you're not coming back down here with us?"

"Nah man," he said, "What I was thinking is that I can handle the legal side of our business with these new ventures that I'm opening and you can handle that side of the business. What I can do is get the entire product bagged up for you here and ready for transport. I can rent some cars to carry the product and you can follow the cars when you go down."

I thought for a moment. That actually wasn't a bad idea.

"Ok," I said, "I'm game with that plan. You stay here and handle those businesses and bag up and transport the product. And, I'll handle business down there. Deal."

And, I extended my hand and we shook on it.

So, I left Slim in New York and took my crew of 8 back to Virginia with me to start cleaning house.

When we got to Virginia, we had to do a little detective work. I took my crew up the hill and we observed the operation of our competition. We saw where they stashed their drugs and once we had the intel we needed, we went in and robbed them. We did the same thing in the apartment complexes. We observed to see where they stashed everything and then we robbed them.

This put them out of business for about a month so we knew we'd have to come up with another long-term solution. My crew was happy with their compensation because not only did I pay them well, but they got to keep everything they took when we robbed these guys.

But, now that they were back in business, we needed to show them how serious we were. We came to the conclusion, that the Jamaicans that were running things in the apartment complexes also lived out there.

So, me and my guys got with some of the girls that we saw rolling with them and we got them drunk, high and sexed them up. After giving them everything they needed, they gave us everything we needed. They sang like canaries.

We ambushed them. One of them got shot and we beat the hell out another one. The way we handled our Jamaican competitors was all about strategy. We raided their apartment with ski masks, gloves, guns and muscle, beating the hell out of them all the while threatening their women and family should they ever try threaten us again. What they didn't know was that we'd never lay finger on their women or children. That was not how we rolled. We know this was a man's game and we intended to keep it that way. But, they didn't know that.

We also rolled into the place with several rental cars to give the illusion that we rolled deep. When we left the apartment, you heard multiple car doors shutting and gunshots. There were really only about 2 guys to a car but it didn't sound like that and we'd already put enough fear into our enemies that they wouldn't dare go outside to check. The reality of the situation was that they really outnumbered us 3-1.

But, we wanted to send a message to these guys. The next time you roll up on someone while they are having a meal and threaten them, be willing to back up your words – with your life!

There was no way I was going to let these fools have all of this money. I've got 4 kids to support. I needed this money! There were a few other dealers in the area, but they were a couple towns over and we had mutual respect for each other's operations so we didn't really overstep. We were at the point where we were ready to die for this money. Just my guys who were hustling for me made $3K - $5K a week.

But, I was always careful to treat the drug trade like a business. When you start to have enough guys working for you, you have to be careful in how you manage things. I've seen many operations go south quickly because one of their guys snitched. To safeguard against this, I had different conversations with all of my dealers, none of them the same. There was no trust or loyalty between the guys because of this and I liked it that way. When you have guys making this kind of money, you have to control the wolves. Otherwise, the money is so good, your dealers will start conspiring against you to figure out how they can get all of the money. My set up worked because everyone played to their position. And, everything ran pretty smoothly for almost a year.

By this time, we'd set up two different places to bag our drugs. We'd go to a girl's house at different times so as not to create a pattern. From there, we'd drive to our spot, bag up, give our dealers what they needed, come back and take our money and go about our business. The way we handled this no one knew who had what, only you and the person working under you. This strategy pretty much protected our guys from getting robbed because no one knew what they had. A thief knew that if he was going to rob someone, he'd have to deal with the consequences of the dealer coming after them, and this wasn't worth it if all he had was weed. So, they didn't mess with us.

We also didn't keep more than $1,500 in cash on us. I know that seems like a lot of money but compared to the money we were making, $1,500 was pocket change. On a slow night, we were pulling in $6k - $8k. We were well past comfortable at this point.

We did what we call fast nights 6-9 times per month. On these nights, we'd clear anywhere from $15k - $20k. Our guys really looked forward to these nights!

When the money came in, I'd always split it into 3's, even when Slim wasn't here. So, after being gone for 8-9 months, Slim decided that he wanted to come down to pay us a visit and check on things. He called me up beforehand to get set up.

"What's up, Cody?" he said, "I know it's been a while since I've been down there. I'd like to come and check you out."

"Okay," I said, "when were you thinking about coming down? I can get you set up."

"I should be down there in a couple of days. Just need to wrap up a few things here at the pet store."

"Alright man, I got you. Call me when you get here."

Slim came down and I made sure he had a good time. I got him a hotel room and hooked him up with three girls so he'd have a good time. After setting my buddy up, I got a call from one of my guys.

"Cody, we think one of the girls you sent in there with your partner is underage. My boy said she is like 17."

"Which one?"

"The short, brown-skinned one."

"Alright. I got it. Thanks."

I hung up and immediately got my partner on the phone.

"Hello," Slim said, the sound of music and girls in the background.

"Yo Slim, you need to get rid of the little brown skinned girl. She's underage."

There was a silence on the phone before I heard Slim mutter under his breath.

"Damn."

"Slim, I'm serious."

"Come on, Cody! She's the freaky one," he said in a pleading voice.

"Slim, get rid of her. You got that fine light skinned chick and chocolate sister in there. You don't need the trouble of dealing with a kid."

I hung up thinking that Slim had taken my advice.

The next day Slim showed up at the spot looking all shiny and new. I'd left $10k for him so he'd decided to go shopping before coming over. He got out of his rental car with shopping bags, dressed nice in his Nike sweat suit. Like I said, Slim was a bit of a show-off. He didn't mind letting people know he had money.

After Slim got out of the car, the little brown skinned, underage girl followed him. I walked over and asked her politely to wait by the car while I spoke with my partner privately.

"What the hell man?"

"What?" Slim asked, acting like nothing was wrong.

"I told you that girl was bad news. That she was underage. Why do you want to be with a child?"

"Don't worry about it, Cody. I've got it under control."

"I don't think you do. What I think is that little girl has got your mind messed up. You're thinking with your head but not the one on your shoulders."

"Whatever," he said, waving me off, "Like I said, I have it under control."

"Well, she can't come in here," I said, "This is where we bag our stuff and handle our business. There are guns in there. I don't even bring your sister around here so she can't come in here man."

"How you gonna bring my sister into this when you sleeping with different hoes every night?"

"Slim, you know good and well that these women around here don't mean a damn thing to me. Everything I do with these girls is all about business and maintaining our operation. When I'm with your sister, I'm with only her. I take care of her. You know that!"

Slim backed down, knowing I was right.

"Yeah, man, I know," he said.

"If you know, then why the hell you bring it up then?"

"I don't know. Just defensive, I guess. I'm sorry, brother."

"Whatever," I said, "get rid of that chick, Slim. She's trouble."

"Alright," he said, and walked back toward the car to talk to her.

They drove off and when he came back to the spot a little later, I thought he'd heeded my advice and got rid of the young girl. I knew he'd gotten a little hung up on this girl so I wanted to make it up to him. I hooked him up with some other girls that night. He got his rocks off then headed back to New York and I continued business as usual.

A couple of weeks later, I was at a girl's house near our spot getting a little head when I got a call from one of my guys.

"What's up?"

"Yo Cody, I know you didn't want to be disturbed, but that chick that your partner was with a couple of weeks ago is here knocking on the door."

"Which chick?" I asked immediately pushing my girl off my junk and pulling up my pants. I had a bad feeling about this.

"The little young chick," he said.

Crap!

"Don't open the door," I said, "I'll be there in a few minutes."

I hustled through the house getting my things together.

"Hey baby. I thought we were going to have a little fun."

Candy was one of the neighborhood girls who has been a good informant on what's going on in the neighborhood. She traded everything she knew for a little head and some money. But, right now she was standing in my way as I tried to go check on my operation.

"I know Candy, baby, but something has come up that I have to go and check on right now. I promise I'll make it up to you."

I gave her a quick kiss and ran out the door.

I didn't want to be detected so I ran through the woods to get to our spot. The girl was standing at the back door so I went in from the front.

Once I was in the house, I gave my guy the go ahead to open the door. I didn't want her to know that I wasn't there.

When he opened the door, I walked up to meet her, blocking her entrance inside.

"What can I do for you?"

"Hey Cody" she said, "Slim told me to come by here and get $5,000 for him."

You've got to be kidding me? Really?

"Slim has $5,000. He doesn't need you to come and get his money for him," I responded coldly.

She rolled her eyes, pretty much ignoring what I said.

"Anyway, he wanted me to come here and get his money."

I looked at her like she was stupid.

"Listen here little girl, you must think I'm stupid. I don't know you from Adam. I know you've been with my partner, yes, but I also know that my partner has money. If he needs $5,000, he can come here and get it. You ain't getting crap from me."

"Slim is not going to like the way you're talking to me," she said, bucking up at me.

I didn't have time for this.

"I don't give a damn what Slim thinks. There ain't no room for you here. Don't come back here again."

Then, I slammed the door in her face.

My crew froze when they heard the door slam.

"If she comes back, don't let her in," I yelled.

I went to the back of the house to start working with some things I had planned for my dealers for the week. It hadn't even been 2 hours before my phone started ringing.

It was Slim.

I hesitated before picking it up, knowing where this conversation was heading. I picked up the phone, and before I said a word, Slim started to lay into me.

"So, I hear you are stashing money on me now," he said.

"Excuse me," I said. I know I did not hear him correctly.

"Yea, Amber told me how you treated her. I told her to come and get that money."

"And, I told you to get rid of that chick. Do you want to go to jail? Because that girl is jailbait. She is under aged, Slim. She is not welcome here. You shouldn't have sent her around here anyway. I don't want her anywhere near my business."

"Well, still you haven't sent me any money?"

"Really, so now you think I'm holding out on you? When have I ever held out on you, Slim? Seriously."

Silence.

"Don't you ever call me like this again! You're not the one out here risking your life every day. You're up there in New York in your cushy apartment, running a damn pet store and watching people work out. Don't talk to me about holding out on you. And, I know the lies you been telling people up there, too. Don't think word doesn't get back down here about you telling everyone that everybody works for you. You want your $5,000, come get it. Don't send your little girl here anymore!"

"Alright, Cody," he said, "you don't need to get so worked up. I know you're not holding out on me. I'll be back in town in a couple more weeks. I can pick up my money then."

"Fine," I said and hung up.

I had a bad feeling in the pit of my stomach after that conversation. I didn't know how much I could trust Slim anymore.

A couple weeks later, Slim came down to Virginia like he said. We were sitting down in one of our spots going over the money.

"I never really understood why you split our money up in 3's like that," he said motioning to the piles I was separating.

"You don't understand why I do that?" I asked, surprised. More often than not, I expected Slim to know more than me. He was much older than me, 32 to be exact. He has business and street smarts well beyond my 19 years, which is why I initially thought we'd make good partners. These days, I wasn't so sure. Slim shook his head.

I placed the piles of money directly in front of Slim to use as a visual aid. "For every $10,000 we make, I take $3,333 and split it into 3 categories. One with your name on it, one with my name and a third for re-up. The money I put aside for us is for bail and a lawyer when we need it. Do you have $50,000 for an attorney?"

Slim leaned back in his chair, a smug look on his face.

"I've got way more than $50,000," he said confidently.

"I know you've got more than $50,000, but do you have $50,000 specifically set aside for an attorney?"

"No," he said nonchalantly, "do you?"

"I do," I replied, "10 times over. So you wanted to know. That's why."

Slim seemed satisfied. We continued to go through our numbers and divided up our shares.

"I'll send you your money to New York so you'll have it when you get there," I said.

Slim looked at me like I was crazy.

"Why can't you just give me my money now?"

"Do you want to drive all the way back to New York with $40,000 on you?"

He just looked at me.

"Ok," I said and handed him $40,000 in cash and he rode all the way back to New York with it.

Things were changing between Slim and me. Nothing about our partnership sat right with me anymore. Ever since he started messing with this young girl, I felt like his judgment was clouded. And now he comes down here trying to figure out more of the ins and outs of the business, things he was never concerned about before. In normal circumstances, this wouldn't bother me, but his latest actions were that of a man who was about to screw me.

I knew that I needed to start making moves to protect myself. I decided to call my girl Tina, Slim's sister. I knew she would be able to give me insight into this situation since he was her brother.

"Hello."

"Hey baby. It's Cody. How you doing?"

"I'm doing good. Missing you though, when you coming home?"

"Hopefully soon, but I got to handle some business first. Your brother has been acting a little funny lately."

I heard a little sarcastic chuckle on the other end of the line.

"That's what happens when he starts to get a little bit of coochie," she said.

"Really?"

"Yes, Slim gets one little piece of tail and it rules his life. He's always been that way. What happened?"

I begin to tell her everything that happened. Also explaining that, "I've warned him a couple of times that she is bad news but he hasn't listened to me. And, now he has started to act real funny with me. I just don't have a good feeling."

"Then, stick with your intuition, baby," Tina said. "Slim will choose a girl over anybody, even his own family. He has even been disrespectful to our mother over a girl and some coochie. Hell, the only reason why he's even been nice to me is because of you."

"Damn."

"All I can tell you, baby is to prepare yourself because he's gonna probably screw you over."

"Damn," there were no other words I could think of. He had no loyalty to his own family. He sure as hell wasn't going to have any loyalty to me. Here was his own flesh and blood telling me that he was going to screw me.

"Alright baby," I said, "let me take care of this so I can come home to you. I'll talk to you soon. Thanks."

I followed Tina's advice and started to prepare myself for what I knew was coming. I started stashing money. If we made $90,000 in profit, I would say that we only made $45,000 and stash the rest. I was also putting another set of money aside in case we got robbed or something. I'd been stashing that money for a year now. Because Slim wasn't involved in the day-to-day operations and was in New York, he had no idea that I'd already stashed $200,000.

The volume of product that we were moving was crazy. At the end of 6 months, we were selling a couple of kilos instead of ounces of crack and cocaine and we were moving 30-40 pounds of weed. Business was becoming more than I even wanted to deal with anymore. As time went on, we were becoming more than just a mini enterprise. There was a saying on the streets back in New York was 'we'll either make a million dollars in this game or a million years.' Looking at the cash flow that was coming in, I realized that we were well past that point in our business. Part of me was ready to bow out, but not just yet. I needed to deal with this issue with my partner. I couldn't be in business with a man I didn't trust.

I called him up one evening.

"Slim, what's up man?"

"Hey Cody," he said, "how's business?"

"That's actually what I called to talk to you about."

"Everything going okay?" he asked, sounding a bit concerned.

I took a pause before my next statement.

"I just don't know if I want to do this anymore. I think it's time we bow out."

"What?" Slim said, shocked, "Nah man. Maybe you just had a bad day or something."

"No Slim, I didn't have a bad day. When we got here, this place was swinging and we've made a lot of money and milked this thing for all we could. But, now things are slowing down. Money is not coming in quite like it used to. It might be good to just quit while we are ahead."

What Slim didn't know was that business had not slowed down. He was never here. He preferred to stay out of harm's way in his nice apartment, running his gym and pet store; and because I'd been stashing money and reporting less income in the last few months, my statement was backed up by our income.

Slim was silent for a minute.

"Has it really slowed down that much?" he said, pondering what I'd said.

"Yeah, man," I said," it's not like it was when we got here a year ago. Here's what I think we should do. I think we should do one last really big re-up, sell everything we got and just get out of this."

"You crazy man," Slim said, "All the money we done made, we need to stay in the game until the well is dry. It's way too early to bow out."

"Alright," I said, "but don't say I didn't warn you."

I got off the phone with Slim that night and proceeded with my plans. I made that last big re-up but did not involve Slim in the process at all. I got some of my best guys together and we started making some money.

During this time, I made a couple of trips back and forth to New York, wrapping up some business. Lena was a chick I was staying with in Virginia while I ran my operation. I'd just came back from New York and was chilling in the house with her eating some lasagna for dinner and watching some TV.

There was a knock at the door and Lena got up and answered the door.

She was at the door for a while but I could not hear the conversation she was having nor could I see who she was talking to. After a few minutes, she came back into the apartment and sat next to me on the couch. I didn't ask her about who was at the door because that was her business.

When she sat down on the couch, she had a wad of money in her hand. I looked at the money and then back at her.

"Oh, I gave some stuff to our neighbors that like to get high and they bought it, so here's your money," she said handing me the money.

I looked at her like she had three heads.

"That ain't my money. My money is in my pocket."

She looked at me and started smiling.

"Come on baby, just take it. I sold some stuff for you. It's yours."

"The hell it is," I said, "I don't bring drugs or guns in this apartment. I come here, pay the bills and have sex with you. That's it. So, why don't you put that money in your pocket because it's not mine."

"I don't have any pockets," she said bashfully looking around her dress that she was wearing.

"Then, put it in your purse or something," I said and then started eating my lasagna again and watching TV.

She continued to sit on the couch next to me quietly while I ate, the money still in her hand.

I look over at her, my gut telling me that something wasn't right.

"We need to get ready to go to the airport. Didn't you say you wanted to go to New York with me?"

She nodded yes.

We sat on the couch for a little bit just chilling and watching TV.

All of a sudden, the lights went out and I heard a big boom at the door.

The door bashed in and I started looking around thinking, what the hell is going on?

Then, I look over at Lena sitting on the couch next to me expecting to hear her screaming or running around, like most women would be in a situation like this. But, she sat on the couch as cool as a cucumber. This girl just set me up.

A crew of men invaded the apartment and slammed me on the ground with excessive force. The house was smoky from the smoke bombs they'd released. I lay on the ground, calm because I knew they couldn't pin anything on me. I was very careful about how I ran my business. What I wanted to know was what gave them the right to invade my place like this. One of the officers began to read me my rights.

"Ty Jenkins, you have a right to remain silent. Anything you say can and will be used against you in a court of law."

I paused for a minute. Something definitely wasn't right.

"Wait...wait a minute," I said as the officer now lifted me to my feet in cuffs, "what did you just call me?"

I looked back at the officer and then to Lena who was still sitting on the couch calmly.

No one spoke.

"How do you know my name?" I demanded, "No one knows my name."

The cop ushered me further into the apartment.

"Let me finish reading you your rights first, and then we can talk."

"I know my rights," I said, "what I want to know is how you know my name."

108

As the officer ignored my requests and continued to read my rights, my mind started racing. It wasn't Lena who did this because she never knew my real name, although the cops clearly used her as a pawn to try to nail me. I had a government issued ID from the Department of Motor Vehicles that said I was someone else. One of my aunts works there and helped me set this up. No one knew my real name except for....Slim. I'll be damned! Baby girl had warned me that he was coming to get me. Alright. Okay. I'll handle him as soon as I get this mess settled.

By now a large crew of cops had invaded the apartment and had begun searching.

"I don't know what ya'll are looking for. There are no guns or drugs in this apartment. What do ya'll want?"

"Oh we know what's in here," one of the cops said as he proceeded to search the apartment.

The cop that cuffed me looked at me smugly, as if he'd been waiting a long time to say this.

"You're going to jail for drug trafficking and a slew of other charges."

"Not me," I said confidently.

"That money on you is marked," he said pointing toward my pockets.

"Not this money," I said gesturing to my pockets, "this money came from Western Union."

At that moment, Lena cleared her throat. She was still sitting on the couch calmly and this was the first we'd heard anything from here since this whole mess started going down.

The $500 that she brought in the house was still sitting on the couch next to her.

The cop walked over to the couch and grabbed the money and then came back over to me and took the money from my pockets.

He held the money together in front of me.

"This right here says that you do have marked money on you," he said.

I shook my head.

"So that's how you gonna play it," I said, "Ok."

At this point, another two officers came into the apartment with a sledgehammer and a German Shepard. But, this dog was not your normal

German Shepard; it looked like a dog on steroids. It was huge and really furry. They started working their way around the apartment and made their way to the bathroom.

They took the sledgehammer and hit the wall right above the toilet.

Crap!

Now, I knew I'd been set up because the only person who knew where I hid the emergency money was Slim. One day when Lena was at work, I cut out a piece of the wall put the money in plastic and put insulation over it and then I called a contractor to come in and fix the hole. I told him that I'd accidentally bust a hole in the wall. When he finished the wall, I painted the bathroom. When Lena got home, she thought I'd just set up a nice surprise for her by painting the bathroom so she never suspected a thing. But, Slim knew. That was our "just in case money" - $200,000.

The cops found that money and the next thing I knew, I was being hauled off to jail.

I sat in jail for a couple of days, thinking about what led to this situation and about what I was going to do to Slim the next time I saw him. I was chilling in my cell when a couple of cops and what looked like federal agents came to retrieve me.

They took me into what looked like an interrogation room, which was much like a conference room with a big table in the middle of it with chairs surrounding it. On the table sat two big black duffel bags with dirt on them.

I sat down at the table and one of the agents gestured toward the duffel bags.

"What's this?" he said.

I chuckled and shrugged my shoulders.

"I don't know," I said, "your dirty laundry?"

The agent walked around to the bags and started to open them. He revealed coke, weed and a little bit of crack.

"We found this buried in the ground not too far from the apartment you were staying at," he said.

"So?" I said, "Why you bringing it to me? I'm not a leaseholder. You found that behind the apartment complex of a girl I been staying with and having sex with. What does that prove? There must be a few hundred people that live there."

110

The agent held up a bag of coke.

"So, you're not going to admit this is yours?" he asked.

I looked at him like the fool he was.

"Hell no," I said, "because it's not."

"Well, as far as we're concerned it's yours," he said.

This is garbage!

"How can you do that?" I said, upset over this injustice, "I didn't do anything. There's no way you can make this stick."

They sent me back to jail and I continued to wait for months for trial. Finally, I got notice of my first bail hearing.

chapter 7
lock up

I appeared before the judge with my attorney.

"Bail is set for $1 million," the judge said.

My attorney looked at me for my response.

"You can tell him what he can do with that bail," I said, "send me back to my cell."

About a week later, I was summoned for another bail hearing.

"$1.5 million," the judge said.

"Take me back to my cell," I said.

I was getting used to this game and started to wonder if I would ever get out of here. That hearing was the beginning of a bad day for me.

I was just sitting outside of my cell, minding my own business. I preferred to keep to myself but today some guys decided to mess with me.

"Yo," one of the guys said, "you need to man up if you gonna be in here. This is no place for pussys."

I was already in a mood. The last thing I needed was some punk coming up to me calling me a punk.

I got up and got in his face.

"Who do you think you're talking too?" I said shoving him.

We got into it, and the fight got pretty intense. He was bigger and stronger than me, but I was motivated so I wouldn't back down. Then, a couple of his crew got involved and just started throwing punches. I had flashbacks of the first fight I had as a kid when I got jumped and just balled up into the fetal position; but I had too much pride to do that anymore. I was a man, so I kept fighting even though I knew it was a losing battle at this point.

They eventually got the best of me and I just went back to my cell, pissed off. Today had just been a bad day.

The next day, I woke up more refreshed, although I still hated the fact that I was waking up in jail and not my own home. I ran into one of the guys who jumped me the day before. His crew wasn't around to defend him this time.

So, I rolled up on him and pressed his head against the bars and tried to stomp him out.

"Where is your crew at now?" I said as I kept stomping him.

The guard immediately got wind of my assault and grabbed me immediately and put me in the hole, which is solitary confinement.

Solitary was meant to be punishment because you were all alone. It was just four walls with a hole in the ground for a toilet, very rudimentary. But, honestly, I liked it. I preferred to be alone. It gave me time to think and I didn't have to worry about anyone messing with me.

Another week later, my lawyer got me another bail hearing. This game we were playing with the judge was getting quite interesting. I was curious to find out what his offer was this time.

This time he dropped it back down to $1 million and I turned around and went back to my cell. Why should I have to come up with an excessive amount of money like that when I was being held for something I didn't even do? They didn't even have evidence to stick these charges against me. This was crap!

Another bail hearing - $750,000. I was starting to get angry. Here I was sitting in a jail cell every day over trumped up charges. While my partner, who'd put this whole thing in motion was probably still in New York running his pet store and gym. I could not wait to get my hands on this fool!

Another bail hearing - $500,000. Well, at least the money was going down. I actually thought about getting out at this point. I knew I had the money, but I still couldn't bring myself to pay that much money for something I wasn't guilty for. So I opted out and went back to my cell.

The funny thing about jail is you find out who your real friends are. There are not that many people that care to come and see you when you go to jail. Either they just don't care, you don't fit into their schedule or they're too embarrassed to admit that they went to see a friend or family member in jail.

Music became my companion while I was locked up. At times it gave me strength and at other times, it served a conduit to my emotions. I loved Jodeci, Red Man, Method Man and Biggie Smalls. It's how I kept my sanity.

I got one letter and one birthday card from 2 of my aunts. But, I talked to my mom, my grandma and one of my aunts every week. All my cousins and friends in the street – nothing. Besides my contact with my mom and grandma, the only person to write or talk to me was my best friend, Redd.

A couple more weeks went by. The judge called another bail hearing. "$250,000."

I called my attorney and gave him explicit instructions on what to do.

"I need to you to go to my apartment."

"Mr. Jenkins, I can't go to the young lady's apartment. Plus, she doesn't even live there anymore."

"No," I corrected, "I understand that. I need you to go to my apartment. I have an apartment of my own. A young lady, Shanice, lives there. She'll sign over the property and give you the keys. I need you to go into the deep freezer and follow these instructions."

I handed him a small piece of paper with instructions to follow.

My attorney came back the next day and sat across from me shaking his head.

"You're either really stupid or you're a genius," he said.

I chuckled.

"I got what you told me to get so we can pay the bondsman," he said.

By going through a bondsman, we only had to pay 10% of the actual bond, so instead of $250,000, we only needed to pay $25,000. However, because I was out of state, the bondsman wanted $50,000 and my mom was going to sign for me. So, while my mom was handling the paperwork with the bondsman, my attorney handled the payment.

My attorney sat across from me still shaking his head in disbelief.

"So, you gotta tell me, how did you hide all that money in different pie boxes?"

I laughed to myself as I thought about how I did this.

I leaned forward.

"A long time ago, I bought a bunch of frozen pies from the grocery store in all kinds of different flavors sweet potato, pumpkin, apple and cherry. I took all of the pies out, steamed them open. I slid the pies out, scooped out the filling and then replaced them with cellophane wrap. The cherry pies had $100s, the apple $50s, sweet potato, $20s, and I put small bills in the pumpkin pies. After wrapping them up neatly, I rolled out a soft crust and baked them in the oven for just a few minutes, just long enough for it to set. Then, I put the pies back in the box and crazy glued them shut."

My attorney leaned back in his chair, an incredulous expression on his face.

"You punk!" he said, "and she never caught on? The girl you were staying with?"

"Nope," I said confidently, "she don't eat pie. Plus, she knew that was my deep freezer and didn't mess with my stuff. She had no reason to. I paid all of her bills. Even before I went to jail, I had her rent paid up for a year and she still worked full-time. She was good."

After all of the paperwork was processed with the bondsman and payment was received from my attorney, I was bonded and went home.

I'd been locked up for an entire year, so it felt good to be back in New York. Of course, I had unfinished business to handle. Slim had to pay for what he did to me. He couldn't think that I was going to come home and act like none of this happened. He ratted me out and I lost a year of my life in prison because of it. His tail was mine!

Problem was, I couldn't find him. He didn't know I was out yet, but after a couple of days he still was nowhere to be found.

A couple of my boys came by the house to see me after I got out.

"So what's it like in the joint?" Sean asked.

I shrugged my shoulders.

"I guess it's not so bad. I mean, I'd much rather be home, but it's not as bad as people say. I got in a couple of fights but mostly just kept to myself. I don't wanna go back."

"So, did you ever drop the soap?" Q joked, laughing with my buddy Sean.

"You guys are idiots," I said, chuckling, "No, I did not drop the soap. My butt hole is just fine, thank you. I would've been locked up in solitary all the time if I had to deal with that crap."

A couple more of my crew came running up to the house like something was going down.

I stood up.

"What's up ya'll?"

"We found Slim."

My tone and mood changed immediately. The time for light conversation was over.

"Where?"

"Cerrato Park."

"I'll meet you there."

I didn't engage in anymore conversation with my friends. I just went in the house. I knew what I had to do.

I went into my old bedroom and started searching the back of the closet.

At that time my mom was walking down the hall and stopped to come into the room.

"Ty, what are you looking for? What are you about to do?"

She could sense that I was upset and she knew something was going down.

"Mom, stay out of this," I said as I continued to rummage through the closet.

My mom threw her hands up.

"You're right," she said, "I don't even want to know what you're getting into. I'm going to your grandmother's house."

She walked out of the room and shortly afterward, I found what I was looking for, my pistol.

I loaded and packed my heat and headed out of the house on a mission. When I came outside, Sean and Q were still sitting there, waiting.

I kept walking and they had to practically run to keep up with my pace.

"Go down to the park and make sure none of our people are there," I said, "I don't want them getting caught up in this. This is between me and Slim."

Q and Sean followed my instructions and ran ahead of me to the park.

But, as I got closer to the park, about a dozen of my crew came running at me. They saw I was on a mission.

"Cody, man, just chill."

"You just got out the joint. Don't do anything crazy man."

I ignored all of their warnings.

"Where's he at?" I demanded.

"He's at the top of the park," one of them said pointing, "gambling and shooting dice."

At that moment I saw him, sitting at the top of the park just as my boy had told me.

We locked eyes.

Fear was in his.

Rage was in mine.

I pulled out my 380 and started firing in his direction.

"Crap!!!" is all I heard from his direction.

His big ass started running. I didn't think I ever saw him move that fast. He jumped over a pole.

I kept shooting.

He ran around bushes, hid behind cars, anything to dodge the bullets I was firing at him.

I emptied out the entire magazine of my 380. I wanted to hit him so bad, but I think he dodged all of the bullets and got away.

The next day, I got a call from Tina, Slim's sister, the first time I'd heard anything from her since I'd gone to jail. I knew what she wanted.

"I need to talk to you," she said.

"Alright," I said, "come on over."

She came to the house and she looked good. After being in jail for a year, my body was longing for the touch and feel of a woman's body.

She walked into the house.

"Okay," she said, "can we talk about my brother?"

"I'll talk to you, but first things first," I said pulling her closer to me, "you gonna give me some, right?"

She hesitated.

I backed away.

"You been giving my stuff away while I been gone?"

Tina lowered her head.

"Well, I been trying to work and go to school," she said before lowering her voice to a near whisper, "and I have been messing around with this dude."

"Really?" I said.

She just stood there silent.

"So, you been messing around with another dude while I been in jail? After I've been taking care of you?"

She looked at me with apologetic eyes.

"I-I…"

"Get your butt in the bedroom," I interrupted.

I was mad as hell with her for messing around with someone else while I was in jail, but my horniness outweighed my anger. A year is a long time to anyone to go without sex, but for someone with my sexual appetite, it was like an eternity.

We made love and it was like the first time. I'd forgotten how good it felt to be inside a woman's body, the feel of her curves, the smell of her perfume and the wetness of her body. She wanted me just as much as I wanted her. There was no denying it. She may have been messing with another man while I was gone but she still wanted me. She loved me. I could feel it. It was time to squash the mess she had going on with this guy. He was history. I wasn't letting anyone back up in this coochie.

As we finished up, we just lay in bed for a moment, catching our breath. I broke the ice.

"So Tina, what did you want to talk to me about?"

She rolled over to face me.

"It's about my brother, Cody. He said he didn't set you up. You gotta lay off him. I know what happened yesterday."

I looked at her smugly.

"It's no secret what happened yesterday," I said, "And if Slim didn't set me up, why was I the only one that was sitting in prison?"

She didn't really have an answer to my question. That's because there was none.

"He wanted me to talk to you, Cody. He didn't set you up to go to prison. He has been running around telling people you tried to set him up, and that's why he wasn't down there in Virginia."

She looked at me expectantly.

I was silent for a moment, and I could tell from her expression that she took my silence to mean acquiescence to her plea.

I sat up and looked her right in her eyes.

"You tell your brother he's a dead man."

"But, Cody..."

"No buts, Tina. I'm done."

She backed down and stopped pleading for her brother.

"And, I want you to call whoever this dude was that you were sleeping with before and tell him it's over. You're not going to see him anymore."

I picked up the phone and handed it to her.

"Go ahead. Do it."

She took the phone from my hand and started to dial a phone number.

"Hey Tony," she said, "I just wanted to let you know that I can't see you anymore."

I couldn't make out everything he was saying on the other line, but quickly figured it out.

"The guy I was seeing before you got out of jail and we are back together so I can't see you anymore."

The rest I could hear because he was screaming through the phone.

"Tina, are you kidding me? This nigga goes to jail and is gone for a year and now you just go back to him. Hell no, forget this crap. Get your stupid behind home so I can deal with you."

Mind you, I'm listening to the whole conversation and can hear this dude blatantly disrespecting my lady.

"Give me the phone," I told her.

120

She handed the phone over to me.

"My man," I said, "what is the problem? There is no need to for you to be speaking to her like that. This is a lady."

"Lady?" he said, "she was just sleeping with me last night and now she with you. That's what you call a lady? She needs to get her butt home now before I come looking for her."

I remained calm. I knew how to handle dudes like this.

"Chill out," I told him, "she's going to be home in about 2 hours."

"And I'll be here waiting for her," he said before hanging up the phone.

I told Tina to get dressed and then got on the phone and called some of my boys.

"Look, I got this dude that has been running up on Tina while I was away. Now, he wanna act all tough and is threatening to hurt her when she goes home. We need to teach him a lesson."

"We got you," my boy Redd told me on the other end, "I'll round up the crew."

I got dressed and went downstairs.

I called her a cab and sent her ahead in the cab while I got in the car with my crew and followed her. We got to her apartment and I was actually surprised to see how bold this dude was. He was there just like he said. We stayed in our car while Tina got out of the cab. As soon as she got out of the cab, he got out of his car. Before he had a chance to raise a hand to her, me and my crew got out of the car.

"I was taught better manners than to ever lay a hand on woman."

He sized me up and then looked at her.

"So, this is the guy?" he said, "the jailbird that you chose over me?"

I just stood there looking at him.

He had no idea what was coming, and I didn't even warn him of the storm that was about to hit him.

He snatched Tina up and pushed her toward the apartment.

"Get in the house!"

I looked at her.

"You living with the nigga, too?"

She just looked at me and shrugged her shoulders.

And, before he had any time to approach me, my boys ambushed him. It was about 4 against one, and that was before I even got involved. We beat him senseless. By the time we were done with him, his face was a bloody mess.

I walked up to Tina while my boys were still kicking and stomping him out.

"Does he have any money in there?"

I'd just got out the joint so I was anxious to get my hands on any cash I could.

"He did give me the key to his safe," she said.

"Sucker," I said out loud. I knew the type. He was one of those dudes that fell in love with chicks quickly thinking it was forever. He was a fool to give this girl the password to his safe. I don't care if I love you or not, I'm not trusting you with my money like that.

We wrecked the house, stealing what little bit of money he did have.

I'd had enough excitement my first couple of weeks out of jail dealing with Slim and Tina, so I laid low for a while and just chilled at my mom's house. Things were cool for a couple of months.

Then, I was due back in court back in Virginia. I thought my court date was on Tuesday, but I woke up on Monday morning and looked at my paperwork and learned the court date was actually scheduled on Monday.

I called the court immediately, because I didn't want them to think I was skipping out.

"Ma'am, I just wanted to apologize. I mixed up my court dates. I thought I was scheduled for tomorrow and just realized it was today. I just wanted to see if we could arrange another date because I don't want you to think I'm skipping or anything."

The lady on the other line was extremely nice.

"You're fine, sweetheart. We appreciate you calling. We can definitely move your date."

I was anxious to make sure they understood that I was cooperative. My blood pressure went down a little bit when I saw how easy going the lady was on the other line.

"I can get a flight out tomorrow to get there when you need me."

"No problem," she said.

122

Then I proceeded to give her all of the information on where I was staying with my mom for their own records. Again, I just wanted them to know that I was cooperative and that me missing my court date was just an honest mistake.

I felt better when I got off the phone, given how nice the lady was that I spoke with.

The next day, I was enjoying some quality time with my 2-year-old son at my mom's house. We were lying on the floor playing together. We heard a noise at the door.

My son ran to the door and turned the knob. I was not worried about him opening the door because we lived in the same building with my grandmother and my aunts so we were surrounded by family so I knew no one was stupid enough to come and try to mess with me at my house. But, I was surprised to find what was on the other side of the door when my son ran to open it. There were a bunch of agents and police swarming the hallway. I got up off the floor. The cops came into the apartment and one of them started to cuff me and read me my rights.

"Ty Jenkins, you have a right to remain silent…"

I'd been through this crap before. I stopped them before they could complete it because I was really confused as to what this was all about but more importantly, I didn't want this going on in front of my son.

"Listen, my son is just a toddler. He doesn't understand what is going on, and I really don't want him around all of this. Please, let me just take him downstairs to my grandmother. Please don't cuff me in front of my son."

The officer cooperated with my request and allowed me to get up and get dressed in some jeans and a T-shirt. Then, I picked up my son and took him downstairs to my grandmother.

When my grandmother came to the door, she saw all of the agents and police in the hallway.

"Ty!" she said, concerned.

I handed my son over to her.

"Grandma, I don't want you to worry. I'm sure it's just a misunderstanding. I just missed my court date. I didn't do anything wrong. It's going to be okay. I promise."

She hugged me and told me she loved me, and I knew she was worried about me.

As soon as the door closed, the officers came up to me and laid cuffs on me. When we got down the stairs, I saw a bunch of agents and cops outside, all dressed in plain clothes like me. What was going on? The officers walked me about a block and a half from my building. When we turned the bend, there were agent and cop cars everywhere. You'd think a serial killer was on the loose.

"What is all this?" I said, in shock, "I ain't no killer!"

One of the agents in my entourage responded.

"We received a phone call from Virginia along with warrants that said you were very dangerous. You're all over the news in Virginia and here in New York. You've gone and made quite a name for yourself Mr. Jenkins."

I just shook my head in disbelief. I'd just missed a bail hearing. The nice lady on the phone yesterday told me that everything was just fine. Now, I'm dangerous?

"I was just selling drugs," I said softly, "I'm not a killer."

So, they sent me back to jail. This time I'm in a New York jail. I wake up the next morning and look at the TV and guess who I see? Me.

"I can't believe this!"

The police want to extradite me back to Virginia since the charges originated there, but I refused to sign the papers. I got my attorney involved. I was told that the most you can fight extradition is just a couple of months but my attorney was good; she was able to fight it for 7 months.

The good thing about being in a New York jail was the conditions were much better. It wasn't overcrowded. Nobody really messed with me, so it was much more peaceful. And, I got to play basketball. It wasn't 23-hour lock up like in Virginia. And, I had my best friend, Redd, with me. He'd recently gotten locked up for hustling. We were chilling together one day just reminiscing over our life.

"Yo man," I said, "we can't be doing this crap no more."

Redd was leaning against a bench outside in the yard, near the basketball court.

"Yeah, I know," he said, "this is no good. We're no good to our family in here. You need to be home with your kids and I need to be home with my mom."

"Yea, I know. But, at least I know mom and grandma are taking good care of them while I'm gone. Still – I shouldn't be here."

"Yea, we should," Redd said, "and what kind of example are we setting for them going to jail like this? I mean, I know our kids are still really young and don't understand what is going on. But, my biggest nightmare would be for one of my babies to start the hustling life, you know?"

I nodded yes.

"It's an attractive and sexy life," I said, "I started…we both started the game young. For me, I wanted more than my mom could afford. I wanted to help. I got tired to being second class to everything else in our family. Then, the money started coming in. And, Redd, man, once you start making the money, it's really hard to turn back."

"Don't I know it?" Redd said lighting a cigarette.

"But, I feel like part of our motivation in doing all of this is to build a life for our kids so that they don't ever have to worry about the things that we did. Isn't that what every parent wants? A better life for their kids than what they had?"

"Oh yeah," Redd said, "For sure. But, our act was cut short. Now we need a plan B."

"You right we do."

"So, what are you going to do when you get out of here?"

I looked at him with raised eyebrows.

"You mean if?" I said. My confidence that I would be able to get out this time had dwindled. They were holding a lot of years over my head, and I honestly didn't know if I could fight it.

Redd came over and sat on the bench next to me and put a comforting arm on my shoulder.

"You will get out, brother," he said looking at me seriously, "So getting back to my question, what are you going to do?"

I shook my head.

"I don't know. I really haven't thought that far ahead, you know. I'm taking things day by day."

I paused for a moment to think. What would I do now that the hustle game was pretty much over for me? Hustling is all that I've known my whole life.

"I guess I've always had pretty good business sense. I think that's why things worked out so well for me in the hustle game. I know how to make money and I know how to help other people make money. My dealers were happy to work for me because they knew I was fair and that I paid well. So, it would be great to own a legitimate business. But, I'm not really sure what kind of business."

"Well that's a start," Redd said patting me on the back.

That's why we were best friends. Redd always saw the silver lining. Here we were sitting in jail, not sure when we'd see the light of freedom and he was encouraging me to dream about the next step in my life. I really appreciated him in my life.

"So, what about you?" I said, nudging him, "what do you think you want to do when you get out of here?"

Redd leaned forward to think for a minute.

"Hmm," he said, "I think I might want to go back to school. I was a pretty decent student in school, you know. Maybe I can get my MBA and go into banking or something."

I smiled.

"Look at us, talking about getting legitimate corporate jobs and crap," I laughed.

"Hey, it can happen," Redd said.

"Yea," I said, "it definitely can."

While I was in New York, I met a couple of female correction officers (CO). Both of them were really nice. The one that was fair skinned with auburn colored hair was pregnant and going through problems with her man. The other one was really cute. She was about 5' 7", with deep chocolate skin and black hair to her shoulders, and was extremely curvy and I really liked her but she didn't want the drama of messing around with an inmate.

But, I really wanted to get to know her, so I sent word to one of my boys in my apartment building, Jerry. Jerry was a CO at the jail I was in and he was a cool cat. He was a big, strong dude and I was always cool with him though he was never involved in any hustling. I asked him if he could talk to Sondra for me, the CO, I was interested in.

A couple days after I sent word to Jerry, Sondra came up to my cell and called me closer.

"What's up?" I said, smiling.

She leaned in.

"When everyone goes asleep," she whispered, "I'm gonna crack your cell so you can come and talk to me."

"Okay," I said and walked back over and started chilling, thinking to myself, Thank you, Jerry!

I kept quiet until my boy Redd came over and started teasing me. I'd told him about her before I'd sent word to Jerry that I wanted to talk to her. He motioned over to her.

"That her?" he said.

I nodded.

"Yea," I said. I was really looking forward to catching up with her and getting to know her better. I'd been a ladies' man my whole life, but going to jail kind of gets in the way of that. Even though I've only been in jail for a few months, that's an eternity to go without being with a woman.

"So, did you get Jerry to talk to her?"

"Yeah, I think he did."

"What did she say when she came over a little while ago?"

I leaned in and lowered my voice to a whisper.

"She said she's gonna come over and crack my cell tonight after everyone goes to sleep."

"For real?" Redd said, then he started grinning devilishly, "You gonna try and get some?"

I started laughing.

"I'd like to get to know her first. Damn man."

"Hey," he said, shrugging his shoulders, "it's not like sex is easy to come by in here."

"That's true. We'll see what happens. I'm looking forward to talking to her. She's cute, right?"

"Oh yeah," Redd said, "and she's got a fat bottom. I'd be all over that."

I laughed at my friend. I could tell he was longing to get some as much as I was. But, I really liked Sondra so I was actually interested in getting to know her a little better before trying to jump right into her pants. Plus, I had no idea how we'd even do that here in lockdown.

I laid back and just chilled in my cell for a little while. Around 1 am, she cracked my cell. I looked around and noticed that everyone was asleep and walked out.

"Come here," she said.

We walked over to the tables where we eat lunch because the cells cannot see you from there. We sat down. She looked at me and flashed a smile. She had a really pretty smile.

"It's Cody, right?" she said.

"Yea," I said.

"I like you, Cody," she said.

"I like you too."

"But, I would be lying if I didn't tell you that I have some concerns about getting involved with you."

"I understand. It's a sticky situation. You're a CO and I'm an inmate. The two don't really mix too well."

She paused for a moment, then she leaned forward and put her hand on my thigh. I worked hard to control myself. Even though we were just talking, just her slight touch started to awaken my body.

"I've heard your story," she said, her hand still on my thigh, "I really believe that you are a good guy that is just in a bad situation. Tell me I'm right."

I didn't really know the answer to that question. Was I a good guy?

I shrugged my shoulders, and fidgeted a little bit and she moved her hand from my thigh.

"I mean, I'd like that think that I am. Like anyone, I've made mistakes, but I try to do the right thing. I guess my whole life, I've known nothing but the streets and a lot of the things I got into was more of a survival mechanism."

She looked at me compassionately, and then put her hand back on my thigh. It was getting harder to control myself, and I think now she was starting to notice. But, she still didn't move her hand. She placed her other hand on my face and started stroking my jawbone.

"I think you're a good guy, and I really do like you."

There was no hiding my physical response to her touch. She looked down.

"And I think you really like me too," she said smiling at the mountain in my pants she'd created.

"I do," I said grabbing her hand and caressing it, "I've been watching you for a little while now. I like your style and the way you carry yourself. You're very attractive. I don't have anyone and I'd really like to get with you."

We sat there looking into each other's eyes.

I could see the passion in Sondra's eyes. She wanted me as much as I wanted her, but we had to figure out how to make it happen.

"So, what's going to happen when this is all over with, when you get out of here?" she asked.

I leaned back on the bench, a little exasperated. I didn't know the end game of my situation.

"I don't know, baby. They are talking about a lot of years. If I get out of this, I'm sure we can work something not. If not, I just don't know."

She leaned forward, real close.

"Well, I'd like to try and make this work," she said.

"I tell you what...why don't we just live in the moment?"

"Sounds good to me," she said as she closed the space between us to give me a sweet, tender kiss.

Her lips were so soft and tasted of her strawberry lip-gloss.

I went back to my cell and went to sleep. It was a good night.

Things changed a little bit over the next couple of weeks. I started to see a lot more of her. Sondra did not typically work the night shift, but after our meeting, she transferred to the night shift just so she could see me every night. Every night, she'd come by to crack my cell and I'd be reading my Bible and praying.

"You always read the Bible?" she asked.

I looked up from my reading.

I'd just circled one of my favorite verses, Philippians 4:6,7:

"Do not be anxious about anything, but in every situation, by prayer and petition, with thanksgiving, present your requests to God. And the peace of God,

129

which transcends all understanding, will guard your hearts and our minds in Christ Jesus." NIV

At times like this, I had to stand on my truth.

"If I can't trust in God, I can't trust in anything," I told her, "I've got to read the Bible. It gives me hope and faith to stand on."

Everyone was already asleep, so Sondra actually took a risk and walked into my cell. I was really surprised by her bold actions.

"I always knew you were a good guy," she said, "but I never pegged you for the religious type."

I closed the Bible and sat it down next to me.

"I never said I was religious," I said, "I do believe in God and having a spiritual relationship with him. That doesn't make me religious."

"Well, I think it's cool that you have a spiritual relationship with God," she said as her hands started to make their way to my thigh, "Like I said, you're a good guy."

Then, she leaned in and kissed me.

I pulled back.

"Sondra, what are you doing?" I whispered, "A couple of the inmates are still up."

She leaned in teasing me with her tongue.

"What?" she asked, "aren't these guys your friends?"

I looked around at the familiar faces smiling back at me with a look that said, "get yours."

"Well, yea."

"Are they gonna tell?"

"Of course not," I said.

"Exactly," she said as she got up and straddled me and began kissing me.

I wanted to do her right there, but I knew that would really be crossing the line. She must have felt me rising as she was kissing me because she moved her hands to my private area and began stroking it. It got to where I couldn't take it anymore without throwing her on the bed. I moved her hand and pulled her away, but that didn't deter her much.

"I want you so bad," she said leaning in on my earlobe, nibbling.

I wanted her so bad it ached.

"I know, baby," I said, "I want you too, but I don't know how we are going to do this."

She pulled back and got up, nearly out of breath.

"We'll figure something out. I promise you."

She leaned in for another kiss.

"Good night, baby."

Figuring out how to be with together without anyone finding out became Sondra and mine's big mission.

We began casing the place. The facility had an upstairs and downstairs and each tier was organized in a horseshoe. There were four of these on each floor and a basketball court separated everything. On the other side was another basketball court and two more tiers. There were four section and within those sections sat a desk and chair where the CO on duty was usually positioned. In between the four squares was what we called the "bubble." This is where the guy sat that controlled the sliding doors and could crack your cell. The cells were all concrete block with flat doors and a little strip of glass. There were not many places you could go without being seen by either the inmates in their cells or another CO on duty.

But, we did find a little section; where we ate lunch, there was a small place behind the wall where no one could see you. Sondra and I began to use that area to spend time together. We'd hang out some nights for almost 2 hours.

But, despite the passion between us, we'd not crossed over into having sex.

One night, she was manning her post while the other CO on duty went to the bubble. Sondra did her rounds before coming to get me. We met in our usual place.

She looked back toward the bubble.

"We don't have to worry about him for about an hour," she said smiling at me.

She had a really beautiful smile. She came over and started kissing me. As I kissed her back, my body awakened again. I was tired of suppressing what I've been wanting for so long. I wanted her right now. I ran my hands through her hair and grabbed the back of her neck and bent her over the table.

I pulled her pants down and started entering her real slowly from behind her.

I was home! She felt so good! It had been too long since I'd felt the sweetness of a woman, and Sondra's was just right.

We finished up in time before the other CO came back around.

I turned her around, kissed her and let her get herself together, then I went back to my cell and went to sleep, satisfied.

The next night, Sondra came and got me like usual.

Of course, I was more excited than usual because I knew I was gonna get some. She cracked my cell and I met her in our usual spot. I grabbed her and started kissing her, moving my hands to her pants. She backed away.

"What's wrong?" I said, concerned, "Didn't you have fun last night? I know I did."

"No, Cody, last night was great, really great. But, we can't do that anymore."

"What? Why?"

"I'm really worried that we might get caught. For one, I'm going to make noise. Baby, you felt so damn good. How am I gonna hold that in?"

I smiled. She was stroking my ego a bit and it was working.

"I'm sure we can figure something out. Get you a pillow to bury your head in or something."

She started laughing.

"Not funny, Cody."

I gave her a comforting rub on the back, then I flashed her my sexy smile. I really wanted to get some tonight. Getting with her had awakened my sexual appetite, and I was hungry.

"Come on, baby," I said pulling her close, "you can be quiet."

She pushed me away and crossed her arms.

"Now what?"

"That's not the only thing," she said, pouting.

I grabbed the stool by the table and took a seat. I had a feeling I was not going to get my way tonight. She seemed pretty adamant.

"Okay," I said, "what else?"

She looked like she was struggling to find the right words to say.

"Well?"

"Well sex is…you know – messy," she said.

132

I started laughing.

She walked over and play punched me on the arm.

"It's not funny, Cody," she said a more serious look on her face, "I can't go back to work all wet and sticky and uncomfortable after we do it. It's not like I have the luxury of jumping in the shower afterward."

I stopped laughing and pulled her closer to me.

"I hear you baby. Those are valid concerns. I get it. We'll figure something out. I promise you."

I gave her a kiss and then got up.

"Where are you going?" she asked.

"Back to my cell."

"Already?"

"Baby, if I'm being honest, I need a cold shower right now. I need to decompress and calm my man down and go to sleep. I was ready for you tonight. But, I know we have to figure a few things out first."

Now it was her turn to flash a sexy smile.

"I promise, we'll figure something out," she said, "and I'll be worth the wait."

And, we did. Thank God! She figured out how to be quiet and baby wipes became our best friend. We'd hook up around 2-3 times a week and it was great. We pretty much had a full-blown relationship, even though I was locked up and she wasn't, because we'd figured out some things. On some nights, she was busy working, but she always made sure I was taken care of. On those nights, she'd come and get me, give me a little head and I'd go back to my cell and go to sleep. We had a great arrangement.

After we'd been seeing each other, a couple of CO's got wind of our relationship. I heard a couple of them talking one day from my cell.

"Did you hear Sondra was going out with one of the inmates? The one up on that big drug charge?"

"Really? The cute, light skinned dude?"

"Yes, but if you ask me, she stupid as hell."

"Well, maybe she just trying to get a piece. I ain't mad at her."

"I think it's more than that. I heard they are spending a lot of time together, more than sex. I think she's falling for that dude."

"Well, it's her life."

"Yeah, I know, but, she stupid. She just setting herself up for a fall. What could she possibly expect to get from this? They talking about giving that dude a lot of years. Plus, I hear they will be shipping him back to Virginia soon."

I laid back on my bed after listening to their pointless gossip. People would always have something to say. But, I couldn't help but wonder if there was some validity in what the one girl was saying. Was I leading Sondra on? She knew my situation. It wasn't exactly like I could hide it or anything. Yet, still, I could see it, too. She was falling for me. And, as much as I liked her, I wasn't in love with her and I didn't know what the future would hold for us.

Shortly after hearing those CO's gossiping about me, I lost my extradition battle after 8 months and was shipped back down to Virginia where the charges originated.

While I longed to be free, I longed more to be in my home state of New York. Being back in the Virginia jail brought back sad, gloomy memories of my first days here. Sondra was a bright light for me in a dark situation, calling me 2 times every week and because she was a CO, she was able to get me to the phone so that I could take her calls. She really was a good woman, and I appreciated her looking after me and checking on me, but I started to think about the conversation those CO ladies had in the New York jail that afternoon. I didn't want to lead Sondra on. I cared for her, but she needed to be free and live her life without me. I decided to let her know this the next time she called.

"Hey baby," she said, voice high with excitement.

"Hey Sondra," I said.

"They treating you okay down there?" she asked.

I looked around the cramped space compared to the more spacious set up in New York and shrugged my shoulders.

"I mean, I guess as much as can be expected under the circumstances."

"I love you," she said.

I paused for a moment.

"I love you, you too, I responded. Though, I really didn't. She'd just been so good to me. I didn't want to hurt her feelings. I did care for her, a lot. But, it wasn't love. Honestly, I was started to realize our situation was more situational. When I was in New York, our little tryst made sense and we were able to work things out, but now, what could we do really? Talk on the phone twice a week? Send letters? I realized that we were both trying to hold on to something that wasn't really even there - or at least she was. She was even sending me money, something I didn't want or need, but another indication of that she was getting too hung up on me. And, I felt bad because I was the one who pursued her. But, she deserved to be with a man that could take care of her and love her fully.

"I miss you so much," she said, "I'm going to figure how I can come down and see you soon, and I'm going to send you some more money too."

I had to cut her off there. Sondra was a good woman. She really needed to let go of me. I had no idea how things were going to shake out in my situation and she had her own life to live.

She picked up on the tension through the silence over the phone line.

"Baby, you okay? You've barely said a word. I feel like I've been doing all the talking."

"Sondra, baby, why you wasting all your time here with me?"

"Don't you know, Cody," she said softly, "I love you. And I believe all of this mess you're caught up in, it'll get cleared up. You're a good man."

I lowered my head. I really hated doing this. I didn't want to break this girl's heart but it wasn't fair to allow her to continue to hold on to this fantasy.

"I know you love me," I paused for a moment, choosing my next words very carefully, "and baby, you've been so good to me, putting your job on the line. You don't need to do that."

She started to say something but I interrupted her.

"Listen Sondra, I need you to do something for me and I really don't want any argument from you on this. I need you to forget about me. Live your life. You deserve so much more than what I can give you right now and I don't want to give you any false hope about my situation. I honestly don't know what's going to happen. All I know is they are talking a lot of years. I may never get out of here. Do you and keep your head up. It won't be long before a good guy swoops your fine butt up. And, please feel free to stay in touch with my family if you like. They really like you. They probably see the same thing I see in you. Take care baby."

And, I handed the phone to the guard and left before even giving her a chance to respond. She continued to call every week and write letters but this time I didn't answer her calls or write back. My heart ached for her because I never wanted to hurt her, but she deserved better. After about 2 months, the calls and letters stopped so I figured she got the message from me or maybe found someone else to move on with.

That gave me some peace of mind which was hard to come by. Back in the Virginia jail, things were much different. I didn't have my best friend to talk to and hang out with and unlike New York; we were locked up 23 hours a day. The hour you were allowed to come out of your cell, you had a few meager options which included going into a little room to work out with no equipment or sign up to take a shower. There was no basketball. In our cells, we had a concrete bowl for a toilet with a metal sink behind it. When we got something to drink from the commissary and needed to keep it cold, the only option we had to was to place it in a plastic bag and sit it in the toilet because that was the coldest place in the room to keep it. Unfortunately, that was also, of course, where we went to the bathroom so every time we went, we had to take the plastic bag out, flush the toilet a couple of times and then place the bag back into the toilet to keep our drinks cold.

I was not in a good place – mentally. I got in a few fights. Of course fighting led me to solitary, which was a reprieve from the chaos of being locked up with everyone else. I looked forward to solitary. The only downside was you didn't really have a real bed in there. They gave you a flat mattress and a pillow and there was just the little hole in the ground to go to the bathroom, but it was peaceful. No one messed with me in there, and it was the only time while I was locked up that I was allowed to be alone with my thoughts. It helped me meditate and pray which I was doing a lot of lately because quite frankly, I was seeing no way out. I was trapped. While I felt like the case they had against me wasn't solid and couldn't possibly stick, they'd found a way to keep in here and I started to wonder if I'd ever see the light of day again. I thought about my children, my mom and my aunts who were all worried about me and wanted me to come home.

All the girls were only concerned about things that just didn't matter when you were locked up.

Then, I just started to wonder how much my family really even needed me in their lives. They'd done just fine without me locked up all this time, so maybe they'd be okay if I was just gone. Life was so dark that I didn't see any reason to go on. I thought about ending it all. How much of a relief would it be not to feel anything anymore? Just to go numb.

A lot of people think about suicide and if you think about something long enough, you will eventually make moves to make it happen.

I'd broken the blade off of a razor, sanded it down and taped it on the back of my toothbrush to use as a weapon in case anyone ever tried to jump me. I'd been jumped a couple times already so I figured the next time something happened; I'd be ready for them. But, this particular day, I had different plans for my razor.

I sat in my cell alone, contemplating the value of my life. Would anyone really miss me? What did I have to live for if I had to spend the rest of my life in this gloomy, miserable cell? No one should be subject to live like this. I started to think of how many people were wrongly accused and placed in situations like mine. Taken away from their children, their families, the only people who really loved them. I was sitting here in this cell, thinking about taking my life while murderers and rapists still roamed the streets. Where was the justice in this world?

I picked up the razor and inspected it for sharpness. It was not uncommon for inmates to try and take their life. There were a lot of people that felt like I did, trapped, like there was no way out. And, there were a lot of suicide attempts. Yet, few were actually successful.

I remember talking to an older fellow during our one-hour break one day.

"It's tough to make it in here. I've been hearing about a lot of guys trying to take their life," I said.

He looked at me.

"Trying," he said, "that's the key word. These guys don't really want to die."

I remember his statement really surprising me because a guy I know had recently been taken to the infirmary for slitting his wrists.

"What do you mean?" I asked, "James just slit his wrists the other day. How much more serious can you get than that?"

The old man leaned in.

"Yeah, he did slit his wrists. But, he cut from left to right," he said demonstrating on his own wrists, "but if he really wanted to die, he would've ripped right down the middle. That way, they wouldn't be able to stop the bleeding."

I remember shuddering at the thought when he told me that. But, it actually made a lot of sense. I'd always thought that if someone was willing to take a blade to their wrists, they were serious about dying. But, the old man was right, a lot of guys that had attempted suicide this way had survived and had the chance to trade their day to day life in their cell for some quiet time in the infirmary.

I stood in my cell alone, inspecting my handmade weapon in my hand.

Just rip down the middle. If I do it fast enough, I'd barely feel the pain. I could do this. It would be quick and over with before I knew it.

I turned my left wrist over, inspecting the green veins running through it, the sign of life and blood flowing through my veins, the life that I was ready to stop. Could I do this? Just end it all? Yes, I needed to do this.

I took my razor and started to slice the middle of my wrist.

"Crap!" I yelled.

A couple of inmates in nearby cells heard my yell.

"Hey man," someone next to me called out, "you ok?"

"I'm fine," I yelled back.

Blood dripped from my wrist and the reality of what had just happened brought me to my knees.

What was I doing? This wasn't right. Already on my knees, I sought the only one I knew could help me in this moment of despair.

"God, please help me! I don't know what I'm doing. I don't know why I'm here anymore. I've lost my purpose and I don't know what is going to happen here. I'm hurting, Lord. Heal me. Help me. I know I have not made the best choices in my life and maybe that's why I'm in the situation I'm in. But, I know you want more from me than this. Please give me the strength to make it through this situation no matter what happens."

"And, Lord, thank you for stopping me from making the biggest mistake of my life. Now, please give me something to live for. In Jesus name, Amen."

I went to bed that night with a calm over me that I hadn't felt in a while. I'd dodged a bullet and for the first time in a while, I really felt like God was working in my life. He didn't want me to end my life. And, my hope was because he'd worked out a way for me to get out of this mess. Either way, I went to bed with some peace that night.

chapter 8
prayers answered

The next day, I was surprised to get a visit from my lawyer. At this point, I'd been locked up for a year and a half so I was hoping he was bringing me some good news. Every other deal he'd come to me with in the last 6 months had been a joke, so I was hoping for better.

I sat down across from my lawyer, expectant, yet guarded.

"Please tell me you have something good to share."

My lawyer smiled tossing his briefcase on the table.

"Actually, I do," he said.

"You not coming here to tell me 20 years or $1 million or some crap like that?"

"No, I've got something better."

I was intrigued now and leaned in.

"Ok, what is it?"

"There is this program, like a boot camp. If you can go into this program for the next 6 months and pass, you get to go home. Now, you'll have parole for the next 20 years, but you'll be free."

"Are you kidding me?"

"No, I'm serious."

I was skeptical. This seemed too good to be true.

"What's the catch?"

"The only catch is you have to pass. This is your only second chance. If you fail, you go back to jail, no more opportunities. That's it."

"Where do I sign?"

My lawyer pulled out the papers for me to sign and I signed them right then. This should be a breeze. I was in great shape. Thank you, God for answering my prayers.

As I was loading my things into the van to depart the jail, I couldn't help but think this would be a piece of cake. Serve 6 months in a boot camp program and go free? Are you kidding me? Why aren't they offering this type of deal to more people? In some ways, it seemed too good to be true, but it was too late to turn back now. I had signed the papers and I was on my way to this place.

It seemed like we rode in the van forever. They were literally taking us to the middle of nowhere. For what seemed like miles, we rode through a thick forest of trees with nothing else around. All of a sudden, we reached a clearing and there I saw where I'd be staying for the next 6 months. There was a fence and some buildings and lots of Hum V's and military-like vehicles riding through the area. Once my van stopped and the guards let me out, I took some time to drink in my surroundings.

During that time several other black vans pulled up as well with inmates like myself, emerged in shackles and chains. The guards took off our shackles and handcuffs and led us to a cafeteria where we'd have our first meal there. Shortly afterwards, I learned that this place was for first time felons and was only offered to inmates between the ages of 18 and 25. The program was designed to keep you from ever going back to jail – a rehabilitation program of sorts.

We were all settling in and eating our meals in the cafeteria while one of the officers took center stage in the room with a microphone and addressed the crowd. He had a deep southern drawl.

"By now, you're probably wondering what you've got yourself into, if this is a hoax or if you really have a chance to earn your freedom back in 6 months. First of all, this is not a hoax. This is a program designed to whip you idiots into shape before introducing you back to society. If you pass my program, you will get to go home."

He paused for a moment.

"However, if you fail, you will go back to jail, no questions asked, no excuses and your sentence will start over from that point. So, if you have a 10-year sentence and you've already served 2, you'd better pass this program or your 10 years starts all over again. The guards are passing out your handbooks that will explicitly go over the rules of the program. I suggest you study that handbook very carefully. Many of you are looking around and thinking that this environment is better than your cell back in jail. After your first couple days here, I challenge you to see if you think different. You are not free men. You are inmates and you're mine for 6 months. We make the rules here and it is your job to follow them. We can do anything we want to you in here but kill you, so I'd suggest being on your best behavior. Enjoy your meal and get settled in fellas because we have a nice long day ahead of us starting tomorrow."

As we finished up our meal, I started to peruse the handbook that the guards had just handed out. We were not allowed to get into any fights with anyone. That would result in automatic ejection from the program with a free ride back to jail. We also had to ask permission to speak. We could not speak unless spoken to and had to address our officers in military fashion, "sir, yes sir or ma'am, yes ma'am." This place was designed to break you all the way down to nothing and then build you back up. The problem was, few people survived the breaking down part. Fifteen people quit the program after the first week. They just could not take it and saw jail as a better alternative. Me, I thought they were fools. This was my one ticket out of this mess and I was going to make it work. I was a couple weeks away from suicide before this offer was made to me so I saw this as God's answer to my prayers. I had to make it work. I could not go back to that place because if I did, I was certain I wouldn't survive. This was my last chance.

And, I had a hard time understanding why some of these other guys in this program didn't seem as desperate as I did. The guy with the least of amount of time in the group had 9 years. But, the vast majority of us had 15, 20 and even 40 years hanging over our heads. Whatever they had to throw at us had to be better than that!

But, it was hard. These guys really tried to break you. I saw them take the thing that you love the most and use it against you. I remember one of the guys in our program. Don. Don was having a really bad day one day and he was by himself in the corner upset, a few tears in his eyes.

Now, don't take Don for a wuss. He was a big boy, a big country boy, about 6'6, 350 pounds. On any normal day, I would say he was no one to be messed with. But, you could tell the strain of the program was starting to break him down emotionally and on this particular day it showed.

One of the guards seemed to show some compassion for him and took him aside.

"What's wrong, Don?" he said.

Grateful to see some compassion being shown in such a hostile environment, Don cracked a weak smile.

"I'm just feeling a bit homesick," he said, "I really need to finish this program. My girl is pregnant and I really want to get home to be there for her and the baby."

Normally, you'd expect a pat on the back or some words of encouragement in this situation, but boot camp offered no such services.

"Oh, you worried about that trick?" the guard said, "That's probably not even your baby. She probably sleeping with Jody."

Jody was a term that all of the guards used in a military context to infer that a loved one was doing something wrong or inappropriate. They used these tactics all of the time whether it was our wife, girlfriend, mother or sister. They knew how to get under your skin.

I could see Don's spine tighten up and his face get really stern. You could tell that he wanted to body slam the officer but he didn't do it. He had too much to lose.

That was our life in the program. The officers did not make it easy on us. They challenged us every step of the way. I guess that was why we started the program with 119 people but only 19 actually graduated.

Our mornings started early, around 5:30 am. We started out with PT (physical training) and then went for a run. At the beginning of the program, we could barely jog one mile. By the end of the program, we were all running 12 miles every morning. Before we went to PT and running, we had to make sure our barracks were squeaky clean, from our fresh made bed to our racks.

Once we finished our run, we could eat breakfast. But, even that was done in a very specific way. We didn't eat until our assigned officer was scheduled to eat. And, when we got to the cafeteria, we did not touch our food until the last man got their food. Then, we'd await the order from our officer, which was usually something to the tone of,

"Eat dogs!" Then, we would eat. Sometimes we'd had 2 or 3 minutes to eat our food but we never had any longer than 6 minutes to finish eating. So, we had to learn how to shovel our food down. If we were caught stashing our food or had any food on us outside of our scheduled time to eat, we were assigned more work, and this would go late into the night, ensuring that we got little to no sleep.

There were also consequences if you got in an argument with someone. If an officer found you arguing with a fellow inmate, they had this giant tree log and the two of you would have to carry that tree log with you all day long from the time you woke up to when you go to bed. The goal was to teach you how to work together. Now, if you got in a physical fight with someone, there was no tolerance or punishment outside of you getting put in cell for the night. The next day, someone picked you up and took you back to jail.

The officers had a file on everyone so that they knew your background and offenses. For most programs like this, things seem to get a little easier the deeper you got into it because you learn routine and your mind and body get used to it. This was not the case with this boot camp. I felt like every day, it actually got harder and harder.

One of the challenges we all had to face was the chief officer just didn't like us. We all came to understand that things were done a certain way at this boot camp. We had no right to demand any respect from the officers but had a responsibility to give it. We'd all accepted this fate. We were inmates. But, the chief officer was excessive in everything he did, so much so that several of us had filed grievances against him by the conclusion of the program. He frequently insulted us, beyond what the other officers did, calling the white inmates "cracker" and calling me a "half-breed nigga." We took serious offense to this slander because there was no need to bring race into this. I didn't care if he called me maggot, dog or whatever. But, to use an oppressive, ugly name with such painful history behind it was unnecessary. And, to top it all off, this man was black! None of the other officers were doing this. He knew that he pushed us to

145

the limit and I came to believe that his sole purpose to try and make us fail the program. He egged us on all the time trying to get a rise out of us so that we'd snap and hit him and he could send us back to jail the next day.

When he knew that he was really getting under your skin, he'd often say, "Come on! We can go. If you win, you can stay."

So many times, I wanted to just punch him in the face and I knew a lot of the other guys felt exactly the same. But, we didn't because we had a bigger goal in mind.

An answer to our prayers, he was eventually replaced by another chief officer, a woman. She pushed our bodies to their physical limits but did not heap on the verbal abuse of our previous officer. She actually wanted us to complete the program. Getting in shape during this period of my life was an understatement. We did sit ups, push-ups and ran obstacle courses on a daily basis.

The silver lining of all of this was the program also offered some level of enrichment for us. During the day, we actually went to class. I got my GED. They taught us a lot and also sent us to therapy to get to the root of some of the problems that had to led our incarceration. Like I said, they broke you down, but they also poured back into you. Despite how hard the officers were on us; they still gave us a sense of normality. As we got closer to graduation, we were given a series of tests. We had to go through an obstacle course, we had to pass a test in school and we had to pass a test in therapy. If we didn't pass these tests, we failed the program and went back to jail. A lot was on the line. 119 people started out with us in the program. By the end, only 19 people graduated. The officers sat down with the remaining 19 to go over protocol before we graduated and were released. Among the 19 was old country boy, Don. He'd made it through and was ripped from all the training, down to about 275 pounds and his confidence was through the roof.

The officers sat us down with clipboard in hand.

"First of all, congratulations," one of the officers said, "you made it. Most of the participants in the program either quit or just couldn't make the cut. But, you did. You should be proud of yourselves. Give yourself a hand."

We all sat there looking at each other. We weren't used to this kind of positive reinforcement.

"Go ahead," he said.

We all started clapping weakly, unsure of what was happening. Our officers were rarely ever this nice or encouraging. I guess we'd started to earn some semblance of respect from them.

"Okay," he said grabbing his clipboard, "back to business. All of you have passed your final tests to exit the program and graduate tomorrow. But, before you can leave the premises, you must have a place to live when you leave here."

For the first time, I felt a wave of concern. I was in Virginia and my home was in New York. I got with one of my officers shortly after our meeting and they reached out to the parole and probation office and they were not willing to release me to New York. I had to remain in Virginia. The problem – I didn't have anywhere to stay! My officer reassured me that we'd figure something out and told me not to be concerned just yet.

Our contact with family had been cut off since we got to the boot camp so it wasn't like I could call my mom and ask her to help me out in this situation.

When we arrived here, there were no TVs, newspapers or phone service so we had no connection to the outside world. They allowed us to write one letter when we first arrived but even with that, they told us exactly what to write.

Dear Mom,

I arrived her safely. I don't know where I am. You will have to talk to an attorney to find out where I am before graduation gets here. If I pass, you will be instructed where I am and what date my graduation is. If I fail, you will be notified and I will be sent back to prison.

We weren't allowed to sign the letter, "I love you" or anything like that and once we finished writing the letter, they took it and mailed it to our families. That was the last attempt of contact I'd had with any of my family in the last 6 months.

My officers contacted the parole and probation office to let them know my dilemma. Their immediate solution was to put me in a halfway house. But, then they called my mother and she was able to get in touch with some of my relatives in Richmond, VA. My grandfather's brother and his wife agreed to take me in and look after me so they signed over custody to them.

As I look back on my experience in this extreme boot camp, if you want to call it that, I don't really know how I made it. They had a no excuses policy when it came to fighting or laying hands on anyone in the camp. I got into 3 altercations where I should have been gone, but somehow the officers always came up with an excuse to let me stay. I even got into a fistfight with the staff sergeant that caused so many problems for everyone. But, somehow, his superior officer stepped in and said I was provoked and that he laid hands on me first. Three times I broke the rules – three times and I'm still here! I just didn't understand it. I should be in jail.

But, when I had some time to reflect on my situation, I remember the prayer I said in my cell before I came to this camp. I remember putting all of my trust in God to please deliver me from this situation. And, I realized it was God. He was granting me favor, when I didn't even deserve it. All I could think is that he must have some kind of plan for me because he knew that if I went back to that jail cell, I would've ended my life.

I'm so thankful for his grace and mercy because there were many people in that program that had more years hanging above their heads and committed lesser offenses that I did and they are in jail today.

The time came for me to finally get out of this place and my uncle came to pick me up. Well, he really was my cousin, not my uncle, but I always called him uncle because he was so much older than me. My mother and son also showed up and we drove a couple hours from the site to Richmond, VA.

chapter 9
free at last

The long drive to Richmond gave me time to think and reflect about the last 2 ½ years of my life. While I'd chosen to live a life on the edge, I'd never imagined that I would have lost nearly 3 years of my life locked up. I looked at my son and could see all of the time I'd lost with him, but at the same time I was extremely grateful. I'd lost almost 3 years of my children's life but it could have been much worse. I could have been locked up for 20 years or longer. I just thanked God for looking out for me and providing a hedge of protection over me during this critical time in my life.

I guess my silence in the car concerned my mom a bit.

She looked over at me, a crinkle of concern in her brow.

"Son, you ok?"

I looked up, shaking my head slightly. I didn't even realize that tears were starting to form in the corners of my eyes. By this time, we'd arrived in Richmond and the car stopped in front of Red Lobster.

Knowing that I would need some time to gain some composure, my mom told my uncle to go on inside the restaurant and reserve our table and she sent my son with him.

She walked around to the back seat and put her hand on my shoulder.

She didn't have to say anything. It was just good to have her there. She reached out to me and pulled me into a close embrace and I broke down, tears flowing. In that moment, I felt like a little boy running to his mommy. The comfort of her arms around me somehow made everything okay.

I pulled away and wiped my eyes.

"I'm sorry, I didn't mean for that to happen."

"What are you apologizing for?" she asked, "You're human, ain't you? You've been locked up for almost 3 years, Ty. You're entitled to have a moment. We've all been waiting for the moment we would have you home with us again."

I looked around at the very unfamiliar surroundings.

"Except this isn't exactly home," I said.

"But, it's not a jail cell," my mom retorted, sending me back to reality.

"No, it's not."

"Then, it's home."

"Yes ma'am."

She reached into the back of the car and retrieved a brand new pair of sweat pants and sneakers and handed them to me.

"Here," she said, "I figured you'd want something fresh to put on after getting out of that place."

I eagerly accepted her gift, anxious to get into some nice clothes again. Then, she leaned over and kissed me on the forehead.

"I love you baby," she said, "Go on and get changed and come have a nice dinner with us."

"Okay mom."

She went inside the restaurant and I stayed in the car and got changed. But, before I went into the restaurant, I still had to take another minute. I know there are lots of people that serve a lot more time in prison than I did, but I was so thankful to breathe the fresh air with no one barking orders at me. No one appreciated their freedom more than I did right now.

I got freshened up in the restroom before joining my family for dinner.

Our server was a cute, light-skinned girl named Amber. She was particularly friendly from the time she came out to take our order. After I placed my order with her, she flashed me a bright smile.

"You smell good," she said.

"Thank you," I said, starting to feel myself a little bit.

Throughout dinner, we talked off and on. Every time she came out to bring food or refill our beverages, she would always gravitate over to me and we'd chat a little bit. We flirted like this the whole evening. Our exchanges started to rebuild my confidence. I was glad to know I still had it, but I had to admit, I was looking pretty good. The new sweat suit my mom brought me looked pretty well on me. I had a fresh baldhead and I was ripped from all of the workouts at boot camp. I was enjoying this attention and wanted to see where it was going to go.

By the time we'd started wrapping up dessert, Amber brought out the bill and handed it to my uncle. Uncle put on his glasses and pored over the bill carefully, and then motioned for Amber.

"Young lady," he said, "my nephew and his son's food are not on this bill."

She picked up the bill and looked at it briefly.

"Oh, don't worry about that. I took care of it," she said and then flashed me a sexy smile.

Once the bill was paid, she brought it back to me with her phone number written on it.

"Call me," she whispered in my ear before we left the restaurant.

My uncle's house was not far from the Red Lobster. I got settled in and we just hung out, talked and laughed for a little bit. It felt good to be home with family. After chilling for a couple hours, I went in my room and gave Amber a call.

"Hello," she said.

"Hey, I didn't know if you'd be home yet or not. This is Cody. We met at Red Lobster."

"Oh, hey cutie," she said, sounding more anxious.

"So, what are you doing right now?"

"Nothing really," she said, "I just got off work about an hour ago, so I'm just chilling at my house."

"Well, I'm just getting in from out of town and I'm staying at my uncle's house for a little while. Why don't you stop by? We can chat and I can get to know you a little better."

"Okay," she said, "what's the address?"

I gave her the address to my uncle's house and she was there in less than an hour. When she got to the house, we hung out for a little bit. My uncle was a jokester and joked around with her and made her feel comfortable around the family.

"Hey," he said, "you are the one who waited on us at the restaurant?"

Amber nodded.

Uncle looked down at his watch.

"Man you didn't waste any time getting over here. You pretty sweet on my nephew, huh?"

Amber stood there, head down, a little embarrassed.

"Don't be ashamed girl," he said walking over and patting her on the back, "I get it. Light skin fellas are back in style. You gotta scoop him up while he's still hot."

Amber cracked a laugh.

My uncle was a crazy dude.

"Seriously though," he said, "it was really nice of you to pick up the tab for my nephew and his son at dinner. It was a real special dinner for the family and I know he really appreciated that."

"It was no problem, really," she said waving it off before flashing me a flirtatious smile.

"Sir, I was wondering if Cody could go out with me for a little while."

Uncle looked at me and then at Amber.

"You two can go out but I don't want you to go far. Stay in the neighborhood. Cody is not from around here and I don't want him getting into anything."

We walked out of the house in the front yard where we could talk more privately.

"What was that all about?" Amber asked.

I knew I was going to have to explain this. I wish Uncle didn't say things like that. He almost made it sound like I was a deviant. What the hell was I going to get into?

"Oh, I'm not from around here," I said, "I've been away from a little while for boot camp doing some training for the military. You know how strict those guys are."

152

I didn't want this girl to know all of my business. I was barely out, plus, it looked like I was about to get some, something my body desperately needed.

"Military huh?" she said, drawing circles on my chest, "I love a man in uniform."

Just as I was starting to feel myself getting hot around the collar, a couple of my family members came out of the house.

"You guys behaving yourself?" one of them asked.

We both flashed a bit of a fake smile, quickly realizing that we needed to have a little bit more privacy to get to know each other better.

"Why don't we just go sit in my car for a little bit?" Amber volunteered.

"Sounds good to me."

We walked over to her car, which was parked down the street on the curb. Once we both got in the car, it was nice and quiet with no interruptions.

"That's much better, don't you think?"

"Yes, it is," I said.

"So, you said you just finished boot camp. Are you going to be sticking around here in Richmond or will you be going somewhere else?"

"I don't really know," I lied, "I know I will be here for a little while, but I'm not sure where they might want me to go after that."

"Cool," she said as she applied red lipstick to her full lips. Her lips were so sexy.

"So, what branch of military are you in?" she asked.

Damn, she was asking a lot of questions about this military thing. Did I just dig myself a rabbit hole? I needed to give her a quick answer. Just spit something out.

"Umm, Marines," I said.

Luckily, she really did not pick up on my hesitation.

"Marines are sexy as hell," she said, "that explains a lot."

Then she leaned over and started to rub on my bald head.

"I like bald guys," she said.

"Yeah?"

She nodded.

"Especially when they are as cute as you," she said still rubbing my head. She stopped rubbing my head and locked eyes with me. She had nice eyes.

Then, she leaned in and kissed me. She tasted good. It has been so long since I'd been with a woman. She smelled so good. As she continued to kiss me, she started to pull down my pants.

I pulled away slightly.

"What are you doing?" I asked, trying to make sure no one was walking past the car.

"Shhh," she said, "no talking."

Once she'd pulled my pants and my boxers down to my ankles, she took a moment to admire my package, and then proceeded to go down on me.

Ohhh – felt so good! Is this what country girls are really like? I'm never leaving this place. All I can say is this girl knew her way around the terrain. Once she'd gotten my rocks off, she wasn't done and I really didn't want her to be. This was the first time I'd been with a woman in over a year. I wanted this. I wanted her. By now, the windows in her little car were starting to fog up so it was harder to see inside.

She jumped on top of me on the passenger side and leaned the seat all the way back.

"I want you, Cody," she breathed heavily.

"I want you too baby."

Then we proceeded to have sex right there in her car. We lost all track of time. And to be honest, I was in such a euphoric state; I could have stayed in that car with her all night.

Little did I know that we'd been gone long enough that my uncle had started looking for us. A knock on the window interrupted our sexual tryst.

I slowly rolled the window down.

"I've been looking all over the place for you boy," he said clearly aware of what was going on, but not commenting on it, "you've got 20 minutes to get back to the house – both of you."

A bit exasperated and a lot embarrassed, Amber and I got dressed and, got out of the car and headed back to my uncle's house.

As we walked into the house, I could tell Amber just wanted to run and hide. How embarrassing is it be caught having sex in your car by your man's uncle? She didn't want to come back to the house, but I reminded her that he asked us both to come back so she reluctantly followed me.

We both stood inside the doorway quiet and awkward. No one in the room but my uncle really knew why.

"Would you like to go to the bathroom, dear?" my uncle asked, motioning toward the bathroom.

Amber didn't say anything. She just looked at me and then looked at him.

My uncle nodded toward the bathroom and Amber followed.

He'd even left a washcloth and towel in the bathroom for her to clean up. I couldn't help but chuckle a little bit as she went into the bathroom. I appreciated my uncle looking out like that, but it certainly did not make the situation any less awkward for either of us. When she came out of the bathroom, my uncle joked around with her, adding a little insult to injury.

Luckily, as embarrassed as Amber was, she was a good sport and relaxed a little bit and laughed at his jokes.

Amber was a pretty cool girl. We continued to date for a few weeks after that. She kept coming by the house to see me and would buy me things. But, in my classic fashion, it didn't take me long to move on to another girl. It was just what I did, what I was used to. And, since I'd gone so long without any female companionship, I wanted a taste of what these Richmond girls were like. And, I had to admit; I really liked the girls here. What I didn't like was where I was staying. As much as I loved my uncle, they were old and their lifestyle did not quite match up with mine. They were up at the crack of dawn every morning and in bed by 8 pm. To make things worse, they gave me a 7:30 curfew. So, here I was a grown man with a curfew every night. Because I was growing a bit in popularity among the ladies, it just made it a little difficult for me to do what I wanted to do.

I had another uncle in the area that was a little younger and had three boys of his own. I approached the parole and probation office to see if I could get moved to his house. I always found the officers there to be really nice to me because they felt I'd gotten a raw deal being on probation for pretty much the rest of my life when I didn't get caught with any drugs, any guns and hadn't been violent with anyone. They'd just accused me of these things and the only reason I'd pled guilty to any charges was to be able to go through the boot camp program they offered so that I could get out. They told me that I could stay with my uncle but I had to have a job. That had been a challenge since I'd gotten out because unfortunately, companies are reluctant to hire ex-cons.

When we presented this dilemma to my uncle, he told parole and probation that he could hire me to work around the house, cut grass and clean. They agreed to put down that I was working for my uncle until I got a better job. As much as I was glad to change my home situation, I was still homesick for New York so I asked when I would able to return home. They told me that it would be at least 6 months. I had to be in good standing for at least that long to be able to transfer. So, I followed their instructions and did all of the right things. I did all of the chores for my uncle as we agreed but I did not get paid for my work. For him, payment was giving me a place to stay and taking care of me while I got on my feet. So, since I wasn't working a full-time job, I found myself with a lot of free time, allowing me to meet lots of girls in Richmond. Before long, I'd started to develop a reputation in Richmond similar to the one I had in New York. All of the girls knew me and they were bold. I was up front with each girl I was with, letting them know that I'd just gotten home and did not really want to be tied down in a relationship. None of them seemed to care. They would come home with me, sleep with me and leave. It became a habit, with different girls all the time and I was really starting to enjoy myself. Not only did the girls sleep with me, but also they brought me things. I came back from the program with only 3-4 outfits and within the first two months of coming home, I had a whole new wardrobe.

I'd developed some good healthy habits as a result of being involved in the boot camp program, most of them fitness related. I got up early every morning and went for a long jog, usually from the east side of town where I lived all the way to the north side of town where my other uncle lived. Most of the times, my uncle would drive me back home at the end of my jog, but when he wasn't available to do that, I would just jog the distance all the way back home.

When I got back to my uncle's house, I would stay outside, grab the water hose and clean myself up before going into the house.

"What are you doing, Cody?" my uncle would ask, "we have a shower in the house."

It was habit. After being locked up for over 2 years, I wasn't used to taking a shower. I just reverted to muscle memory which told me to clean up outside. It took me an entire year before I took a bath.

I'd also gotten used to the habit of sleeping on the floor. My aunt and uncle would come into my room to find me asleep on the floor beside my bed. They couldn't understand why I'd sleep on the floor when I had a soft, warm bed to sleep in. To be honest, after 2 ½ years of sleeping on a hard surface, sleeping on the floor was actually more comfortable for me because it was what I'd grown used to.

I was thankful for my uncle's hospitality but eventually, I was allowed to go back to New York.

It felt so good to be home after being away for over 2 years. But, what I quickly learned after coming back home is that nothing really changed. Everyone was happy to see me and was glad that I was home but all they wanted to do was party. But, I didn't want to party. I wasn't in that mode anymore. The drug game was still running strong.

"Here Cody," one of my buddies told me as he handed me about 50 vials of crack, "take this and make yourself some quick money."

I stood there and just shook my head. I did not just get out of jail to fall back into the same cycle that got me there in the first place. I handed the drugs back to him.

"Nah man," I said, "I don't do that anymore." I'd made a promise to God that if he'd get me out of the mess I was in that I'd never sell drugs again and didn't plan to break that promise. But, despite the promise that I made, the offers kept coming in. I was surrounded by people selling drugs because this environment is all I'd known my entire life. My friends got tired of me turning them down and finally made me an offer.

"Look Cody," one of them said, "I'll sell it for you and give you the money. How about that?"

I wasn't about to turn down free money.

"I'll take the money if you're offering," I said.

Despite all of the peer pressure surrounding me, I stuck to my guns not to sell again, but eventually I became a product of my environment and fell back into some of my old habits. I started drinking and partying again. I was "the man" in the neighborhood again, minus selling drugs.

When I had my meetings with the parole board, a lot of my friends just told them that I was working for them and that kept them satisfied. I chuckle to myself when I think about the fact that they thought they'd confiscated all of my money. What they didn't know was I was a very smart businessman. I'd stashed money all over the place for occasions just like now. I'd left money with my mom. I'd asked my uncle Trevor in Bluefield, VA to hold a bag of money for me. I had one of my ladies stash some money for me and I also stashed some money in the back yard of my aunt and uncle's house and planted a fruit tree over it. So, I was doing ok. I was living like I did when I was actively selling drugs.

About a year after I got out, I got some of the money from my mom and got myself a house. I had a young lady I was seeing at the time and we had her put the house in her name and I made all of the payments. After making the commitment to buying the house, she started having doubts because she couldn't understand where the money was coming from.

"Cody, I don't know how comfortable I am with this. How can you really afford to do this?"

I kept reassuring her.

"Don't worry baby, I got this."

But, she kept nagging me about it.

"How are we going to afford to pay the mortgage? You don't really have a job. Where is the money going to come from? The house is in my name and I don't want anything bad to happen."

"If you have so many reservations about this, why did you sign the papers in the first place?" I asked.

"I don't know," she said, pacing the living room exasperated, "you told me that you were going to take care of it and I trusted you, I guess."

"And you don't now?"

"It's not that I don't trust you. I just don't know how you're going to pay for this place. I don't want to get stuck with a house I can't afford."

I grabbed her by the arm and took her into one of the smaller bedrooms in the house. I opened up the safe and showed her a healthy pile of money. I thought this would ease her uncertainty but unfortunately, it opened up another bag of worms.

She backed away from me.

"I don't want to be a part of anything illegal, Cody," she said.

"This was illegal years ago," I explained, "but not anymore. This money is clean now."

She wasn't convinced.

She put her hands up in the air.

"I don't want to be a part of it," she said.

"Fine," I said, shutting the safe, "go back and live with your parents. But, this is my house. I pay all the mortgage and all the bills here."

She left and had a bit of an attitude. I guess I couldn't really fault her for standing up for her own morals. She had a right to do that. But, she ended up coming back to the house a couple days later.

"Look," she said, "I really didn't mean to come at you that way. I was just a little frustrated, I guess. I know you will take care of the house."

I appreciated that she came back and apologized, but I already knew the house was taken care of.

"That being said," she continued, "I just don't feel comfortable living here with you."

I was sitting on the couch when she'd walked into the house. I got up and walked over to her.

"I understand," I said, "do whatever makes you feel comfortable. Would it make you feel better if I paid for the house for year in advance?"

She nodded.

"Done."

She had her little attitude in the beginning because she didn't like where my money came from and despite her moving out, like all women, she came right back to me – if for anything to have sex. She came by the house about every other day to see me. One afternoon, we were both lying in bed after making love and I gave her a bit of an ultimatum.

"I understand that you don't want to stay here, but you can't just keep coming in and out of my life like this," I said, "I need someone who is going to more of a constant fixture in my life. If you're not going to be in my life every day, I'm going to find another woman who will."

She looked over at me, a look of surprise on her face.

"Well baby, if you want me that bad, all you had to do is ask," she said leaning in to kiss me as we rolled in the sheets for another round. What she didn't know was that I was just running game on her. I didn't really want a permanent relationship. I just wanted to have my cake and eat it too, and I'd learned how to get my way with women.

chapter 10
in love

Amidst all of my sexual experiences, I did find a girl I liked and started kicking it with for a little while. Jasmine was very positive and forward thinking. She was fixing me something to eat in the house one day and asked me a question that really challenged me.

"Cody, have you ever thought of doing something positive with your money?"

I thought about her question. Up until she asked me that, I thought that I'd be able to live off the money I'd saved forever. I realized now that was more of a fantasy.

"What did you have in mind?"

"Well," she said as she placed a plate of food in front of me, "you're really good with your hands. You're a great carpenter. Why don't we open up something?"

"Open up something? How am I supposed to do that? I can't even put nothing in my name."

Jasmine sat down calmly at the table.

"Yeah, I know, but you have capital. I'm sure we can figure something out."

"Ok," I said.

I put my trust in her and she went to work. She called some of her relatives to get some advice and help setting things up. I ended up setting some things up in my sister's names. In this day and time, there was not much security on identity so I had no problem using her information to set up my business. No one knew she was a 13-year old kid. And, just like that, I had a construction business.

I was so proud to have a real, legitimate business. I tried to invest back into the community by hiring other black tradesmen, or at least I thought. I ran into all kinds of problems with the guys I hired. Some lied and said they could do things they really couldn't do and other nickeled and dimed me for everything, trying to get over and get as much out of me as they could. It was a disaster.

I sat at my desk one day and just buried my head in my hands because I wasn't sure how to resolve this issue. I really wanted to help these guys out and give them jobs, but they were making it really hard.

Jasmine walked in and saw the frustration on my face.

"What's wrong baby?"

"These guys are all whack jobs. No one is doing what they are supposed to do. How are we supposed to build a successful company without good people?"

Jasmine walked around the desk and took a seat on my lap. She caressed my face with her hands and looked me in the eyes.

"Here's what we're going to do," she said, "we're going to just fire everyone and start over with new people."

I pulled back a little bit.

"Everybody?"

"Everybody."

I was a little hesitant at first because I didn't want to put anyone out of a job, but Jasmine reminded me that this was a business and these guys had not been pulling their own weight. So, I listened to her and we cleaned house. We realized that our previous recruiting methods clearly were not working for us so we decided to try something new. We went out to job sites and started recruiting guys from there. These were guys working off the books that had real skills and you could see the fruits of their labor. This strategy worked and we hired our-

162

selves a pretty good crew. Things were going well for a while and our business thrived for about 2 years.

I eventually found myself falling back into my old habits, running the streets with my friends and partying. I had to be "the man." As I ran the streets, messing with different girls every night, I left Jasmine alone to run the construction business all by herself. Naturally, she did not appreciate this and she really hated that I was messing with other girls after everything she'd done for me. We ended up shutting the business down which relieved her because she was no longer vested in it when I abandoned her.

This gave me some time to really reflect on my life and the self-destructive habits I'd developed. How is it that good things keep happening to me and I always find a way to mess it up? I realized that I needed a change in my life, so I started going to church with my mom. My eyes were opened to things I'd never seen before in a church. There is this image you have of church, a perfect image. It's God's dwelling place so nothing should ever go wrong there, right? There was a young pastor at the church, about my age preaching. I could really relate to him because he was my age, but also because this man was really anointed by the Lord. But, the senior pastor who'd pastored the church my entire life, didn't let the young pastor preach that often and get the shine he really deserved. I couldn't really understand this. My expectation was that when you're a pastor, you're supposed to be a certain way. Pastors are leaders in the faith, in the community. I'm supposed to look at you and want to model my life after you and the things you do. But, that wasn't what was happening in the church. I heard the gossip among the people, between my mom and my aunts and everyone really liked this young pastor and really wanted to see him preach. The problem was, the senior pastor felt threatened by him and was more concerned with losing his spot in the church than let this man preach the word for the Glory of God. He was so concerned that the church would forget him. But, how could we ever forget this man? He'd pastored this church for over 30 years!

Then, there was the gossip that our senior pastor was out there messing around with different women and even had a baby outside of his marriage. Now, I'm not inclined to believe everything I hear. Gossip is gossip. But, then I saw it with my own eyes. These things were happening right here in my church! This was supposed to be the safe place, where you go to get cleansed and repent and our leader was out there doing these things. That's when it became very apparent to me – pastors are not perfect. They make mistakes too. That doesn't absolve the things that our pastor did but I think we put people like him on a pedestal when they are subject to the same temptations as us.

What impressed me the most though, was this man's wife! I'd never seen a better demonstration of a strong woman. She stuck by her man. Through all of the rumors and gossip, which I know she heard, she stood with her head held high. She never bought in or said anything that would tarnish her husband's reputation.

We were just leaving church one day and I caught up with the young pastor. His name was Donald. We were just kicking it by my car and discussing the Word and some of the things the church was doing.

"Pastor, I really just wanted to let you know that you are doing the right thing. I feel like I can really relate to you and I like what you're doing. I'll follow you anywhere," I told him.

Pastor Donald cracked a smile. He was a humble man, which I really respected.

"I really appreciate that, Cody – really," he said, "I know you don't really know me that well, but your family, your mom and your aunts have been a true blessing to me and my family since we joined this church. I've heard a lot about you and I'm really glad that you told me that. You have no idea how much that means. I really do appreciate it. I'm working on some things and I definitely want you to be part of it. But, no matter what you hear, I want you to promise me one thing."

"What's that pastor?"

"I want you to keep coming to church, keep worshipping. No one is responsible for your salvation but you. Come here and get what you need and just filter out any negative that you hear. Remember, this is the place of the Lord and as long as you treat it as such, he'll give you what you need."

I nodded and gave him a bro hug before getting into my car.

"Bet."

"I'm proud of you Cody. I know life has not always been easy for you and you've been through some things but I'm so glad to see getting your life together."

I remembered what pastor told me and upheld my promise. I continued to come to church every Sunday, and the rumors kept circulating. It got to the point that it was nearly impossible to filter out the negative and even Pastor Donald couldn't take it anymore. He finally decided to break away from the church.

He talked to some people in the church and started to coordinate a small service, which would be his initial church plant at the Camen Lodge. At the first Sunday service at the Camen Lodge, there were only about 13 people, included my family, pastor, his wife and 2 kids. This small group of people became the charter members of Kingdom Baptist Church.

We grew quickly. By Bible study the following Wednesday, our small group had grown to over 20 people. By the following Sunday, we'd grown from our small group of 13 to over 30 people. Within a couple months' time, the Camen Lodge could no longer accommodate us. We moved to a local recreation center and began meeting there. We continued to grow, and as the church grew, so did my personal relationship with God. I was seeing about 10 different women. Prior to this point in my life, women were as dispensable to me as a new pair of pants. Once I was done using them for what I needed at the time, I pushed them aside and moved on to the next once. My new association with the Lord started to expose these bad habits and I started to notice a pattern, an unhealthy one. So, I decided to cut down the amount of women I was seeing down to 2-3. I thought I'd done a good deed. I mean we've talking about a 75-80% cut. That's significant. Proud of the positive changes I made in my life, I decided to counsel with Pastor Donald about this.

I approached him after church one Sunday.

"Pastor, can I talk to you for minute? It's kind of private."

"Of course," he said.

We walked over to a more private area of the rec center. We found a couple of chairs and sat down.

"What's going on Cody?"

"I know that I haven't talked to you about every detail in my life, but I've always had a reputation with women and when I started coming to church with you, I was seeing a lot of women, up to 10 at a time. Please don't judge me."

"Not at all," Pastor said, "please continue."

"Well, being around you and the church has really impacted me. I'm in the Word more and I really feel myself drawing closer to God."

"That's great Cody. I think you are a valuable asset to the church. I'm glad you're growing and learning."

"Thanks," I said, "Well, I guess I realized after going to church and being in the Word that I didn't need to be seeing all of these women, that it was wrong. So, I decided to make some changes. I'm now only seeing about 2-3 women. Do you think that is okay?"

"What do you think?" he questioned back.

"I don't know," I said, "but I thought I was doing a good thing narrowing it down."

"Let me ask you this question, Cody. It's great that you made the decision to see less women. But, since you are still seeing more than one woman, how fair is it to them to only have half or a third of your attention?"

"I guess it's not fair to them at all."

"I think you know the answer to your own question. This is not my decision to make for you. I'll never tell you what you should do. It's your life and you have the freedom to navigate through it as you choose. But, as your spiritual mentor, I will say this. The fact that you felt prompted to talk to me about this and ask me about it tells me that you are not completely settled with this decision. You know the right thing to do."

"Ok."

He put his hand on my shoulder before heading out of the room.

"Pray about it. God will help you make the right decision. I think he's already prompted you."

And, he was right, I knew what I had to do. I had to narrow down my choice of women to 1 which wasn't the easiest thing for me to do. I decided to stay with my daughter's mother, Debbie at the time. Things were going pretty well with us for a while until I met someone who literally stole my heart, Camille. She was not only beautiful, but she was just a nice girl, different from the girls I was used to seeing. Thinking about my pastor's words, I know I would have to break things off with Debbie if I wanted to pursue a relationship with Camille.

Debbie and I were chilling in the living room one day. I was sitting there trying to think of an easy way to break things off with her. She really was a sweet girl and I didn't want to hurt her, but I knew there was not a long-term future for us. She actually started the conversation before I had a chance to say anything.

"Cody," she said turning to me, "we need to talk."

Perfect! I knew 'we need to talk' was almost always code for 'I wanna break up.' This means that we were in the same place.

"That's good," I said, "cause I was thinking the same thing."

"I'm pregnant."

There was an awkward silence between us. I know she didn't say what I just thought she said.

"Excuse me?"

I just wanted to make sure I didn't mishear this.

"I'm pregnant," she repeated.

"Oh. Ok," I said processing the information she'd just shared, "don't worry. I've got some money, so what we're going to do is I'm going to take you to the clinic and we're going to get an abortion."

"No," she said standing up from the couch, "I'm not getting an abortion, and I'm not going to let you make me."

I sat back on the couch, covering my face in my hands, exasperated.

"But, I don't want to have a baby by you."

"Why?" she asked.

"Because you're an atheist."

This was not the only reason I didn't want to have a child with her, but with my newfound faith, it was an easy excuse. Truth was, I had enough children. I didn't need anymore, and I didn't want any more with this woman.

"But, I don't believe in abortions," she said.

"But, that doesn't make sense," I said, "you're an atheist. You don't believe in nothing. What do you care?"

"That's not fair," she defended, "I care about this baby – our baby."

Then, she walked over and tried to place my hand on her belly, hoping to get an emotional response out of me. I got up and walked away. I was pissed. I didn't want to be with her. I wanted to be with Camille.

"How you gonna trap me like this?"

"I'm not trying to trap you, "Debbie said, sounding hurt, "Cody, I care

167

about you. I thought this might be a good thing, that it might bring us closer together as a family."

"No Debbie, I don't want to have a child by you."

"I'm not getting rid of my baby. You're not making me get an abortion. It's okay. I'll stay away from you and do whatever I have to do. I can raise this child on my own."

Memories of my past flashed through my mind. I didn't want this child but I'd be damned if I was going to allow a child of mine to grow up fatherless like I had. It just wasn't' fair.

"How far along are you?"

"Three months."

"Debbie, we've only got a couple more weeks left to do this. Come on stop playing with me. You want me to pay you to get an abortion?"

"It doesn't matter what you say, Cody. I'm not getting rid of this baby. I'm keeping it. Now you can choose to be a part of this child's life or not but I'm having this baby."

Then she left the room.

I was left there sitting in the living room in a daze. This was crazy. I didn't want to have a baby by this girl and now I had no choice. Why did I have to have a child by someone I didn't want to have a child with? I ended up talking to my mom about this and she was actually surprised that we were splitting up because we were getting along so great. And, we were, but I knew she wasn't my future. I told her about Camille and how much I liked her. Now she is a girl that I would have a baby with.

Camille and I ended up getting an apartment together. I got rid of the house I had with the other girl, much to her relief since she was never comfortable with our little arrangement. I agreed to be there for the child and took Debbie to all of her doctor's appointments. I just couldn't believe that I was 25 years old about to have my 5th child. What was I out here doing? I needed to slow it down.

I felt like Camille was a great change of pace for me. She was a good girl. I told her about the situation with Debbie and she was okay with it, no drama at all. Camille was a nice Muslim girl with a good job and she loved herself some Cody, which was all good because I loved me some Camille. She loved me in a way that I wasn't used to being loved. The care and attention that she gave me was different that any of the other women I'd ever been with. I started feeling like she could be "the one." Camille even talked to Debbie and was willing to develop a relationship with her for the sake of our child and me. I don't know many women that would do that.

She was afraid of dogs, so I got us 2 pit bulls to help her work through her fear of dogs. I really felt like we were starting to build a life together. She had two sisters, one who was sweet like her and another who was mean to her and couldn't stand that I was with her. The mean sister actually lived across the hall from us, and the only time I saw her being nice to Camille was when she wanted something from her. She despised me. Part of the reason she couldn't stand me was because she saw me bringing other girls into the apartment while Camille was at work.

I wasn't proud of this but I'd always had a problem with sex. It was an addiction for me and I really didn't know how to control it except to just give in to my urges. Sex wasn't a want for me; it was a need. I would meet girls in the neighborhood and bring them back to the apartment to have sex. But, that was just it – sex. There was no emotional attachment. I had an itch and it needed to be scratched. It got to the point that if I didn't have sex every day; I'd literally start to feel sick. I started having headaches. Lucky for me, I had so many options; I never really had to worry about that too much. I always fulfilled that need.

My actions were in no way a reflection of how I felt for me girl. I loved Camille. I was in a good place. I was still going to church on a regular basis. And, our church had now grown to where we were now meeting in the YWCA. Life was really good. I was the happiest I'd ever been. Camille and I had a great relationship and we spent all of our time together. When she wasn't at work, we were together. She was just so good to me. I could really see myself marrying this girl.

Of course, that still did not change my habits in the streets. Other girls were just part of my life. A fly chick moved into the neighborhood from Cali. She was model tall, about 6'1", dark skin, long dark hair and banging body. I had to hit that! She made it easy because she took a liking to me quickly as soon as we met so we'd get together and have sex while my girl was at work.

With all of these girls I messed with, there was a particular arrangement.

169

They all knew that I had a main girl and if they ever came in contact with her, they knew to keep their mouth shut. I threatened to have my cousins and sister beat them up if they ever threatened to tell Camille about what we were doing. But, it never came to this, probably because when I was with them, I always made a point of making them feel like they were the only woman in the world. This was just how I was raised treat a woman and I'd always adopted this philosophy. Make them feel like the only woman in the world when you are with them. And, because of that philosophy, none of my side chicks every caused me any problems with my girl.

One afternoon, I was hanging out with my buddy Mike. He needed to go and see his daughter's mother. She was a little older than us, in her thirties. I went with him to meet her. We caught up at a local club not far from our house. I waited around at the bar and grabbed a drink while my boy went to go see his daughter's mother.

About 5 minutes later, he came back.

"That was quick," I said, sipping on a Long Island.

"She brought her aunt with her," he said, "She's sexy. I think you should meet her."

"Eww," I said, "I'm not into old ladies like that."

"Nah man," he said, "it's not like that. She's her aunt but they are close to the same age. She's only about a couple years older than her. I think you might like her."

"Okay," I said as I grabbed my drink and followed my friend.

When I came around the corner and met the aunt, I was pleasantly surprised. She didn't look like an aunt at all. She actually looked younger than my boy's girl.

"Hey, I'm Cody."

"Kendra," she said extending her hand.

She was sexy.

We hung out for a while that night, getting to know each other, joking around and having a good time.

The next day my boy called me up.

"Cody, my girl's aunt wants your phone number. Should I give it to her?"

"Yea, give it to her," I said.

She called me shortly afterward and we started messing around a little bit. Kendra was about 11-12 years older than me, so this was unlike any other relationship I'd ever had. Because she was older, she was established. She lived about an hour away so she'd come into town, pick me up and we'd sometime have sex in the car and other times we'd get a hotel and she'd just keep it moving. It was perfect for my lifestyle. She knew I had a girl and would even give me money to buy stuff for Camille. This was a perfect relationship. I had it made. Here this woman was coming into town, hitting me off and then giving me money to buy stuff for my girl? Seriously? But, I learned that there is some truth in the saying, "if it's too good to be true, it probably is."

Kendra was dropping me off one afternoon and my mom and one of our long time neighbors were outside.

"Hold it down for me daddy," Kendra said after kissing me good-bye.

"For sure," I said before walking toward my mama's house.

"You keep playing with fire and you're going to get burned," I heard my mother say as I approached the house.

"Mom, what are you talking about?"

Mr. Barnes, our neighbor, was sitting outside with my mother.

"She's talking about this older woman you're running around with, Ty. Now, nothing good is going to come from that."

"You don't know what you're talking about, Mr. Barnes," I said, agitated.

"First of all," my mother said, raising her hand to me, "this man is much older than you, so show some respect. And second, Ty, you have a good woman in Camille. Why are you messing around with this older lady?"

"Mom, I don't expect you to understand," I said, "but I've got it under control. Don't you worry about me?"

She sat back on her stool and just shook her head.

I leaned in, smiled and kissed her on her cheek.

"Did you cook?"

"Yea, I cooked."

"Okay, I'm gonna grab me a plate."

A few months into my affair with Kendra, I was growing tired. This was different than what I was doing with the other side chicks in my neighborhood. I felt like I was managing to two different relationships and I was becoming exhausted. Camille was the girl I loved and who I wanted a future with so I knew I had to change what I was doing with Kendra.

She came in town one afternoon and we hit each other up. I was going to miss the sex with this woman because it was unbelievable, maybe something that comes with a little age. She'd gotten us a hotel this time and I was getting up from the bed and getting myself dressed.

"Kendra, this has been great, but I think it has run its course. We need to stop doing this. I need to spend more time concentrating on my girl."

I did not expect the reaction I got.

"Your girl?" she said, "you mean the girl I bought that nice necklace for last week?"

"Kendra, you always knew I had a girlfriend. I never tried to hide that from you from the beginning. Why are you so upset?"

"Because you think you can just quit me whenever you feel like it. It doesn't work like that, Cody."

"Well, then tell me exactly how is it supposed to work? I think I'm a little confused."

"Clearly you are," she said walking closer to me, "it's simple. Our little relationship here hasn't run its course. It's still very much alive and when I'm ready for us to be done, we'll be done, and I'm not ready to let you go yet."

I started shaking my head.

"Oh hell no," I said walking away from her.

She stalked me to the other side of the room.

"What did you think? That you can just keep hitting me off every week and not have to deal with me?"

"Pretty much. Yeah."

"Well this lady is done giving the milk for free."

"This is nonsense. I'm done with you," I said walking toward the door.

"You think it's going to be that easy. I'll tell your girl what we've been doing. I don't think your precious Camille will be too happy to learn that you been tapping this tail."

I stopped at the door and turned around.

"You don't want to play this game with me."

"Don't I? I think I do want to play," she teased.

"You're going to mess around and get your tail beat. Keep Camille out of this. She doesn't need to know anything."

"I don't have no time for your petty threats. Send whoever you want to send. I don't give a damn. It still won't change the fact that I will call her and I will tell her every juicy little detail about everything we've done together."

This woman had me backed in a corner. I couldn't tell if she'd actually tell Camille what we'd done or not, but I was not going to let her bully me into being with her. I did not roll like that. I walked out of the hotel room and left her there, making a statement on how I felt about the matter.

As I walked out of the hotel, part of me thought that maybe she was just bluffing. She really wouldn't follow through with her threats. We started getting calls at the apartment.

"Hello."

"Can I speak to Camille? I want to tell her about all the hot, nasty sex me and her boyfriend have been having?"

"Whore, don't you ever call here again, you hear me?" I said, slamming the phone down.

"Baby, who was that?" Camille asked from the living room.

"Telemarketer," I lied.

"You sounded pretty upset for it to be a telemarketer," she said looking concerned.

She walked over to me and started to stroke my face. God, I loved this girl.

"Are you okay?"

I grabbed her hands and kissed them.

"Yea, baby, I'm fine. Those damn telemarketers are just so annoying. They never know when to stop calling. Come on, let's eat some dinner."

I distracted Camille and we sat down and had a quiet dinner together. But, the calls kept coming. I did not know how long I would be able to intercept them before Camille was the one who picked up the phone. As many women as I'd been with, I had no experience with situations like this. I guess my mom and Mr. Barnes were right. I should have left this woman alone. I talked to church friends about my situation, but no one could offer a viable solution to help me out of this mess. I started to realize that I'd made my bed, so I'd have to lie in it. Maybe the best thing to do would be to face the music and tell Camille myself. It would be much better coming from me than from that no good Kendra.

"You ready to eat baby," Camille interrupted my thoughts.

She was so beautiful. I took one look into those brown eyes and realized it could wait. She was so happy and I didn't want to ruin our good night together. Intercepting Kendra's calls became more and more difficult as they days went on. She was crafty and changed up the times she called each day, trying to catch Camille on the phone. My hope were that she would just eventually get tired and give up. I mean, I didn't even want to be with her so I don't know what she thought she would accomplish by doing this.

Eventually, I lost the battle. I was preparing for what I hoped was going to be a romantic evening for Camille and me. I was in the kitchen cooking a special dinner and had planned to dine with her via candlelight.
I heard the lock turn on the door and got ready to greet her with a kiss.

"Baby, have I got a surprise for you," I yelled out as I came around the corner to greet her.

But, I was the one who would be surprised. She looked at me, he beautiful brown eyes puffy and stained with tears. It looked as if she'd been crying for hours.

"Really?" she said, "I think I've had enough surprises for one day."

I walked up to her and touched her tear stained cheek.

She slapped my hand away.

"Don't," she said angrily.

"Baby, I don't understand. What's wrong?"

"You've been playing me for a fool all this time?" she said just shaking her head.

I started to speak but no words came out. I realized that my biggest nightmare had now come true. Kendra must have found some way to get to her.

"I thought you loved me," she said as the tears began to flow.

I took another step toward her and she took two steps back.

"I do love you," I said.

"You do?" she yelled, "then why'd you cheat on me, Cody? Is it true?"

174

I didn't know how to respond to her accusations so I decided to play dumb.

"What are you talking about, Camille?"

She rolled her eyes.

"Don't patronize me, okay?" she said, "I know. You other girlfriend, your sidepiece, whatever you want to call her, called me at work today. She told me about all of the nasty little things you have been doing."

She'd caught me. I felt like there as a frog stuck in my throat. I didn't know how to defend myself because there was 100% truth to everything she was saying.

"So, what do you have to say for yourself? Cat got your tongue?"

"I love you, Camille," I said.

"Well, you have a really funny way of showing it," she said walking to our bedroom while she sobbed softly.

I gave her a few minutes before appearing in the doorway. She had a suitcase on the bed and was packing.

"Please," I said, pleading, "don't go."

She looked up at me, her heart clearly broken.

"I just can't do this, Cody," she said, "it hurts too much. I love you, but I've gotta go."

I walked up behind her and wrapped my arms around her waist.

"I love you," I said, "how can we fix this?"

She turned around and kissed me softly on the lips before picking up her suitcase and walking to the door.

"I don't know if we can."

Camille went to stay with her sister that night but shortly afterwards, moved to Florida to stay with her stepsister. That was the last time I saw her.

My heart was broken. She was the first woman in my life that I truly loved, that I could see a real future with. She didn't deserve the way I treated her. She was definitely too good for me, but I loved her and really wanted her back in my life.

After she left, I couldn't take care of the apartment by myself so I approached the landlord and explained my situation and he was more that gracious to me. He gave me 2 full months to get myself together and get my things moved out, not charging me one single dime. I was grateful for the time to figure something out because I had more than myself to consider since we'd gotten a couple of dogs along the way. While I was getting myself together, I spent many lonely nights crying over my failed relationship with Camille. It had never hurt so much to lose someone.

As I was getting ready to move, Kendra re-appeared in my life wanting to mess around again. I guess I could have felt bitter and blamed her for what happened between me and Camille but I was the one who'd chosen to sleep with her in the first place so I really had no one to blame but myself. Looking at my own situation, I decided it wasn't a bad decision to get with her again. I was in between apartments and Kendra had a good job, good credit, a car and an apartment. She helped me get another place and maintain it, plus she gave me the keys to her place and let me use her car when I needed it. I almost looked at it as a good business decision to help me get from point A to point B. I'd lost my girl and didn't see any hope of getting her back, so I made the most of my current situation.

After getting over my break up with Camille, things started going pretty well. I was very active in the church and found myself getting closer to God each day. I was in the process of studying to be a deacon and I was also on the welcoming committee of the church, helping new members and guests when they attended service. As I got more involved with the church, it became evident that though people claimed to be Christians, everything wasn't perfect in the church either. In some respects, I'd learned that from my old church and the skeletons our pastor had in the closet, but I viewed this church in a different light as I aligned with the pastor to help him grow and build it. But, even our church had its share of flaws because in the end people are going to be people. The church had begun to form cliques and within those cliques' gossip and banter started to flow about various things. Now, I tried to avoid idle gossip as much as possible because the church was a place to serve the Lord and to worship; anything outside of that just wasn't important. Plus, there wasn't much they could say about me other than the fact that I dealt with a lot of women. But, I already knew this was an issue for me and it was something I was working out with God to figure out why I felt this need to be with different women. Because I was upfront and honest about my life, most people respected me for my honesty. But, like anywhere, there are always haters who will still talk behind your back no matter how honest you'd been with them. This was just something I had to learn about people in general. The church did not necessarily shield you from those naysayers in your life.

After getting with Kendra, I made a decision to just be with one woman for a while. For a while things were good. We decided to move down south to Virginia Beach for almost a year. Kendra and I got a house and tried to settle down a bit. She already had 3 kids. Her oldest son really liked me and we got along great. She had two daughters. The middle child got along fine with me as long as I didn't tell her what to do. If I tried to tell her anything, we usually had a problem. Her younger sister was worse. She didn't like me at all and walked around the house with an attitude all the time.

One afternoon, Kendra's middle child, Destiny had just finished eating her lunch at the table in the kitchen. I was in the kitchen cleaning up. Destiny got up from the table and left her plate sitting on the table.

"Destiny," I said, "I need you to throw away your trash and put your plate away, please."

She stopped in her tracks and just gave me a sour look.

"I'm serious little girl. Pick up your trash and throw it away. I didn't spend all this time cleaning up the kitchen for you to leave you mess there on the table."

She walked past the table into the kitchen where I was standing by the sink.

"I ain't no little girl!" she yelled at me.

"Whatever," I said, "you need to throw your stuff away."

I didn't have time for this child and her little games.

"No," she said.

I turned away from the dishes in the sink.

"What did you say?"

"I said no," she said crossing her arms with an attitude.

I took a pause as I felt my temper flaring. I didn't have the time or patience to be dealing with this kid. I had my own kids to worry about without having to deal with Kendra's rude kids.

"Destiny," I said slowly, "you're going to pick up your trash and throw it away like I told you."

"I said no," she yelled at me and before I knew it, this kid was throwing a punch at me.

Are you freaking kidding me?

I grabbed her by the wrist before she landed a punch and swung her around on the floor.

"What the hell is wrong with you?" I yelled at her.

Hearing the commotion in the kitchen, Kendra ran down the stairs.

"What the hell is going on down here?"

I just stared at Kendra's 14-year-old daughter still sitting on the floor, looking at me like she wanted to kill me.

"Your little angel here just tried to take a swing at me because I asked her to throw away her trash from dinner," I said shaking my head.

Just saying it out loud sounded incredibly ridiculous. That child had issues.

"Destiny, take your butt upstairs," Kendra ordered.

She huffed and ran upstairs, eyes still on me. I felt like I needed to sleep with one eye open that night.

Kendra walked up to me and placed a hand on my arm.

"You know how teenagers can get," she said, "attitudes about everything."

But, that was like the last straw for me. I really didn't want to be there anyway. I still missed Camille like crazy and this situation with Kendra and her kids was not working out. I wasn't happy.

I took a step away.

"Kendra, this is not working. We can't live in this house together anymore."

"What do you mean?" she said chasing after me as I walked away.

I stopped and faced her.

"What are we doing here? Are we really happy? We're at each other's throats all the time. Your kids don't like me. It's just not working. This thing we have here has run its course."

"You can't just walk out on me," Kendra demanded.

"Why not? What ties do you have on me, Kendra? What relationship are you going to threaten to end now? You already drove away the girl I really love. What could you possibly take away from me now?"

She was silent for a moment because she knew that there was truth in my statement. As much as she wanted me to, she knew I didn't really love her.

"Well, it's not just your name on the house," she said.

"I need to get some air," I said, "I'm going to take a walk. We'll sort this out when I get back."

I grabbed my coat and left the house. I needed to clear my head. The whole situation with Destiny was messed up but was a wake-up call more than anything. I had to ask myself, "why am I even here?" I don't love this girl. If there's any emotion that I feel toward Kendra, it's resentment for messing up what I had with Camille. I still missed her so much, and I was starting to realize that being with Kendra was not the way to move on with my life. I needed a fresh start.

After a brisk 15-minute walk, my head was cleared and I felt much better, more equipped to deal with Kendra and her crazy kids. When I got back to the house, the police were there.

The officer met me outside.

"What seems to be the problem officer?"

"We received a call about a disturbance. You didn't call?" he asked.

"We had a situation with one of the children where I thought I might need to call if we were not able to get her under control, but then she calmed down. So, no I didn't not call you."

"I called."

I heard Kendra's voice as she was coming out of the house.

I looked at her puzzled. What the hell?

"I called the police because he," Kendra said pointing at me, "threatened me."

I couldn't believe this crap.

"Really?" I said looking at Kendra, "you're going to play that game."

I directed my attention to the officer standing between us.

"Officer, that is not true. I'm from New York and told her that I was going to leave and go back home because things were not working out with us. It's time to go. I just need to go into the house and get my stuff."

"Nothing in there belongs to him," Kendra said blocking my way.

I was really getting exasperated. All I wanted to do was leave but she was making it more and more difficult.

"Officer, ½ of everything in that house belongs to me, from the stereo equipment to the furniture. Let's go get the paperwork and I'll show you."

I knew exactly where we kept all of the paperwork on everything in the house. I told the officer where to find everything and he went inside to retrieve it. He walked out of the house a few minutes later shaking his head.

"Sir, there's no paperwork where you told me to look."

That chick had moved it. Damn!

"Whatever," I said, "I just need to get my clothes and my stereo equipment and she can have everything else."

I really wanted my stereo equipment because it was a really nice system and I'd spent a couple grand on it.

"That stereo equipment isn't his," Kendra said, hands on her hips.

I looked at the officer and then looked at her.

"Really?"

The officer just shook his head.

"I'm sorry, but there's no paperwork to prove otherwise."

"So you just going to side with her?" I asked, "You know this isn't fair that you guys are just siding with her because she's a female. There's no paperwork to prove that any of that stuff belongs to her either."

The officer just stood there, silent. He knew I was right but couldn't argue it either way.

"Fine," I said.

I grabbed my phone and called my cousins in Richmond about an hour and a half away.

"Hey Tony, I need your help. I got a situation here with Kendra in Virginia Beach. It's not working out and I need to get out of here ASAP. How soon can you get down here with a U-Haul?"

"We can be there tomorrow morning," Tony said.

"I'll be ready."

I left and stayed in a hotel that night. As soon as my cousins arrived, we rolled over to the house and I got my clothes, my dogs and a few other things and we rolled to Richmond. As soon as I got settled into my cousins' house in

Richmond, I called the power company and the gas company and had everything turned off. Of course, I received a call from Kendra shortly afterward.

"Why you being so petty?"

"I don't know what you're talking about. You said it was your house, remember?"

"Well, who's going to pay the mortgage?" she asked, sounding concerned.

"Did you forget your own words? Let me remind you again. You said it was 'your house.' Your house means your bills. Don't ask me for anything because I don't owe you a damn thing."

"But, Cody, I love you. We can work this out," she pleaded.

I just snickered.

"You don't love me," I said, "you love you, and you only want me for what you can use me for. I'm sorry – we're done."

"But baby…."

"But nothing," I said, "what could I possibly have to say to you after what you did? I don't even know why I came down here with you from New York. You caused the woman I love to run away and you can never replace what she meant to me. I'm done with you, Kendra."

I hung up the phone. I really didn't want to deal with this woman again. She was toxic, and truth is, I knew this about her when we got together. I don't know what possessed me to want to move to Virginia with her. I think the hurt and pain from my break up with Camille more than clouded my judgment.

A month went by and I got another call from Kendra.

"What do you want, Kendra?"

"I'm pregnant," she said.

"What you calling me for? It ain't mine."

"Cody, it's your baby."

"No, it's not," I argued, "I ain't been with you in 2 months."

"Cody, I'm almost 3 months pregnant."

I hung up on her. There was no way this chick was pregnant with my child. She could have been with any dude in the last couple of months. I didn't believe her.

A few minutes I got another call.

"Is this Cody?" a female voice asked on the other line.

"Yes," I said, "who is this?"

"This is Dr. Smith. I'm here at the clinic with your wife."

I interrupted immediately.

"Hold up, doctor, this woman is not my wife."

"Well, she is pregnant."

Click. I hung up on the doctor. I wasn't ready to process this information. Was Kendra really pregnant? She was the last woman in the world I wanted to have another baby with. The doctor had told me which clinic she was calling from so I looked it up and it was legitimate. Damn!

I called Kendra back.

"How far along are you?" I asked.

"11 weeks."

"Get rid of it," I said.

"No, I want to keep this child."

"But, I don't," I said, "so here's what we're going to go, we're going to go to a clinic and get an abortion. It's not too late. We still have a couple of weeks to do this."

"Maybe you're not hearing me right," Kendra said, "I'm keeping this baby."

No matter how hard I tried, there was no convincing Kendra to get rid of this child, so here I was with another child on the way with a woman I didn't want to be with. I knew the right thing to do was to stand by her so I went back to Kendra even though I didn't want her. We moved out of the house in Virginia Beach and headed back to New York. We were 'working it out' if that's what you want to call it, only I didn't care about being loyal to Kendra because I didn't really want to be with her. So, it wasn't long after I got to New York before I slipped back into my old habits of seeing multiple women.

In the meantime, I tried to stay in contact with Camille in Florida. I missed her so much. One of my friends was actually dating her sister and he was keeping me up to date on what was happening with her.

"Have you heard anything about Camille lately?" I asked him, anxiously. We were outside on the corner, like always. He was smoking a blunt and I was just chilling.

"Actually," he said taking a puff, "yes, I have. Her sister said she met someone and it's pretty serious. I think she said she is engaged now."

"Engaged?"

I couldn't believe it. I always held out hope that Camille would one day come back to me, and now it looks like I might have lost her forever. But, despite my hurt in hearing this news, all I really wanted is her happiness. She was the sweetest, kindest, most beautiful spirit I'd ever know and all I wanted was for her to be happy. She deserved that.

"You alright man?" my friend asked.

"Yea," I said, "It was just a big blow. Wow, engaged, huh?"

"Yeah," he said as he took another puff, "sorry to be the bearer of bad news. I can tell you really loved her."

"Yeah, I did," I said, taking a pause, "But, I messed up. I really don't deserve her. I don't know that I ever did. Can you please send a message to her? The next time she comes up, can you tell me? I just want to apologize to her. I'll take her and her fiancé out to dinner; I just want to her to know that I never meant to hurt her."

"Alright man. Bet."

Learning that Camille was engaged was a really humbling experience for me. I didn't feel jealous or upset because the only person I had to blame for our failed relationship was myself. I know she loved me and I loved her, but I messed that up. As much as I wanted to be with her, I just wanted to let her know that I was sorry more. She deserved to live a happy, fulfilled life, even if it wasn't with me.

A couple weeks later, my buddy came running up to me on the corner.

"Guess what?"

"What?"

"Camille's coming to New York."

"Are you serious? When?"

"She's going to be here in about a month."

I'd moved back with my mom and went back to the house, excited about seeing the love of my life. I knew that she was engaged and had no intention of breaking up her relationship, unless of course, she told me that she wasn't happy. But, if she was happy, then I was happy. I was just excited to see her beautiful face again after all this time. I was so excited that a month seemed way too far away.

About a week before Camille was due to come into town, I checked in with my boy to make sure everything was still a go.

"Hey Mike," I said, "Camille still coming up next week?"

He looked at me, a big grin on his face.

"What you smiling so big for? You just get some?" I laughed.

"No, but you might," she said, nudging me.

"What?"

"Yes, Camille is coming next week. And – she broke up with her fiancé."

"You lying!" I said.

"Nah man."

"For real?"

"For real, man. She's back on the market."

Yes! Now I had another chance!

Every night leading up to her arrival, I could hardly sleep. I just had so much I wanted to say to this girl. I made a promise to God that I was going to get it right this time. I knew she was the one and I was going to do my best to convince her to give me another chance.

Finally – it was the day she was scheduled to come in town. I'd gone to the barber and got a fresh haircut. I put on my newest pair of sneakers and a fresh sweat suit. I wanted to look my best when I saw her. I came outside and noticed that everyone was hanging out on the corner, as usual, some of them getting their hustle on.

Then, I spotted my boy, leaning on his car on the corner. He looked like something was wrong. Everyone around him seemed to be in a somber mood. Even though I sensed something was going on, I didn't want that to mess with my mood. Nothing could spoil today. My baby was coming home to me today.

I approached my boy.

"Yo, where she at?" I asked grinning from ear to ear.

My buddy looked at me, surprised.

"No one told you?" he asked.

"Told me what?"

He took a deep pause, hesitating to even say anything.

"Told me what? Where's Camille?"

He moved me away from the car and the crowd surrounding him. Now, I was starting to feel a bit concerned.

"Last night, Camille was out walking her dog back at her place in Florida. A kid started messing with her but she ignored him and went home to her apartment. He came through the window and attacked her. He tried to rape her but she fought him off. When he couldn't rape her, he stabbed her over 20 times and killed her. She's gone."

I couldn't breathe. There was no way this was real. She couldn't be gone. I couldn't access my vocal cords to even form a response to this news. I didn't know what to say, how to respond, what to feel.

My buddy reached over and grabbed my arm.

"Cody, you okay?"

I shrugged my shoulders and tried to shake it off.

"Yea, I'm okay," I said. Then, I walked away before he could say anything else.

I went home and went upstairs to my room and just let the tears flow. In all my life, I don't think I'd ever felt a pain so deep. I really loved this girl. We were supposed to be together and now it would never happen. I didn't understand why something like this would happen to a sweet girl like her. It just wasn't fair. As I lay in my bed, grieving my lost love, I went through the gamut of emotions and eventually landed at guilt, guilt because I'd done her wrong, because I'd broken her heart and never gotten a chance to apologize. Guilt because if I'd done right by her, maybe she'd still be her in New York with me instead of going to Florida where this happened to her.

I felt this ache in my heart, an empty hollow feeling. But, this time it was different. Our break up was painful, but at least I knew she was okay and that I could pray for her to have a good life, which was all I really wanted for her. But, there was no coming back from this. Her life wasn't meant to end so soon. She was such a bright light in this world. I loved her so much. I didn't sleep a wink that night. No one could console the pain I was feeling.

I learned about her funeral from my friend. Her family and I were not on good terms because of how our relationship ended but I was not going to let that keep me from going to the funeral. I needed to say a proper good-bye. She was Muslim so her service was held at a nearby Muslim temple. When I walked in, I expected to get some dirty looks from her family but they were so caught up in their grief, they didn't devote any of their energy to that. The casket was in the front of the church. Even in death, she was still beautiful. I approached the casket and just looked at her. It was so hard to believe that she was gone. It looked as if she was just sleeping, the way she used to sleep next to me every night. I wanted to tap her on the shoulder and see those beautiful brown eyes. It pained me to know that I'd never see that smile or those bright eyes again. I reached into the casket and touched her hand.

"Camille, I've waited a long time to tell you this, and I hoped that it would be under better circumstances. But, I'm sorry for what I did to you when we were together. I didn't understand what I had and I'm ashamed of that. I loved you then, but I love you even more now. You were the best thing that ever happened to me, and I'm so sorry that I took that for granted. You're with the angels now, but I always thought you were an angel here on earth. I'll love you forever."

I walked away from the casket, tears in my eyes. Saying good-bye to her was the hardest thing I ever had to do. As strong as my faith was, it was rocked with her death. I couldn't understand why something like this would happen to someone as sweet and loving as Camille. She didn't deserve this.

chapter 11
back in the habit

It took me a little while to get over the death of Camille. She was my heart and the first girl I ever really saw a future with. But, before long, I was back on the prowl, the only way I knew to deal with the horrible ache I felt inside. I met a new girl from Jersey. But, she was different than all of the other women I'd dated. She was thicker. And, most of the women I dated were what I'd call thick in a good way, coke bottle shape, nice butt. Shanda had a nice shape, but she was the first plus size girl I'd ever hooked up with. What attracted me to her was that she was a big girl but she was in shape. All of her weight was in her butt and her boobs which were at least 40DD. But, she had a small waist and no stomach. She kept herself up. I liked that. She had hair down her back and was very attractive.

When we first met, she was very serious. A sweet girl, but a little bit uptight. I helped loosen her up and before long she was comfortable with me and cracking jokes back at me. I liked her so we started kicking it. She'd come back and forth from Jersey to see me and sometimes I'd stay up there with her. She had a good job making over $100,000 a year. She had a house and she gave me anything I wanted. Things were good. I felt grounded and focused for the first time in a while. Shanda even went to church with me, which meant a lot.

As time passed, I found myself traveling back and forth to Jersey to see Shanda more often. I stopped going to church as regularly as I used to. And, something interesting happened when I stopped going to church. The more I was away from the church, the less I noticed my phone calls getting answered by my brothers. The guys that I talked to on a daily basis went to weekly. Then weekly became every other week. I started feeling some type of way. What had I done to deserve this kind of treatment from my brothers? Did I do something to offend them? Did I have to attend church every week to receive the encouragement and association of my brothers in Christ? They were treating me different and I didn't like it. Church became a turn off to me. If I couldn't count on my brothers in Christ when I wasn't at church, how could I count on the church at all?

The more I analyzed the situation, the more agitated I got. I came to the conclusion that there was a lack of leadership in the church. I understood that the pastor could not control everyone and their actions. But, someone should be directing the people leading the flock when he can't. I just realized that we were no longer that tight, close-knitted group that we were when we started to build this church. And, just because you're growing as an organization and have more people, that doesn't mean that you forget where you came from and the people that supported you to get you where you are today. Now I found myself upset with my pastor because things had changed in the church and it was his organization. He's in charge so he should be able to control or prevent things like this from happening. But, then I realized that pastor never, at any point in time, treated me differently. He never called me less than his brother. I had no reason to be mad at him. The actions of these few men were in no way a reflection on him. We were grown men, not children. If these men were not returning my calls, it was their fault, not pastor's. But, I still let my anger grow inside of me because my utopic view of my church was flawed. As a result, I just stopped going to church all together. I didn't want to stir up mixed and angry emotions every time I went.

Unfortunately, as I stopped going to church and harbored resentment towards those brothers, my bitterness started to trickle down into my relationship with Shanda. By this point, we'd been seeing each other for a year now and she'd watched the challenges I was having with my brothers in the church and it began to cause a rift between us.

I realized that it had been a while since I'd been to church and was craving some spiritual food from my heavenly Father so I encouraged her to come with me.

"You need to come to church with me, Shanda."

She looked at me from the couch in the living room and just rolled her eyes.

"You must be playing. I'm not going to be driving back and forth from Jersey to New York for church and Bible study for those damn hypocrites."

Now the problems I was having with the brothers in the church were my problems, not hers. So, I took offense to her comment.

"You don't even know the people in my church like that to be calling them hypocrites. Plus, you don't go to church for the people anyway. You go for the word."

"I don't know why you want to go back to that church anyway the way they been treating you. They don't even answer your phone calls."

"Some of them do," I yelled at her before storming out of the house.

Her words made me angry partially because she was right because it wasn't her business or her place to be calling out the church like that. It wasn't her issue. It was mine and I had to deal with it. She should've just kept her mouth shut.

I went to church a few times after that without her but I was still irritated by her words. She had no reason to judge. No one was doing anything to her. The funny thing was when I went to church; it was like nothing was wrong. Those same brothers embraced me the same way they always did, even though they weren't taking my calls.

It got to the point that I knew who was phony and who was genuine which was a shame that I had to make that distinction in the church, but I did. I reached a point where I was just fed up with my entire situation, with the drama in church, the drama at home with Shanda. I needed to get away so I decided that it was time for me to dip out of New York and move to Virginia.

I came home and had a conversation with Shanda about my plans.

"I need a fresh start," I told her, "and I'd always told myself if there was anywhere that I ever wanted to settle down, it was going to be in Virginia. So

189

that's what I'm going to do."

"How you going to do that?" she asked.

"I'm just going to leave. I don't have anything keeping me here anymore. I've got some money so I'm just going to bounce."

"That's not exactly true."

"What's not true?" I asked her.

"That you don't have anything keeping you here anymore."

"What? Do you mean you? Shanda, you know we haven't been getting along that great for a while now."

"I'm pregnant," she said.

"Excuse me. What?"

"I'm pregnant."

I threw my hands up in the air.

"No, I can't deal with this right now. I just had a baby a couple years ago with a woman I didn't want to have a baby with."

"What are you saying? You don't want to have a baby with me?"

I just stood there and looked at her for a minute as I tried to digest this information.

"I'm not ready for another kid right now, that's it. Are you sure you want to keep it?"

She looked at me like I was crazy.

"Of course I'm keeping it. I don't believe in abortion."

"Fine," I said walking out of the room.

I needed some time process the fact that I was about to become a father, yet again. I was hoping to be free from the drama and just make a fresh, clean start, but I didn't see that happening anytime soon. If there was anything I believed in, it was being a father to my children. If my baby's mama insisted on having my children, I was not going to be an absentee dad. So, I decided to stick it out.

When I made the decision to stick around, I didn't just have to deal with Shanda and our deteriorating relationship but her disrespectful daughter. Shanda had a 13-year-old daughter with a host of issues and some definite attitude problems. Part of her problem was her low life father and then I think she resented me because Shanda listened to me when it came to her. But, as time went on and Shanda progressed in her pregnancy, things became even more out of control with her daughter, to the point that I think she probably needed psychiatric help. I think the way Shanda disciplined her really contributed to a lot of this little girl's issues. She pushed this little girl so hard and whenever she did something that Shanda didn't approve of, Shanda would strip this little girl down to her bra and panties and wear her behind out. I'm not talking about a 30 second whipping; I mean she would wear her behind down! I didn't approve of how she disciplined this little girl because here was this thick 220-pound woman beating a 90-pound kid. It just wasn't right and I told Shanda that time and time again.

I think these harsh beatings began to cultivate hatred in this little girl's heart. I could see it in her eyes every time her mother whipped her. I tried on several occasions to get through to her because I knew the little girl was suffering. I would talk to her, spend time with her and would constantly jump between Shanda and her when she went to discipline her. The little girl appreciated my advocacy but I don't know if it was possible to undo the damage that had already been done.

It became clear to me one day that something had changed after observing this little girl for a couple of months. Something had changed with her and I wasn't sure what it was. My gut told me it wasn't good. Her behavior changed. She was usually a pretty talkative kid and would sit down and watch TV in the living room every afternoon. But, the last couple of months, she'd become very quiet and had stopped watching television, but would instead just go in her room and sit. I was from the hood and could see the writing on the wall. Something was up.

One day while she was at school, I grabbed Shanda.

"Come on, we're going to raid your daughter's bedroom," I said.

She looked at me hesitantly.

"Cody, that's an invasion of privacy," she said pulling away.

"What privacy? She's a kid. She has no privacy. What bills is she paying?"

Shanda still wasn't convinced.

"I don't know."

"Shanda, for all I know, she could be doing drugs in there. Now, come

191

on, we're doing this."

So, we raided this child's room and I'm glad we did. As we searched through the room, we found a giant butcher knife in between her mattress and box spring. I thank God for my intuition and keen observation. I don't know if this child planned on harming herself or us but it was clear that she needed some help.

All of this pushing from her mother had sent this little girl to a breaking point.

"What are we going to do?" Shanda asked, frantic.

I looked at the large knife in my hand, thinking about what could've happened with this kid.

"First of all, we're going to hide this, and you're going to lay off this kid."

"You saying this is my fault?" Shanda copped an attitude.

"I'm not blaming you for anything. I'm just saying that you ride that little girl too hard. I've told you that time and time again."

"I only ride her because she's smart and I want her to make something of herself," she defended.

"And, that's fine, but you have to let her find her own way. You can't keep forcing these extracurricular activities on her and expect her to just love it. Just lay off."

Shanda backed down.

"And don't say anything to her about this. She doesn't need to know that we were in her room."

But unfortunately, I was too late.

"What are you doing in my room?" I heard a little voice behind me yell.

"What the hell were you planning to do with the knife we found under your bed?" Shanda yelled back at her daughter.

I just rolled my eyes, wishing she'd just kept her damn mouth shut.

The little girl just glared at her mother, a fierce look of hate in her eyes I'd never seen before.

"I was going to use it on you," she said, not blinking an eye.

Shanda was just silent, in shock that her daughter had just threatened to kill her. I looked at her, compassion in my eyes, although this little girl actually scared me.

"Can I talk to you for minute? Just you and me," I said.

"Just me and you?" she asked softly.

"Yes."

She nodded.

Shanda stood there for a moment in disbelief before leaving the room in a huff. The little girl's name was Chastity.

We both sat down on the bed. She looked at me wide-eyed.

"Are you going to send me away now?"

"Chastity, why would we do that?"

"Because of what I just said."

I looked her in her eyes.

"Did you mean what you said?"

"Yes" she said definitively.

I felt chills up and down my spine.

"Why would you want to harm your mother?" I asked.

"Because she makes me miserable. She doesn't really love me," she said piddling with her hands, head bowed.

"Chastity, look a me."

The little girl lifted her head.

"Your mother loves you," I told her.

"She has a funny way of showing it," she said sarcastically.

"Yes, she does sometimes. But, she thinks you're brilliant. She tells me that all the time. And, I think she just sees so much in you that she gets carried away when she gets you involved in all those activities. That's all."

"What if I don't want to do all those things?"

"I've talked to you mother. We're going to work on shaving some of those things down. Would that make you happier?"

She nodded.

"Can you promise me that nothing like this will happen again? Can we move forward?"

She looked at me and shrugged her shoulders.

"Chastity, I want to help you, but I need you to work with me, too. I don't want anything to happen to you or your mother. If you ever feel overwhelmed or upset about anything, you know you can always talk to me, right?"

She nodded.

"So, do we have a deal? You won't try to harm your mother or yourself?"

She looked at me and smiled.

"Deal."

I gave her a hug, realizing that as crazy as this situation was, this child just needed love and affection.

Things were good for a little while after that. I saw Chastity perk up and settle back into her old habits. I convinced Shanda to let her drop one of her activities and Chastity was grateful. We started to spend more time together and she felt free to open up to me more.

One evening we were hanging out after she got out of school. I noticed that she seemed a little sad.

"Chastity, what's wrong?"

"I miss Jamal," she pouted.

"Who's Jamal?" I said, thinking that maybe Shanda was stepping out on me.

"He's my big brother," she said.

"Ok," I said. I didn't ask her any more questions.

My mind started to race, trying to figure out who Jamal was. If Shanda had another son, she would have told me about him. We'd been together for over a year now. But, I just played it cool. I knew how to get what I wanted.

That night, I cooked us a good dinner, we watched a movie together as a family and then sent Chastity to bed. Once she was in the bed, we decided to go to the bedroom and mess around a little bit.

Shanda was about to climax, I stopped.

"Cody, what you doing?" Shanda said, out of breath, "don't stop."

"Who's Jamal?"

"Seriously?"

"Seriously. Why is Chastity crying and mad that she can never see her brother? Is that your ex man's child?"

"You really want to talk about this right now?"

"Yes."

"Can I at least get off first?"

194

"After we get this settled, I'll please you however you like."

"Fine," she said as she rolled over.

"Yes, Jamal is my son"

"But, I don't understand. I've been with you over a year and you're halfway through your pregnancy with my child. You mean he's your stepson?"

"No, I gave birth to him."

This was shaking me up.

"Your daughter is 13. How old is your son?"

"He's 15 going on 16."

"How come I've never heard of him or seen him?"

"I let his father have him after he was born."

I shook my head.

"I'm sorry – what? What kind of mother gives her son to his father?"

She didn't flinch.

"I was young and wasn't ready to be a parent. His father wanted him. So, we went to court and I awarded custody to him and his family."

"And you never went back to check on the kid?"

"I just thought it would be better if I let his father raise him."

I just shook my head.

About a month went by and things seemed to be going okay at home. There were no more incidents with Chastity and she seemed to be somewhat happier despite her questions about her older brother.

Shanda ended up getting a call from her long lost son at work one day.

She came home and told me about it.

"So what did he say?" I prodded.

"He just said that he wanted to get to know me and try to see if we could build a relationship together."

"That's great," I said, "He's giving you another chance to be his mother. He's not angry with you but wants to be in your life. You need to call and talk to him."

Shanda stood there uneasy about the whole situation.

I was sitting on the couch at the time and got up to confront her.

"Shanda, he needs to know about his mother."

"I know, I know," she said reluctantly, walking away from me to go in the kitchen and start working on dinner.

"Even if you don't want to deal with him, at least call him and tell him why you did what you did. You do owe him at least that," I suggested.

"Yeah, you're right," Shanda agreed, "I'll call him."

I was satisfied because I didn't believe any child should grow up without knowing who their parents are. Growing up without my dad had made me really sensitive to this situation. My mom did a great job of raising me, but there was always a longing in my heart for the father I never had. I could only imagine how this kid felt without his mother in his life.

Shanda called and talked to her son. She invited him over to the house. When he got there, I introduced myself to him, but excused myself so that they could have some one-on-one time together because this was really none of my business. I came home a couple hours later.

"How'd it go?"

Shanda smiled which surprised me given her reluctance to meet with this kid in the first place.

"It went great," she said, "He wants to be a part of our lives. I told him that he could come and visit once a month."

"Okay," I said as I took a seat on the couch, "how far away does he live?"

"Oh, he lives about 15 minutes from here," Shanda said casually.

"15 minutes?" I said, "And you told him that he could only come by once a month?"

Shanda avoided eye contact and walked into the kitchen.

"Yea, he gets in trouble at school and I don't want him bringing those problems around my daughter."

I sat on the couch in disbelief. This woman was ridiculous and she was about to be the mother of my child.

"Yea, cause we both know that if she doesn't do her lessons, you gonna whip that tail. You jump on that child for every little thing. You know what — you actually might be doing that boy a favor by not letting him come around here."

She didn't have any words for my response, just huffed and walked into the bedroom.

Another month went by and Shanda's son actually called the house. He had an event at school and wanted to know if Shanda could make it. She told him no. She didn't have anything else planned that evening, she just told him she couldn't go.

I started to see this woman's true colors with each passing day and I didn't like what I saw.

Her son reached out to her again to ask for shirt and slacks for school. I think he had a recital or some type of formal event he had to attend. I was in the living room watching TV when Shanda took the call and just overhead pieces of the conversation.

"I don't think every time you call me that you should be asking me for something," she said and hung up shortly afterward.

"Was that your son?" I asked.

"Yes," she replied shortly.

"It sounded like he needed something for school," I said.

"He always needs something," she said angrily.

"That's because he's a child and you're his mother."

"I may be his mother but I don't take responsibility for him. He has his father for that."

Wow. I heard all that I needed to hear at this point. She didn't give a damn about this kid. She'd done nothing for him his entire life and now a shirt and slacks for school was too much to ask. I realized at this point that it was time to get out of here. I didn't want to be here anymore. I was ready to leave. But, I realized that I had an obligation to my unborn child. So, I made a decision to stick around until my kid was born. But, I reverted back to my old habits. I was no longer faithful to her. I traveled back and forth from New Jersey to Virginia messing around with a bunch of different girls to fill my needs and keep me out of the house.

A month later, Shanda had our baby - a little boy. For the sake of my son, I decided to stick around for a little while longer. As a result, Shanda and I ended up messing around a little bit and I got caught up with her.

After we'd finished making love one night, she crawled up the bed and wrapped her arms around me.

"I'm so glad we're back together, Cody," she said.

I didn't really think we were back together but I didn't really want to hurt her feelings so I remained silent.

This didn't seem to faze her. She continued on.

"We just have such great chemistry together," she said, "baby, you might be the best I've ever had."

She was saying all of the right things to make a man feel good and swell his head up. Sex was my thing and knew I was good, but it always felt good to have your ego stroked. I smiled rolled across my face.

"I want to have another baby by you," she said.

And then the smile was gone.

"You what?!"

"I want another baby, Cody," she said moving closer and grabbing me by my pants that I'd just put back on, "have you seen how cute our son is? Imagine a little girl."

I got up and pushed her away.

"No Shanda! No," I said and started getting dressed. I definitely needed some air now.

"What's your problem?" she said, turning up her nose.

"Shanda, you not getting any more babies out of me, okay? I don't want any anymore kids."

"Okay," she said rolling over in the bed, "we'll see."

I walked out of the bedroom mad. There was no way I was going to let her trap me. I'd wear three condoms if I had to.

I stuck around for a few more days and then decided to roll to VA to get away for a little while and I took my son with me. While I was away, I realized that it was time to really end this. There was no sense in dragging this on any longer. It was getting painful for both of us – but most of all, me.

I called her up.

"Hey baby, when you coming back home?"

"Shanda, I don't think this is going to work," I said.

Tears started flowing.

"Why?" she said.

"I think we both know why. I'm just not happy and it's just not working."

"Can you at least come home and tell me goodbye?" she asked.

I was surprised that she didn't ask about our son once.

"Yea, baby, I can do that."

I went back to Jersey to say a proper good-bye to Shanda, which just meant a couple rounds of hot, sloppy sex. I think she thought this would change my mind but sex was sex to me. I never turned down a good roll in the hay but I'd already made my decision to leave.

chapter 12
wedding bells

I stayed there in Jersey with her for a couple of days, and she never spent more than an hour with our son who was only a couple months old at the time. This was further proof that I didn't want to be in a relationship with this woman, so I cut the ties and headed back down to Virginia.

After I'd been down there a couple of days, I got a call from one of my boys, James.

"Hey Cody, I need you to take a ride with me?"

"Take a ride with you? Where?"

"I need you to come with me down to this apartment complex," he said.

"Why? I'm not looking for an apartment."

"I know, but there's this fine chocolate girl that works there. She's thick and sexy. Our boy used to go out with her and said she is good."

"Okay," I said, "I still don't' understand that this has to do with me."

"I want to push up on her," he said.

"And?"

"And I need you there as back up. I don't know if I know how to talk to her."

"Oh, I see now," I said, "alright, let's go."

We rolled to this apartment complex. There was a big window to the office so we could see inside. There she was, cute chocolate girl sitting at her desk. It looked like she was alone.

"My buddy said she's the assistant manager here," James said, "what am I supposed to say?"

James was clueless. You would think he'd never talked to a girl before.

"Okay, just tell her you're getting ready to move and that you're interested in a 2-bedroom apartment. Just start with that."

So we walked into the clubhouse of the apartment together.

"Good afternoon, how can I help you guys today?"

I looked over at James, waiting for him to say something.

He just stood there silent, looking stupid. So, I took over.

"Yea, me and my boy are going to be roommates. We're looking for a two bedroom. Do you think you can help us?"

She smiled. She had a beautiful smile.

"I think we can figure something out," she said.

She led James and me into the leasing office and started going over the different options for two bedroom apartments. I kept waiting for James to jump in and say something to the girl since he was the one who wanted to hook up with her. But, he barely said two words the whole time. So, I just took over to keep us from looking stupid.

"Which of these plans do you think would work the best for the two of you?"

I looked at the floor plans she'd shown us and decided to play around and joke with her a little bit.

I pointed to one of the plans she showed us.

"I'm thinking about this one, because I'm going to need the bigger bedroom to fit my king sized water bed. A brother needs his space."
She laughed.

I liked it when she laughed.

She finished showing us the model apartment along with amenities like the fitness center and the pool at the clubhouse.

"We'll have a couple of these floor plans available around the time frame you and your friend are looking to move," she said, "just let me know when you'd like to put your application in."

"Thanks for showing us around," I said, "do you have a card? We've got a couple more places we planned to look at but we really do like this place and I'd like to get back to you with our decision soon."

"Absolutely," she said, flashing that smile again as she handed me her card.

When we got in the car to leave, James leaned in anxiously.

"Did you think she was into me?" he asked.

"She ain't pay you no mind, man," I said waving him off.

"Really?" he said, surprised.

"James," I said, exasperated, "you didn't say two words to her. What did you expect?"

"I know, I know," he said, "I chickened out. She was so fine, I just didn't know what to say to her."

"I told you what to say."

"Yea, but still…Imma go back tomorrow and talk to her."

"Okay," I said as I flipped her card back and forth in my hand.

I knew James wasn't going to go see this girl the next day, but I'd determined at this point that I was definitely interested so I decided to call her the next day, which was a Saturday.

I was the morning, around 10:00.

"It's a great day at Foxcroft Apartments, this is Stephanie, how may I help you?"

"Hi, I wanted to talk to you about an apartment."

"Okay," she said, "what size were you looking for?"

I heard all of the pep seep out of her voice. She sounded almost solemn now.

"You sound sad. You alright?"

"I'm fine. I was just thinking about something," she said.

"You want to talk about it?"

"With you?" she said, almost with an attitude, "I don't mean to be rude, but I don't even know you."

"Do you have anyone else to talk to? I'm coming over there already to look at an apartment. You might as well talk to me."

She sighed before speaking.

"I was just hoping it was someone else on the phone," she said.

"Who you thought it was? Your man?"

"I don't have a man."

"Then who?"

"Somebody I met yesterday."

I smiled.

We talked a couple more minutes about some various apartment options, and then I decided to go over there. When I walked in the door, she smiled and buried her head in her hands.

"That was you on the phone?"

"Yep," I said walking toward her.

"Now, I'm actually a little embarrassed," she said.

"Don't be embarrassed," I said, "I'm here, ain't I? Are you busy?"

"No, it's been pretty slow this morning."

I took a seat and we began talking. She told me a little bit about herself and I told her about me. Right away, I realized there was instant chemistry between us. We ended up talking for a couple of hours that day.

The next Sunday, we spent the morning together hanging out and getting to know each other. I offered grab us some lunch from Olive Garden. She could shut down the office for about an hour for lunch, so when I came back, we got to spend some uninterrupted time together. She was only supposed to close the office for an hour but we ended up spending almost 2 hours together for lunch. I'd planned to leave after lunch so that I didn't interrupt her workday anymore but we ended up spending the entire day together. I can't put my finger on what it was exactly, but I genuinely enjoyed her company. I wanted to spend all of my spare time with her.

At the end of the day, I was getting ready to leave. I'd been staring at her full lips for 2 full days now, eager to find out what they tasted like.

"So, can I have a kiss?"

She blushed. It was cute.

"Sure," she said, smiling, "you can give me a little peck."

She was still sitting behind her desk.

I'd continued to keep up with my running routine and work outs since boot camp so I was still in pretty good shape.

I walked over to her, and anticipating the peck she asked for, she leaned in a little bit. I picked her up out of her chair, sat her on the desk and slobbed her down for a good minute, running my fingers all through her hair. By the time I finished, she was breathing hard, hardly able to speak. Then, I just walked out of the office. No good-bye or anything. Just gone.

The next day I called her up.

"So, you just going to leave me like that huh?" she said.

I laughed.

"I didn't want to move too fast for you," I said, "and I definitely don't want to bother you while you're working."

"You're not bothering me."

"I don't want you to think I'm just trying to get into your panties."

"I don't think that," she said, "You've told me about your kids and your family. Unless you're lying to me, I don't think that about you."

I chuckled a bit over the phone.

"No, I'm not lying. I'm not like the other guys you've been messing with."

"How you know who I've been with?"

I sighed.

"I just know," I said, "I've been with enough stressed out and hurt women to know. Trust me."

I ended up spending another day at work with her. This time we kissed and touched a little more.

Things were progressing nicely with us and we really started dating. After our third date, I met her at the leasing office, as we'd become accustomed to doing. She was wrapping up her work for the day.

"Hey, you want to grab a couple of drinks and head over to one of the model apartments and just chill for a bit?" she asked.

"That sounds good to me."

"Great," she said, "I've got some things to finish up here. Why don't you go ahead and grab the drinks? By the time you get back, I should be wrapped up and we can head on over."

"Bet."

I went out and grabbed some drinks, came back and we headed over to

205

the model apartment.

I grabbed my portable CD player and put in one of my favorite mixed CDs to set the mood. A little Teddy P, Gerald Levert, and Luther... now we're getting somewhere.

She was sitting on the couch and by the time we'd had a couple of shots, she was really getting relaxed.

I turned the lights down low, and came back over to her and started to sing softly in her ear, while I kissed her earlobe and the nape of her neck.

"Turn off the lights, light a candle...."

The more I kissed her, the more she leaned in to me.

"If you want me to stop, I'll stop," I said, already knowing the answer because her body was already telling me the answer.

She looked at me, intense desire in her eyes.

"I want you to stop," she whimpered, "but I want you to keep going."

I caressed her face while I gently kissed her full lips.

"If we do this, we're going all the way."

I could feel the quivers in her body.

"Now I really want you to keep going."

I had all the permission I needed. I started taking off her clothes, little by little, stopping to admire the work of art that was before me. When I'd stripped her all the way down, I laid her down on the couch.

"You're beautiful," I said.

Then, I did something I rarely ever did with any other woman before.

I put her legs in the air and I put my mouth on her. Her juicy nectar was sweet to my lips and the more excited she got and, the more exhilarating the experience was for me. By the time I was done, she'd climaxed a couple of time and was out of breath.

I got up and went to the bathroom to clean myself up, then came back and sat down next to her.

"What are you doing?" she asked.

"What?"

"Come here so I can..."

"No no no," I said, "this isn't about me. It's about pleasing you. You can please me next time."

She sat there for a moment, bewildered. I can tell she wasn't used to that.

We continued to hang out, listen to a bit more music, drank a little bit more and just chilled. It was a great night. But, the next thing I knew, we were kissing and touching again and before we knew it, we were both lying naked on the floor having intercourse. But, this time was different. I'd been with so many other women before, but there was something special about Stephanie. About the way she made me feel when I was with her. I don't know if it was the way she looked at me, or the way she held on to me so tight. I just knew it was different. It wasn't a new experience for me, but it felt brand new. It was a more pleasurable, more sensual, softer experience. As I was with her, I was already thinking about a future with her and I'd only known for a few days. Of all the women I'd ever been with, this had never happened to me before.

That night was a pivotal point in our relationship, not only because we made love but also because we continued to connect on a deeper level. We laughed, we talked, and we joked.

Stephanie looked at me seriously after we played around for a little bit.

"Cody, I've never experienced anything like this before," she said.

"What do you mean?"

She looked around at the candles, pointed to the music.

"This," she said, "no one has ever taken their time with me like you have tonight. How long have we been at it now? 3 hours?"

She bowed her head and laughed a little bit to herself.

"I mean, I don't even know if I thought that was possible," she said.

I leaned in and kissed her.

"Oh, it's possible."

"And, something else I realized, something that I never even really knew until tonight..."

"What's that?"

She paused a moment before speaking, a look of embarrassment almost flushing across her face.

"Until tonight, Cody, I don't think I've ever had an orgasm."

"Really?"

I was shocked to hear this. Stephanie was a beautiful woman. It was unthinkable for me to not please her. But, then I realized that despite my history with women, I was not like other guys. Being raised by women, I'd always learned to put a woman first when I was with them. I was always in tune with their needs, and it made me happy to see them satisfied.

She smiled at me sheepishly.

"Really. I guess there were a few times that I thought I'd experienced it but since I had nothing to compare it to, I never really knew. Tonight, with you, there was no comparison. Cody, the way you make me feel…"

I leaned in and stroked her face and started to kiss the nape of her neck.

"I told you, I'm not like other guys. Most guys when they are with a woman think about their needs first. That's all they care about. That's why you've never experienced an orgasm before."

I smiled.

"So, technically, you were an orgasm virgin and I popped your cherry."

She laughed. Then, I took her in my arms and got serious for a moment.

"Baby, I can promise you this. As long as we are together, I will always put your sexual needs first. You don't ever have to worry about going back to scraps again."

We had a beautiful night together and our relationship just blossomed from that point. We went from going on our third date to me seeing each other every day. When I wasn't with her, I missed her. I couldn't remember the last time I felt this way about a woman.

Stephanie had a 4-year-old son and he was great. In all of the time Stephanie and I spent together, I didn't see his dad much. The funny thing was her little boy even resembled me a little bit, making it easy for me to pass him off as my son and blend him with my own family. He fit right in. And, he took to me quickly so it wasn't long before we became like a small family. Before I knew it, I found myself picking up her boy and hanging out with him and my son from Shanda in New Jersey.

The first few months of our relationship, I was heading to New York almost every week for a day or two to see my mom, handle some things and let my son see his mom in New Jersey. Every time I made a trip home, I brought more of my clothes and things back to Virginia. After I'd made a few trips, I knew it was time to definitely draw a line in the sand with Shanda and let her know that I wasn't coming back. I'd been breaking her off every time I went to

Jersey and I started to realize that this needed to stop as I was getting more serious about my relationship with Stephanie. So, I called Shanda up.

"Shanda, I'm not coming back anymore," I said, "I'll bring your son there to see you, but this is it. I'm done."

I could hear her waving me off on the other line.

"We'll talk about it when you come up next time," she said.

"You're not getting it. There is no next time. We're not talking about anything. We're not doing anything anymore. Virginia is my home now. And the only relationship you and I have is for our son."

I could hear her huffing on the other line.

"I'm serious, Shanda. And, you should know, I'm seeing someone now. It's serious."

"What?" she said, "I couldn't tell you were seeing someone the last time you were up here tapping this body of mine."

"That's why I'm telling you now. We've become more serious, more committed to each other. And, I've realized that it is time to let go of the past and move into the future."

"So, I'm your past now?"

"You have been for a while now," I said, "It was a mistake being with you the last few times I've come up there. It wasn't fair to you because I didn't feel anything. It was just sex. I never wanted anything more. I'm sorry. It's time for both of us to move on."

I could hear sobs on the other line.

"Shanda, are you okay?"

"So, you're saying you never loved me at all?"

"Shanda, you know I cared for you. We were together for over a year. Why would I have stayed if I didn't care about you?"

"Because I was pregnant."

She was right about that. There were a couple of times that I just wanted to leave but stopped short because I knew I needed to do right by my child.

"Yes, I did have a responsibility, but I did care for you. But, our relationship ran its course a long time ago. We've both been holding on to something that's not really there. You deserve to be with someone who does really love you and that wants to be in a relationship with you."

She was silent for a while.

"So, this girl you're with. She really make you happy?"

"She does."

"I guess I wish you the best. I do want you to be happy. I just wish things would have worked out for us."

"I know, Shanda."

"Good-bye."

Click.

I'm glad that she was at least lukewarm to my new relationship. She was still my son's mother and we'd always have to maintain some level of relationship so the more peace we kept between each other, the better. With her job, she still needed me to care for our son, so I considered that a blessing because I always thought he was better off with me.

Stephanie and I were spending so much time together that her son had started to call me daddy and my son was now calling her mommy. If Shanda knew this, I knew I'd be in for some drama, but as it was, she didn't really see her son that much so it was fine. The same was true of Stephanie's son. His dad just wasn't around that much and he'd grown attached to having me around. I was happy to be the father figure he needed in his life. He was a good little kid.

I was staying my aunt and uncle and that had helped me get on my feet after I graduated from boot camp. But, I was getting a hotel a couple nights a week so that Stephanie and I could have some alone time together. My aunt and uncle had three sons, my cousins. We'd go out to the club and party, have a good time and then come back to the house. Stephanie would follow us in her car so we could hook up when we got back. But, then my cousins would start acting crazy, running into the house, cutting off all the lights and locking the door and acting like they were sleep. No matter how loud I pounded on the door, no one would answer, even though they'd just gone in the house minutes before me. So many nights, I found myself sleeping in my car.

In the span of about a month and a half, my cousins did this to me 5 different times. None of these times, did anyone come out to let me in. My uncle wasn't home. He drove tractor-trailers for a living so he worked late nights. But, my aunt was home. I have a hard time believing that no one in that house could hear me pounding on the door each night.

I had my own car and just got used to sleeping in it when this happened. Stephanie was with me most of the time when they did this to me.

"Why do your cousins treat you like that?"

We were sitting in my car together one night after they'd done this to me – again.

I just shook my head.

"Because they're idiots."

"Why don't you just tell your uncle?"

"Because they take advantage of him too, babe. All that man does is work, and they just take advantage of him. All three of them are grown men, living up in their parent's house, doing nothing. Only one of them holds down a real job. The other two don't even work."

"So, your uncle just takes care of them?"

"I don't think he really wants to, but as much as I love him, he just doesn't have it in him to stand up to his kids or his wife. He's the only real working person in the house. My aunt doesn't work. She's retired and collects disability from an injury she got on the job a long time ago. The two dead beats live more off of her than anything because anything they ask for, she just gives them, even though she's on a fixed income. Now, mind you, we are still talking about grown men."

Stephanie shook her head now.

"That's a damn shame, Cody."

"I know, but what can I do? They've given me a roof over my head, even though my cousins do stupid crap like that. I appreciate what my uncle has done. I just wish they wouldn't let my cousins take advantage. He's too good of a man and works too hard to be dealing with that."

Stephanie kicked it with me for a while that night and I was able to get into the house in the morning once my uncle got home. I never mentioned anything to him about what my cousins were doing because I didn't want to cause any drama. I just tried to stay in my lane and do my thing, but it was hard sometimes because my cousins and my aunt didn't treat me that same.

There were times I'd get into the house late after being with my girl, nights they didn't lock me out, and my aunt would be in the kitchen.

"I hope you got something to eat where you were tonight, because we didn't have enough food for you."

I just chuckled to myself, because these kinds of situations happened quite often. Then, I'd look over at the plate that my aunt had prepared for my uncle and it would be a mountain of food.

"That's fine, "I said, and walking toward my bedroom.

"I saved you a hot dog," she said.

But, I just kept walking. She knew I didn't eat any damn hot dogs. They cooked out on the grill a lot. I had a hard time believing she couldn't save me a sausage link or something like that. When things like this happened around the house, I thanked God that this situation was only temporary and was ready to start making some moves to get out of there. I was just biding my time. What no one knew was that I had $90,000 saved in a suitcase from a long time ago. So, I had no problem clothing and feeding myself, but I knew it raised some questions in their minds since I wasn't working yet.

After being there for a couple of months, my aunt and cousins called a house meeting. The funny thing was I was the only one that needed to be there and they were the ones asking all of the questions.

We all sat in the living room. Of course, my uncle was not there because he was the only one who would vouch for me.

"So, Cody, you've been here for a couple of months now, and we think it's about time you start pulling your weight. There is no such thing as a free ride."

I'd been pretty laid back to this point in dealing with them, but my aunt's attitude and her comment about a free ride actually got under my skin.

"Wait a minute, auntie," I said, "I appreciate you letting me stay with you, but I never expected a free ride from anyone. From the beginning, I've always asked what you need from me so that I can do my part in the house. That's why Uncle had me cutting the grass and doing chores for him. I've always done whatever you ask me to do."

She sat there silently and then one of my freeloading cousins decided to chime in.

"Well, that's good. We just think that maybe you should do a little more," he said.

It really pissed me off that he had something to say when his lazy butt didn't do anything but drink, party and play video games all day.

"That's fine," I said, "I've never objected to anything you've asked of me. Let me know what you want and I'll take care of it."

"We need a new shed in the backyard," my other cousin said, "Dad has a lot of tools and we are running out of places to put them. Plus, it would be a good place for him to work on some of his projects."

"Okay."

As irritated as I was with this situation, I knew it was only temporary, so I played along and honored my aunt's wishes. I spent a couple thousand dollars on a shed for them and even put it up. Do you think my lazy cousins even offered to help? Of course not. But, it was okay because I had a plan. I continued to help out around the house.

Another project that my uncle actually asked for my help on was more construction related. He and my aunt owned another house that was pretty old and decrepit and it needed a little TLC. I think they were planning to rent it out but the house was built in the 1940s and everything about it suggested so. My uncle knew I was good with my hands and had some experience working in construction, so he asked me to go in and gut the place before we got ready to do some work on it.

I was happy to do something with my hands again so I jumped at the opportunity. I spent about a week or so gutting the place and getting it ready for renovation. One of my cousins, the one who has a job, came by and helped me a couple of times.

We both stood and looked around the place. It was much improved from where we started but was still in need of a lot of work. Most of all, there was dust and dirt everywhere. But, it was a 2-story home and was a pretty decent place to use as a get-away.

"You know cuz," I said, "I think we might be able to use this place as a little sanctuary with the ladies when we can't get a hotel room. What do you think?"

He looked around at all of the dirt and dust and frowned.

"You think any girl would want to stay in this dirty, dusty place?" he asked.

"If she's down with you, she will," I said.

Then, an idea sprung in my head. I'd bring Stephanie here to see if she was really down with me. Things had been going great so far, but if she was willing to stay with me in a place like this, I knew she would be a keeper.

I smiled real big.

"So, what you think, cuz?"

He looked around the place again, and shrugged his shoulders.

"It sure beats bringing a girl back home," she said, "Crap, why not."

And we shook on it.

The next day I was on the phone with Stephanie.

"Hey baby, I got a little surprise for you," I said.

"What?" she asked.

"My aunt and uncle have an old house that I've been doing some work on. I've actually been crashing there some nights when my cousins have been acting funny instead of sleeping in my car. Why don't you come there with me tonight? We can listen to a little music over candlelight and have a nice quiet, romantic evening."

"That sounds nice," she said.

"Great, I'll see you tonight."

We met up after she got off work that evening and headed over to the house. I could tell that she seemed excited but I wasn't sure how excited she would be once she really saw this place. We walked in and I could tell she was just taking in the place so I started talking first.

"Okay, so there's no heat or AC. So, I figured if it gets hot, we'll just open up the windows. If it gets cold, we can close the windows and cuddle up close. There is working electricity and water. What do you think?"

Stephanie started walking through the living room of the house carefully like she didn't want to touch anything. Dust and dirt was all over the place. She attempted to sit but then thought twice and kept moving.

"Are you sure you want to stay here?" she asked.

"Oh, I see. You only want to go out with me when we're going out to nice dinners and staying in nice hotels?"

She didn't know, but I was definitely running game. I just wanted to see how far she was going to take this.

"No, no," she said, "I'll stay with you."

But, I could tell she had her reservations about the place. My next move,

214

I think probably just made her even more uncomfortable. There was a mattress up against the wall.

"I figured we could sleep on this," I said as I threw the mattress down on the floor.

When the mattress hit the floor, dust went everywhere.

Stephanie's eyes were huge. I could tell that she couldn't believe we'd be staying in this dirty place, but she composed herself well.

"I love you babe, it'll be alright."

I just smiled because I couldn't believe she was actually going along with this.

"There's some sheets we can lay on the mattress," I said and then ran off to the bathroom, leaving her in the room with a bewildered look on her face. When I came back in the room, Stephanie had swept the room out and had put a sheet on the mattress.

It looked 10 times better. I was impressed.

"Do we have any pillows? I wasn't able to find any."

I walked over to the corner and picked up a couple packs of sheets that were still packaged.

"We can use these," I said.

"Okay," she said taking the sheets from me and laying them on the bed, "I closed all the doors and the windows so that should keep the dust out for the night."

I was so impressed with her. We made the most of our night. I'd brought in my boom box and we played a little soft music and made love. It was really a perfect night and she seemed so comfortable.

The next day after work when I came to see her, she asked me if we were going back to the house. At that point, I knew this chick was really down with me.

Things were going well, and they continued to go well with us as we dated over the next couple of months. One night we were chilling together after I'd gotten us a hotel room. We'd had a really nice dinner and had just finished making love, but I could tell something was on Stephanie's mind. She'd seemed a bit distant all night.

"Baby, you gonna tell me what's wrong?"

She looked at me, surprised by my perception.

"Am I that obvious?" she asked.

"To me you are."

"Something is bothering me."

"What is it?"

"Well, a couple days ago, I noticed that my period was late, and it's never late. So, I took a pregnancy test....and it came back positive."

I paused for a minute. I wasn't ready for this kind of news. I had too many children already and didn't really want another one right now. But, things were different with Stephanie. I knew from the beginning that she was special; different from all of the other women I'd dated. So, I did not want to react rashly to her news.

"Okay," I said calmed after processing what she'd said, "what do you want to do?"

She looked at me, confused.

"I don't really know," she said, "I don't think now is a good time to bring a child in this world. Things are going great between us but the relationship is still new and I don't want to mess it up."

"So, you don't want to keep the baby?" I asked.

"Would you be upset if I said no? Be honest. Tell me."

I leaned back in the bed and laced my hands behind my head. I knew that I really didn't want to keep this child but I was glad that it came from her and not me. It made the conversation much easier.

"No, baby," I said, "I wouldn't be upset. I guess I feel like you do. Our relationship is going great but it is still new. The way I feel about you, I think we will have children together some day, but right now, it's just too soon."

I could see a wave of relief sweep over Stephanie's face. The next thing I knew she was throwing her arms around me.

"Thank you for understanding," she whispered in my ear.

A couple days later, we went to the clinic together and she had an abortion. I could tell this was not an easy decision for her to make, so I was there for her the entire time, comforting her and holding her hand.

Meanwhile, I continued to deal with the same issues at my aunt and uncle's house. After I'd bought the shed and put it up, I didn't hear much from my aunt or my cousins for a little while. But, that only lasted so long. But, my aunt made the mistake of making a smart comment to me while he was home one day.

To my surprise, he stepped in and defended me.

"Hey, hey, wait a minute," he said, "don't you be treating my nephew like that. He is family and you will treat him like family. He has more than paid his way around here. Tell me one time you've asked him to do something and he didn't do it."

My aunt just sat there in the living room, stoic. That's because she couldn't say anything.

"That's what I thought," my uncle said, "now leave this kid alone. He does more around this house than any of our own sons."

Then he walked out of the living room. I stood there a minute and smiled at my aunt until she just looked away. I was so glad to see my uncle put her in her place. But he was right; I was carrying my own weight around the house, paying my way and my lazy cousins too.

I continued to work on mapping out my plan to leave this place so that I could get my own place. With the way things were going with Stephanie, I was starting to think she would be a big part of my plan.

Even though my cousins were a huge annoyance, I decided to take them with me up to New York when I made one of my trips home. When we got there, I took them out to some of the local clubs and we drank and partied together. They were in 7th heaven because that's all they liked to do anyway. We hung out most of the night when we first got in town. Later that evening when I got back home, I found myself sick as a dog. I was on an off the toilet at least 12 times that night.

I was miserable. So, I started thinking about what I ate that may have disagreed with me. Was I food poisoned? All I'd had that night was pizza and Hennessey and though that wasn't a winning and nutritious combination, I'd eaten like that most of my life.

At about 4 am, I was emerging from the bathroom for about the 12th time. My skin felt pasty and when I looked in the mirror in the bathroom, I noticed that I was starting to look pale. I was getting concerned.

When I came out of the bathroom, I keeled over leaning on the hallway.

My chest was hurting so bad; I thought I might pass out. Was I having a heart attack? Something wasn't right.

At about that time, one of my cousins' best friend walked by. He put his hand on my shoulder.

"Are you alright man? You look a little bugged out?"

I could barely catch my breath.

"No man, something's not right with me. I need to go to the hospital."

"Okay, brotha, hold on for a sec. I'm gonna go get your cousin."

He went into the bedroom to wake up my cousins to tell them what was going on with me, but they didn't care. They just said they were sleep and rolled back over, which didn't surprise me one bit. They never gave a damn about me. My cousin's friend, Nick, came back to me.

"I'll take you," he said, "but I don't know my way around New York. Do you think you can help me find the nearest hospital?"

I nodded, barely able to catch my breath between the pains I was feeling in my chest.

"Yea, St. Joseph's in Yonkers. It's not far from here."

"Okay," he said, grabbing his coat, "let's go. Can you walk?"

I nodded.

Then, he came over to me and helped me into the car.

By the time we got into the emergency room, it was around 6 am.

I went straight to the registration area and told them that I thought I was having a heart attack.

They immediately called for a nurse and doctor to attend to me, but while they were going to get the doctor, the pains started to hit me again and I dropped to my knees right there in the middle of the emergency room.

A nurse and one of the security guards immediately came to my aid and took me to a little room where I could lie down. After they'd settled me in the room, the nurse went to go and get the machine so that they could do an EKG and check the condition on my heart.

As the nurse left the room, I fell off the bed to my knees and just started to throw up on the floor. I threw up so long and so hard that by the time I'd finished, the entire floor of the room that I was in was covered. Then, I passed out because I'd expended so much energy and oxygen in the process.

Following the episode, the doctors got oxygen on me and wheeled me into another room while they got that room cleaned up. They gave me a bucket to keep by my bed and I still threw up a couple more times but nothing as severe as the first time. They ran a bunch of tests on me to try and figure out what was wrong. I ended up staying in the hospital for a couple of days and in that short period of time lost about 10 pounds. My mom came to the hospital to see me and Nick never left my side. But, my cousins never once came to check on me and see how I was doing. They were too busy drinking and partying.

After running several tests on me, the doctor came into my hospital room to talk to me. My mom was there along with Nick, who'd stayed with me through this entire ordeal.

"What's the verdict doc?" I asked, "Did I have a heart attack?"

The doctor smiled.

"Did you think you were having heart attack?"

I sat up in the bed a little bit. I'd started to feel a little bit better, at least to the point that I didn't have to vomit anymore.

"Well, I figured when I started to feel that pain and tightness in my chest, that's what it had to be, right?"

The doctor pulled up a chair and sat next to my bed.

"Not exactly," he said, "So, I've got good news and bad news."

"Okay," I said, "Let's start with the good news I guess."

"The good news is you didn't have a hard attack."

"And the bad news?"

"The bad news is you have a condition called GERD disease."

"GERD? What the hell is that?"

"Gastric Esophogeal Reflux Disease. You ever had heartburn before?"

I nodded.

"That times 20. And, it sticks with you. It's a condition that you're going to have to learn to live with and that starts with changing your diet. I'm guessing you have a lot of junk food in your diet now – pizza, hamburgers, fries, alcohol."

"How did you know?"

"Because that is what triggered this attack. You're going to have to change your diet overnight if you don't want to go through this again. You've got to cut the junk food from your diet and start a clean eating regimen. Fresh fruits and vegetables and lean proteins."

I leaned back in my hospital bed with my hands over my head. Why did these things always have to happen to me?

"Okay doc," I said, "whatever I need to do to get healthy."

"That's what you need to do," he said, "your vitals look good but we're going to keep you one more night to make sure you're in the clear. Your nurse will also give you a suggested list of foods to incorporate into your diet. Look son, I know this is not going to be easy to change everything so suddenly. But, it beats having you back here in my emergency room."

After the doctor left, the reality of my situation really hit me. All my life, all I'd know was beer, liquor and pizza. How was I going to change my eating habits overnight? I had a flashback of the pain I was in when I came to the hospital just a couple days ago and I knew what I had to do.

And I did good, too. Over the next three months, I completely changed my diet just like the doctor told me. No pizza, greasy foods or alcohol. When I got home, Stephanie was so great and attentive after I told her about what happened. After doing so well for a few months, I decided to test the waters. A few drinks couldn't possibly hurt. I was doing good now.

I went out with my friends and my cousins and drank about 20 Coronas. I turned down all of the liquor because I thought if I stayed away from the liquor I'd be okay. I was wrong.

The next day I was writhing in pain, sick all over again. Stephanie was great. She was an excellent caregiver. She got me an apartment at her complex and then got an air mattress for my son and me. She had no idea that I had money saved. She just wanted to take care of me. Then, she would lay beside me each day and just help nurse me back to health. She never left my side. If I needed anything, she was there.

It was at that point I knew; I'm never leaving this girl. She is really down with me. While I was with her, I never even thought about another woman. She was my focus. I wasn't cheating anymore or even thinking about it. She was all I wanted. I really changed my diet overnight at this point. Two bad episodes of being sick for days weren't worth it.

Seven months later, Stephanie and I had completely furnished my new place. We had dishes and it was starting to look lived in. And, I was looking for a new job. A couple days before my birthday, I was lying in bed with her.

"Do you love me?" I asked.

"Yes, I love you."

"Would you spend the rest of your life with me?"

"Yes."

"If I told you let's get married right now, would you marry me?"

She sat up in the bed, eyes wide, smiling.

"Are you serious, Cody? Don't play with me."

I looked at her, seriously.

"You're the best woman I've ever met. Why wouldn't I want to marry you?"

She leaned back in the bed.

"You're not serious," she said.

I was offended at her response.

"Get up," I said.

She just sat up in the bed and looked at me.

I got up out of the bed and got the kids ready and dressed. We took them to her mother's house.

While we were riding in the car, she looked at me, surprised.

"We're really doing this?" she asked.

"You said you love me right?"

"Yes, I love you."

"Then, yes, we're doing this, unless you have any objections."

She shook her head.

We went to city hall and got our marriage license.

"Cody, I don't want to get married at the Justice of the Peace. It doesn't have to be an elaborate ceremony but I do want it to be special."

I leaned in and kissed her softly on the lips.

"We'll do whatever you want to do. I want this to be special too."

"But, I need to make a run to New York real quick. I will be right back and we're going to do this."

I drove her back to the apartment and I hit the road. Even though we had our marriage license, I don't think the reality of everything had hit her.

As I drove to New York, I talked to her on the phone almost entire way,

221

letting her know that this was real and it was going to happen. When I got off the phone with her, I called one of my brothers in Christ from my church in New York. I told him what was going on and that I was planning on marrying Stephanie, picked him up in New York, stopped and picked up some wedding rings and then drove all through the night back to Virginia on my birthday.

The next morning, I got dressed and drove to her uncle's house, he was a pastor, and we set the stage for our wedding. We got married in her uncle's living room that day. Our witnesses were my brother in Christ, her aunt and a couple of her cousins. Her uncle married us.

After we got married, I kissed my new wife and hit the road again to take my brother back to New York and get my family so that they could celebrate with us.

When I got back to Virginia, I took a 3-4-hour nap to recover from all of the traveling I'd been doing up and down the road to New York. When I awoke, I got with Stephanie and we set up the recreation room in our apartment complex so that we could celebrate the occasion with our family.

All of our family came in and cooked to the nines. My mom cooked; her mom cooked. We had all of our family there with us but they did not have a clue what they were there to celebrate. Well, they thought they did.

After we'd eaten and partied for a little while, I asked the DJ to turn the music down.

"We'd like to make an announcement," I said.

Before I could say anything else, my uncle piped in.

"We know, we know, you two want to get married," he said.

We both smiled.

"No, that's not it."

All of our family looked at each other, puzzled.

"Oh," Uncle said, "It's your birthday party."

"No," we said in unison.

Now, they were really stumped.

"Then what the hell is it?" my uncle asked, a little frustration showing in his voice.

We smiled, pulled our new wedding bands out of our pockets and putting them on our fingers.

"We're already married," I said.

Uncle was speechless, probably the first time in history. Everyone ran to us and hugged and congratulated us. Everyone was happy for us except her father and her cousins. They'd always been haters since we got together. Her father always told her I wasn't crap when I never gave him any reason to think that about me.

In addition to celebrating our new marriage, we celebrated my new job that I'd just gotten the day before. I'd gotten a new construction job paying $20/hour.

Life was good for the first 3 years. I never thought I'd find a girl that would make me feel the way Stephanie did, that I could love the way I loved her. Shortly after we were married, Stephanie got pregnant again. Timing was right because we were in love and had a long, bright future together so there was no question as to whether or not we wanted to keep the baby.

Even though I was happy about this child because it came at a great time in my life, I couldn't help feeling some anxiety because this was going to be my eighth child and I was only 32 years old at this point. But, I was happy.

After weeks of self-reflection and prayer I realized I need God's forgiveness for not only the mistakes I have made, but for the wrongs I have done towards the women I was previously involved with. Also I asked God to forgive them for the wrongs they inflicted against me. I decided getting along with all of my children's mothers was in the best interest for my children. I decided I needed to apologize to them for the mistakes I had made when I was younger, and they had accepted my apologizes, allowing us to be successful co-parents. Knowing I had a clean slate with God and my exes, excluding Kendra who refused to talk to me, I was able to only feel excited and happy about Stephanie and I's baby on the way.

Stephanie had a bit of a rough pregnancy. Her morning sickness was pretty hard on her and the baby grew quickly, making her very uncomfortable.

When my daughter was born, she was 9 pounds.

Things were great. We were a family. I loved Stephanie's son as if he were my own and I found that I spent more time with him than my own son who was in New York. My family loved Stephanie from the first time we started dating. For the first time in a long time, I was really happy.

But, things started to change about 6 months after our daughter was born. I can't really describe it but sex just wasn't the same. Stephanie did not have the insatiable drive and passion to make love to me like she once did. Before the baby was born, I was used to getting sex every day or at least getting head. But, now, it just stopped and I was lucky if I got it once or twice a month.

Stephanie even went to the doctor to see what was wrong. She thought it might be postpartum depression or something like that but when she came back from the doctor and they confirmed that her sex drive had just gone downhill and just asked me to give her some time.

I agreed to give her some time but felt it was important to remind her of a conversation we had before we got married.

"Stephanie, do you remember what we talked about before we got married in front of your mother?"

I thought back to that evening when we were sitting down in a café grabbing lunch with Stephanie's mother. At this point, I was pretty sure I was going to marry this woman.

"I love your daughter," I told her mother, "I can picture myself being married to her one day. But there are a couple of things I need to know that she can do."

Her mother laughed a little bit and sat back in her chair.

"And, what is that?"

"First of all, I need a woman that believes in God. I need her to do that for both of us because I know sometimes I stray away and don't live right. I'll always take care of my family but one of us has to be constantly in prayer."

Stephanie nodded.

"No problem," she said and her mother nodded her approval.

"What's next?" her mother asked.

"You gotta stay in shape. I need a woman that cares about the way that she looks. I don't mess with any big, out of shape chicks and I have no intention of changing that standard."

Stephanie and her mother laughed.

"Okay. Go on."

"You gotta keep the house clean."

Stephanie's mother started shaking her head.

"You might have a problem there because my daughter can be pretty messy. Baby, you're going to have to work on that," she said to her daughter. I waved it off.

"It's okay. I can teach her that, no problem. But, there is one more thing."

"What's that?" Stephanie asked.

"You've got to give me sex all the time. I've been with a lot of women and I'm used to having sex on a regular basis. I've never really considered marriage before. But, you, I can see myself being married to. These things are very important to me."

"Do you have any problems with what I'm doing now?" Stephanie asked.

"No, you're doing great."

I was unhappy with our sexual relationship so I knew we had to do something. We first tried role-playing but that didn't work. Because I'd been with so many women, when she thought I was thinking about one of them she would get mad, and I'd get mad if I thought she was picturing another guy. It was just a bad idea all around. So, we were back at zero.

One day the construction crew and I were out in the Tidewater/Virginia Beach area doing some work. We stopped at the gas station to fill up and get some snacks. One of the guys tapped me on the shoulder.

"Cody, that girl over there keeps looking at you," he said.

I looked up to see this thick, brown skinned honey stealing a few glances my way. She had the kind of butt you just wanted to wrap your hands around, about 5'5, 180 pounds with curves in all the right places.

My buddy caught me stealing a few glances at her.

"I bet you can't get her," he said.

"Are you serious? You guys know I'm a married man. Plus, she looks really young, like 20 or something."

"But aren't you having problems at home?" my boy asked.

There he was throwing salt in my wounds. I didn't need to be reminded that my wife was not satisfying me sexually anymore.

"Yea, but that don't mean I want to run out and cheat on my wife. I love my wife. We're just working though some issues right now."

"Okay," my co-worker said, leaning against the truck, "then do it to see if you still got it."

225

"What's in it for me?" I asked.

"If you get her, we'll all buy you lunch this week. If you don't, you buy us all lunch tomorrow."

"Okay. Bet."

I walked over to the girl. She was still pumping gas into her car. She had a cute little, sporty sedan.

She looked up at me, expectantly.

"That's a cute little car you have there," I told her, "is this your work car?"

"No," she said flatly.

"This is your car? This little car?"

"Why? Is my car too little for me?"

I looked at her large backside.

"With all that you got behind you, I don't know if you can fit in there," I joked.

She laughed.

Her name was Sandra. I told her how attractive she was and that I'd like the opportunity to get to know her better.

"I saw you looking at me while I was over there with my crew in my work truck," I said.

"Oh you did?" she smiled.

"Oh yeah. That's why I had to come over here."

"Cute as you are, I figured, I had to get your number so we could hook up some time."

She flashed me her cute smile, and then wrote her number down and handed it to me.

"Well then, I guess you better call me," she said.

I took the piece of paper from her hand and when I did, our fingers brushed each other slightly, instant chemistry between us. We both felt it.

"I will," I said smiling as I walked back to the work truck with the fellows.

"Well?" one of the guys asked.

I held up the paper with her number after I'd gotten in the truck.

"I guess lunch is on you guys the next week," I said, "I still got it."

We laughed as we pulled off from the gas station and hit the road back to Richmond.

"You gonna call her?" one of the guys asked.

"I don't know," I said, tucking the piece of paper in my pocket, "I just might."

I did. We ended up talking a lot over the phone for the next few weeks. She was a great distraction to take my mind off of all the problems I was having at home with Stephanie. We really hit it off. I really liked this girl and the relationship we were developing reminded me of how things were when I first met my wife. She made me feel like the 'old me', in a good way.

After a few weeks, it was finally time for me to go and see her. I couldn't wait any longer. It just wasn't happening at home and my body needed this.

I packed up some clothes and told Stephanie that I was heading to Tidewater to go and see some of my boys and that I would be back late that night or early the next morning.

She looked at me and smiled.

"If you want to spend time with your boys, go and have a good time. Don't worry about the kids and me. We will be fine. Plus, if you're tired, I'd rather you just stay there with them instead of trying to get on the road late at night anyway."

"Okay," I said, kissed her and headed out the door.

Part of me felt horrible. I hated lying to my wife. But, I needed to do this. I couldn't remember the last time Stephanie and I had even attempted to make love and lack of sex was starting to take its toll on me, physically. I know that sounds crazy but I used to get sick if I went longer than 3 days without sex. I even went to a doctor to find out if something was wrong with me and he told me that I was fine. I just have always had an insatiable appetite for sex, and right now, I was starving.

The more I rationalized my actions as I drove down the road, the better I felt and my guilt began to subside.

I called Sandra up and told her that I was getting a hotel room for us that night, but that I had to leave early in the morning to go back home.

She met me there and we made love. It was great. I'd forgotten how great it felt to be inside a woman and I didn't want it to end. She was so young and willing and I enjoyed every minute of it. Being a young girl, she was so used to dealing with young guys that only cared about getting themselves off. She wasn't used to a man that took his time with her and focused on pleasing her needs.

When we finished up and were laying in the bed after a few rounds, I felt it was time to me to confess things to her.

"Sandra, I have a confession to make to you, baby. I'm married."

I waited a brief moment to see if she was going to react harshly to this new before continuing.

"I'm so sorry if I led you on in any way. That is not what I meant. I would like for us to continue seeing each other because I really do like you. If you want to leave, I completely understand. But, if you decide to stay with me, I promise that I'll treat you far better than anyone else that comes around so you won't need no one else."

She lay there and contemplated my proposal for a minute. No drama or yelling. She wasn't mad at me. Just calm.

Then, she put her hand on my chest.

"I really like you too, Cody. And, I'm glad you were honest with me. Most men wouldn't even do that. I want to stay with you."

I leaned over and kissed her.

"I promise to take good care of you. And, I do want you to come to Richmond and meet my wife. I'll call you and let you know when we can set something up."

She nodded.

"Okay."

As I was driving home the next morning, I felt recharged, energized. It had been so long since I'd had sex, that I'd almost forgotten how much I needed it, how much more complete I felt when that appetite was satisfied. Then I started to feel guilty. I'd never cheated on Stephanie. I loved her that much. But, up until lately, I never had a reason to. She used to pay attention to me and all of my needs. Now, I just wasn't sure what was happening to us. We were losing what made us, us, and I didn't like it. I desperately wanted to save my marriage. I just didn't know how.

Then, I got this wild and crazy idea that maybe was a little bit self-serving, but maybe could spark something in our relationship.

I got home and my wife was in the kitchen drinking her morning coffee.

"Hey baby," I said, leaning over giving her a kiss.

She looked up at me from her phone.

"You're home earlier than I thought," she said.

"I told you that I'd leave first thing this morning," I said.

"Oh yeah," she said and went back to playing with her phone while sipping her coffee.

I know I was only gone for a day but did she even miss me while I was gone? Some emotion would be better than what I was getting now. I almost wanted to yell at her, "I cheated on you last night" just to get some kind of reaction out of her.

"Baby, we need to talk," I said.

"Okay," she said never looking up from her phone.

I sat down at the kitchen table and took the cell phone from her hands.

"Hey," she said.

"Will you just look at me for a minute? I said we need to talk."

She leaned back in her chair and crossed her arms.

"Fine," she said, "what do you want to talk about?"

"Really?" I said, "that's the attitude I get? I've been gone for the last day and I didn't even get so much as an 'I miss you baby.' It's like you don't even give a damn if I'm here or not. Do you want our marriage to work? Do you want to fix what is going on with us because I'm not happy baby?"

She leaned forward immediately and her face softened.

"Of course, yes, baby. I want us to work. I'll do anything."

I was getting her where I wanted her now.

"We need to find a way to reconnect," I said, "and we've tried role playing, different positions but none of those things have seemed to work for us." Stephanie put her head down, disappointed.

"I know."

"So, I was thinking, maybe we should think a little bit out of the box. Try something totally new, like maybe get someone else involved. Somebody that nobody knows to come in and help pick up the slack."

I paused.

She looked up at me, incredulous.

229

"You mean like another woman?"

"Well, yeah."

"And, how are you going to pick someone that nobody knows? I don't know how I feel about this."

Okay, less resistance than I expected. If her biggest concern was who the other chick was, I'm pretty sure I can get her to come around.

"Okay, well how about I do it in front of you, or we could just do a threesome?"

She wrestled in her seat, looking uncomfortable.

"You mean to tell me that you've never thought about a threesome before?"

"No," she said, "that's something men fantasize about. It's not necessarily my thing. I just don't know, Cody."

"Well, we need to figure something out baby because I'm miserable. I want to try and fix us because I love you."

"We can try it once."

She buckled.

"Who are you going to get?"

I was silently celebrating this victory in my head and missed her question.

"I'm sorry, what?"

"Who are you going to get? That nobody knows like you said."

"I don't know. I guess I have to go out and meet somebody."

I paused – for effect.

"But, there is this young girl I met at work. She seems nice, but I don't know. We'll have to see."

"Well, you need to let me know who it's going to be so we can get this over with. I'm agreeing but I can't say I'm going to like it."

"Come on baby," I said, caressing her arm, "keep an open mind."

"And, I ain't putting my mouth on her," she said getting up from the table.

"You don't have to. We can just get her to put her mouth on you."

She walked over and got in my face.

"If you ask me to put my mouth on that girl, it's going to be a problem," she said.

230

"Okay, baby."

"And, if I catch you looking at her in a different way than you look at me, it's going to be a problem."

"Alright baby."

She walked out the room.

"I love you," I yelled after her.

I was so excited that she went for it. Now it was time to put this plan into action. I planned our little tryst on a weekend. I'd called Sandra up and she was set to come to our house on Friday night. I'd made arrangements with a babysitter for the kids so they were out of the house for the weekend.

Sandra arrived and I was still working out in my head how I was going to facilitate this because she had no idea what I had planned for us to do. She thought she was just coming to meet my wife.

I came out and met her in the parking lot and told Stephanie that I was helping her find a place to park.

"Hey baby," I said.

She smiled real big.

"I'm glad you came. Dinner's ready and Stephanie is looking forward to meeting you. We're going to go in, have a nice dinner together, have a few drinks and just see what happens from there, okay?"

She started fidgeting and looking uncomfortable.

"Cody, I don't know. I…"

I put my hand on her shoulder.

"Trust me," I said.

She smiled immediately at the comfort of my touch.

"To please you, ok."

We walked into the house and I introduced her to my wife. To my surprise, they hit it off quite well.

We sat down, ate and enjoyed each other's company.

Then, I pulled out the wine and we all drank a few glasses.

It started getting late.

"I think I'm ready to turn in for the night," Sandra said, "where's your bathroom? I'd like to freshen up."

I directed her to our guest bathroom and showed her where to put her things. By this time, Stephanie had decided to turn in for the night as well and went into our master bath to shower. While the ladies were in the shower, I was making sure the bed was all made up and ready.

Sandra peeked around the corner at the door.

"Hey," she said, "should I just sleep in one of the kids' rooms?"

"No, no" I said, "you don't need to sleep in there. Why don't you sleep in here with us?"

She looked at me, uneasy.

"It's okay," I said, walking toward her. "What did I tell you earlier?"

"To trust you," she said.

"And do you trust me?"

"Yes."

"Then come to bed with me."

She walked into the bedroom cautiously.

By this time, my wife emerged from our master bath, ready for bed.

"Sandra is just going to sleep in here with us tonight."

She looked at me and then looked at her.

"Ok."

My wife crawled into the bed and slept by the wall while Sandra slept on the end with me in the middle. Everyone fell asleep and I went to work with my master plan. Earlier, I'd stopped by the adult toy store and bought a couple of those vibrating eggs just for this occasion.

While the girls were sleeping, I crawled under the covers, and started eating my wife. At the same time, I grabbed the vibrating egg and started using it on Sandra. Neither of the ladies were complaining at this point; they were too caught up in their own sensual pleasure to even object to what was actually happening.

Now that they were both clearly awake, I put the vibrating egg aside and pulled Sandra down to me and started having sex with her while I continued to eat my wife. Now, it was getting real.

When they both climaxed, I cleaned myself up and started kissing my wife. I pulled Sandra closer to us so that I could kiss both of them. Before I knew it, I had them kissing each other. I felt like I was living a real life porno at the moment and honestly loved every bit of it.

The next morning, the three of us sat at the kitchen table, eating breakfast.

Silence.

We had definitely done things last night that made it hard to look each other in the eye.

I broke the silence.

"Look, I know things seem a little awkward between us after last night, but you have to admit, there was real chemistry. And, now we have a secret between just the three of us. Nobody is going to know about this but us."

Sandra smiled weakly, showing a feeling of relief.

I looked over at her and reassured her.

"We all share something now. Sandra, you're part of this family now because this is a secret that all of us are going to keep."

Stephanie chimed in.

"Yeah, because we ain't telling nobody about this."

Sandra ended up staying with us another night, and something happened with us again. But, this time it was more comfortable because we were growing used to each other and had learned how to please each other.

After the weekend, Sandra went home, and things went back to normal in our house.

We continued to date and stay in touch. She called me a couple weeks after our sexual rendezvous.

"Hey baby, how's it going?"

"Not good," she said, sounding upset.

It sounded like she'd been crying.

"What's going on?"

"It's my parents," she said, "sometimes I just can't take living here. They are trying to run my life and want to know every little thing I'm doing. Just driving me nuts. I'm not a kid anymore and I just want to leave."

"If you need to get away for a few weeks, you know you can always come and stay with us. Stephanie likes you and would have no problem with it. Pack up your son and come on up."

Sandra had a young son, about a year old.

"Are you sure it's okay?"

"Yes, I am. It sounds like you really need a break, so come on."

"Thank you, Cody."

Sandra stayed with us for a few weeks. We told the kids that she was their cousin and they called her auntie. For the first week that she was there, I slept on the couch, while her and Stephanie slept in our room.

Then, I would sneak into the room in the middle of the night and come back out to the couch by the time the kids woke up.

Sandra's stay went from a few weeks to 1 ½ years. For me, life was good. I had my cake and was eating it, too. Whenever my wife was not in the mood for the three of us to get together, she'd always say, "that's what #2 is for." That's all I needed – permission to sleep with another woman.

And it was nice because unlike my wife, Sandra would do anything I asked her to do. But, I had one golden rule. I told her never to try and come before my wife. Know the place of order in this house, because as much as I enjoyed being with her, my wife always came first.

Even if we were out shopping, I always took care of my wife first. And, things went well for a while, until Sandra started to challenge her place in our home.

She started making sly comments to me like, "I can do everything your wife does."

She was slowly trying to shift the power to her side. During her stay, she'd witnessed a couple of arguments between my wife and me. Afterward, she'd approach me.

"Daddy, I would never argue with you. Whatever you say goes. She has to learn to appreciate you more."

I should have taken these queues as an invitation to make a change in my house, but I really enjoyed the sex, so she continued to stay.

One night, Stephanie and I had another argument, over something stupid. I think I'd forgotten to do something she'd asked me to do, so she ran out of the house in a huff to cool off

I went downstairs to the basement and started working out in the gym. That was always a great remedy for me to relieve stress and cool off.

Sandra came downstairs, and sensing that I was tense after the argument, got to her knees and gave me head. She knew that would help to relax

234

me, and it did, for a while.

"Your wife really doesn't appreciate you, baby. She complains about everything. She has to learn that you are the man of the house."

I immediately saw where this conversation was going and pushed her away.

"I appreciate what you're saying, baby. But, even though you're young, you're really old school. You think the world is promised tomorrow. It ain't. I'm never leaving my wife. I'm not going to make you queen B and her number 2. That's never happening."

She stood up, pouting, hoping to score more points with me.

"But, I do more for you."

I quickly clarified her statement.

"You do more for me sexually. You can never do more for me emotionally and mentally."

Now, she was offended.

"What am I then? Just some piece of meat to you?"

I walked over to her and put my hand on her shoulder gently.

"Of course not. I care about you. I have the utmost love and respect for you and will do anything for you. But, I don't' care or love nobody like my wife."

Sandra clearly didn't like my answer because she backed away and swatted my hand.

Then, she got in my face, lunged at me and pushed me.

I was actually shocked that she was that bold. I quickly pushed her away.

"Don't you ever put your hands on me," I told her, "I don't hit women, but women don't hit me."

Then, she slapped me.

"What you think about that punk?" she taunted, "I hit you."

At that moment, Stephanie walked back in the house to find me standing there with Sandra yelling and screaming in my face.

I was fed up.

"You don't like the way things are? Then, get out of here."

"Fine," she said, "I'll go right now."

"No, you're not going to go right now because you're not going to get that boy out of bed at 1:00 in the morning. But, in the morning, you can leave and go back to your parents' house."

"And I won't ever come back," she yelled at me.

"Fine, don't come back."

I didn't need any more of this damn drama in my house, so I welcomed her departure.

The next morning, she got up and left. Before she left, I gave her some money for gas and she threw it out of the car window as she drove off.

If that wasn't crazy enough, after all that drama, she ended up coming back the next week. We spent the day together and messed around and kind of made amends. We fooled around a few more times after that, but she decided to call it quits. She really had feelings for me and each time we were together, she had a harder time with me going back home to my wife. She just couldn't take it anymore. So, we eventually just stopped seeing each other.

The funny thing is she and my wife actually became pretty good friends while she was staying with us. Despite the fact that I was out of the picture, she kept in touch with Stephanie, mostly through just email and text. They never caught up for coffee or anything, but stayed in pretty consistent communication with one another.

chapter 13
trouble in paradise

A few months later, the company I worked for got a construction gig with VCU, a local university, to replace all the windows and doorframes in their dorms. The dorms were 7 floors, alternating between guys and girls. Prior to our work, we had to leave notices on all of the floors to let the residents know that we'd be doing work on their floor. Naturally, I chose all of the floors with the girls.

I was amazed at how bold these girls were when we came to do the work. Girls were answering the door in towels, or asking us to come in while they were showering. Mind you, we'd already left notices telling these girls exactly when we'd be on their floor doing work.

One of the first girls I met was an African girl. I started talking to her friend.

"Can you do work in the evening?" she asked.

"Nah, I have to be out by 6:00, per our contract,"

"When you're not working, can you come over?"

I smiled.

"Now that I can do."

Her name was Megan. I did come to see her after work one day. Her two friends were gone, and we had sex. She was straight and to the point on what she wanted and I had no problem giving it to her.

The next day, I was in their dorm, finishing up my construction project on that floor. Megan was there with her boyfriend, just like nothing ever happened between us. It didn't faze me at all. I got a wife.

What was really crazy was that she acted like she didn't even really know me.

"What's your name?" she asked, while she sat on the bed huddled up with her boyfriend.

I laughed to myself. Okay, you want to play this game?

"Cody," I played along.

By this time, her friend, Tamika came in, went into the kitchen and got something to drink. I could tell by the look on her face that she had an idea what was going on here.

She motioned for me to come into the kitchen.

"Look," she said, "I know what happened last night. I should have warned you about Megan. She's trifling."

Then she started running her finger up and down my arm seductively.

"But she did tell me how good it was."

"She told you?" I asked, a little surprised.

"Oh yeah. She said you knew how to work that thing. So, when we going out?"

Heck, as long as these girls were willing to give it up, I was going to milk this. I wasn't getting anything at home.

"When you want to go out?"

We ended up messing around the next day. And, we fooled around for a little while. She called me every day after we got together.

One week later, she asked me to come up to Fredericksburg at her family's place. They were going to be out of town. So, I rode up there and we messed around at her parents' house and then I rode back to Richmond the next morning.

The week after that, I met a cute, white girl, Brittney. She had long blond hair and a cute little shape. Brittney lived down the hall from Tamika and her roommate was this girl from Bangladesh, Chara, who seemed to give me dirty looks every time I saw her.

Brittney and I struck up a conversation while I was finishing up some work in her room. She seemed pretty shy and quiet, but perked up when we started talking about my dogs. She handed me her phone number.

I looked at her. She looked so innocent.

"Sweetie, you don't want to go down this road with me."

"I want to see your dogs."

I met her and her roommate at the park one day with my dogs. Her roommate sat on a bench a distance away from us and just glared at me like she couldn't stand me.

"What's your friend's problem?"

Brittney just waved her off.

"Oh, she's like that with everybody. Don't pay her any mind. She a Bengali princess and comes from wealth. Frankly, she's a little stuck up."

"But don't you?"

"Don't I what?" she asked, "I'm not stuck up."

"No, what I meant to say is don't you come from wealth too?"

"We're alright," she said flippantly, "I'm no princess or anything like her. But, I guess my dad makes about $600K."

She was definitely all right. After meeting to play with the dogs, she convinced me to come back to the dorm one evening and hang out when her roommate wasn't around.

She leaned in and tried to kiss me. And, typically I don't kiss girls I don't know that well because I'm a bit germ-a-phobic. But, that wasn't the problem. This girl didn't know how to kiss. I pulled away from her.

"Have you ever kissed a guy before?"

She shrugged her shoulders.

"Once."

I was confused.

"So, how do you mess around?"

"I don't" she said innocently, "I'm a virgin."

We hung out for a little while after that, but I pulled away from her a little bit. This girl was really innocent and I didn't want to be the one to take her virginity. I shouldn't be that person for her.

A few weeks went by and Brittany calls me.

"What are you doing?"

"Nothing," I said, as I looked at my wife sitting in our living room playing on her phone like she always does.

"Why don't you come and see me? My roommate is gone."

My better judgment told me that I should have stayed home that night, but just looking at the pathetic situation of my home life exasperated me, so I wasn't really thinking clearly.

"Okay."

"Oh, and stop by the store on your way," she said.

"What do you want? Something to drink?"

"I want you to get some condoms."

Reason kicked in.

"Sweetheart, you don't want to do this. I'm not the guy you want to be your first."

"Yes, I do."

Who was I to argue with her? I'd already warned her and she still wanted to do this. So, I went over to her place.

She wanted me to show her how to give head, so I showed her. Then we had sex. About 40 minutes into it, she started bleeding everywhere. At first, I thought this was because she was a virgin, but there was a lot of blood and when we tried to have sex again, it happened again.

I told her to get checked out to make sure she was okay. She went to the doctor and ended up discovering that she had a problem with her cervix and had to have a small procedure to correct it.

After that, everything was fine.

This girl was eager to please me. I kept teaching her how to give me head and she was a very eager student. Some nights, she'd be down there as long as 1 ½ hours – no joke! She was determined to master this craft, the entire time, interrogating me on my pleasure meter. Am I doing it right? Does it feel right? What do I need to do?

But, I had to admit, her hard work and determination paid off because she mastered giving head like no other. I'm just glad I was the happy recipient of her mastery!

After we'd been kicking it for a while, my conscience really started bothering me. What I was doing wasn't right. I knew things were not right at home, but at this point, I wasn't even trying. And, I did love my wife. I needed to do the right thing. So, I tried to break it off with Brittney. She knew I was married which was something I always disclosed to any woman I got involved with so they didn't have any unrealistic expectations of me.

The next day I get a call from her roommate and her father.

"I'm looking for Cody." The voice on the other end was a man and he sounded like an older white man.

"Who is this?"

"I'm Brittany's father. My daughter is in love with you and has attempted suicide."

What?!

"Excuse me?" was all that I could muster. This chick was crazy!

"She drank a bunch of liquor and took a bunch of pills."

I was stupefied.

"Sir, I'm really sorry to hear about this. But, what do you want me to do?"

"I'm not asking you to date my daughter. All she keeps doing is crying and asking for you. I'm just asking that you please talk to her."

This was a strange request, but I didn't want the girl to try and kill herself again so I complied.

"Okay."

I called and talked to Brittney, hoping to just convince her that she'd be okay without me. But, unfortunately, talking led to "can you come over and visit me one time?"

So, again, against my better judgment, I went to see this girl. She tried everything to try and get me to stay with her. She gave me money and gifts even though I told her I didn't need her money. I was stuck between a rock and a hard place. How do I pull away from her without her trying to kill herself?

So, I crafted the most devious plan that I probably ever came up with in my life. I faked an accident. But this scenario was very carefully planned because I needed it to work. I consulted my aunt and a friend of mine who were doctors and had a long talk with them about various medical conditions and scenarios to make sure I had my facts straight.

So, here's what I did – I faked a head injury and had some friends call and tell her that I had to have surgery. I would only be able to communicate via text as a 3rd party and my sister was handling all of my communications during my recovery. Because I'd researched with my aunt and friend, I knew what my symptoms had to be and everything. They were told that after surgery, there could be some potential memory loss. I really had to be on point because a third girl that I'd met that hung out with Brittney and her roommate was an EMT, Amanda.

We'd actually kicked it a little bit before I faked my accident. She'd told me how much she liked me and that her other roommate had told her how I be putting it down in the bedroom. Amanda was one of the sexiest white girls I'd ever met. She had long blond hair to her butt. She was 5'5 and was built like Serena Williams.

So, after my fake surgery was completed, my sister texted the girls to let them know that I was recovering but had some memory loss. My long-term memory was in-tact and I remembered things from a long time ago, but I couldn't remember things within the last few months.

After a month and a half, they wanted to come by and visit. I told my wife that they wanted to come and visit and she said that if they were going to come to our house to have them do it where we were staying now because we were getting ready to move in a couple of months.

My wife didn't really want to be involved in my little scheme but she ended up helping me out anyway.

So Amanda and Chara came over to my house. Brittany did not come.

When they knocked on the door, I just sat in the room real quiet while my wife went and answered the door.

"Can we come in?" they asked.

They introduced themselves to my wife.

"We just want to see him and take him out for some fresh air and talk."

My wife let them inside the house.

"Well, talk to him here first and see if he's comfortable going out with ya'll cause he really doesn't know who you are. You're going to have to take your time with him."

"Yea, I'm an EMT," Amanda said, "so I've actually seen this before with

242

my work. We'll take our time with him and see what he wants to do. Thank you."

"Yea, I'm his wife and he don't even remember me like that," Stephanie said, "I'm going upstairs but if you need me, just call me."

So they both walked over to me cautiously and sat down.

The hardest thing for me to do in this situation was not laugh, because they looked so serious and all I wanted was to just get rid of Brittany. But, it was easy for me to keep up my facade because I really didn't know either of these girls that well.

One of the girls got up to get snacks while the other stayed with me.

"I was thinking that maybe we could go to the botanical gardens. You could get out for a little bit and get some sunlight and enjoy the flowers. Would you like that?"

I looked at her strange and backed away.

"Stephanie," I yelled, "Stephanie!"

She backed away.

"What did we do wrong?"

Stephanie came running down the stairs and just looked at me.

I could tell she was a little pissed because she did not want to play along in my little charade but she did anyway.

"Is it okay to go with them? Do I know them? I don't know. I'm real nervous."

Stephanie rolled her eyes but played along.

"If you want to go out and get some fresh air, you can go. But, you know you gotta wear your baseball cap and keep the sun out of your face."

"Okay," I said, and Stephanie went up the stairs.

The two girls were just standing there, looking a little confused about what to do next. They were afraid of setting me off again.

"I'll go get my cap," I said.

So, I went with the girls to the botanical gardens. I wore my cap and even had a little scully on my head to hide my scar.

As we were walking through the gardens, one girl was on each side of me, trying to support me.

I looked at them like they were crazy.

"Why are ya'll trying to hold me up? I lost my memory. I didn't break

243

my legs."

They backed away a little bit.

When Amanda wasn't looking, Chara, held on to me real tight.

"I really like you," she said, "I've always liked you."

I was quiet, but in the back of my mind I was thinking about how she always treated me.

Chara ran to the bathroom and left me there with Amanda for a little while. She started to tell me about how we were supposed to get together before the accident.

"What about her?" I asked, pointing in the direction of Chara who'd just gone to the bathroom.

"I don't know about her," Amanda said, "I just know we talked about getting together."

I stopped and sat down on a bench, talking slow and confused.

"I don't know. I've got a lot to think about."

The girls brought me back home and left.

My wife came down the stairs.

"Let me guess," she said, "they both want you, right?"

"Yeah," I said, feeling myself a little bit, "it's crazy though. These girls come from money. They can't really be this stupid."

"Well, what you gonna do?"

"I'm just gonna chill right now," I said.

"They gonna drive you crazy," she said.

"I know."

"And I don't want them coming around here ever again."

"Ok."

I wasn't concerned about that since we were moving in 2 months anyway.

A couple weeks later, Brittney got a hotel room and we met up.

When I arrived, she came up to me and hugged me.

I backed away.

"Do you remember me?" she asked.

"No."

Then she proceeded to tell me a pack of lies, saying that she has been my girlfriend for 3 years when we'd only known each other a year and a half. She

244

said we were planning a future together and that I was planning on leaving my wife.

"Don't let you wife tell you that everything is okay between you, because it isn't. I'm the one you love."

All I could think was, you conniving whore. You just going to try to take advantage of me to get what you want.

I just looked at her, disgusted.

"I don't know how me and you gonna get along. You could be lying for all I know."

She leaned in and caressed my face.

"I'd never lie to you, baby. Just ask my friend."

I was thinking, they really ain't your friends since they were plotting how to get with me too.

"I would do anything for you," Brittney said.

She scooted a little closer to me on the bed. I was sitting on the edge.

"Would it be okay if I hugged and touched you?" she asked.

"I'll be fine, but why would you want to touch me. Touch me how?"

"Did the doctor say your memory would come back?"

"The doctor said my memory could come back in a day, or 5 years from now. We really have no control over that if it comes back at all. It was just my short term memory that I lost."

She kept moving closer and closer to me on the bed.

"I want to be close to you. You know we used to lie in the bed naked together and just watch TV. You want to do that with me?"

"I guess," I said hesitantly.

So, I lay in bed with her but kept my t-shirt and underwear on because I told her I was not comfortable taking all of my clothes off. We got under the covers and started watching TV, and I pretended to fall asleep.

She'd started stroking me while we were watching TV. When she thought I'd dozed off, she slipped under the covers and started giving me head. Then, she proceeded to crawl on top of me and try to have sex, with no condom or anything. This woke me up from my fake slumber real quick.

"What are you doing?"

"I just miss you and I love you so much," she said, "this is what we used to do."

"But, why would you try and do it without a condom?"

I was disgusted that she would try to have unprotected sex with me.

"Oh yea, I brought condoms," she said, "I see you losing your memory didn't change how germophobic you are."

"Never gonna happen," I said.

So, I put the condom on and we had sex.

Later than night, her girlfriend, Amanda called me up. She said that Brittney went out of town and she realized that she hadn't seen me that day.

She got a hotel room, said she was going to be in town for the weekend and wanted to see me.

I agreed. My wife was with her mother for the weekend so she picked me up. As soon as we got into the hotel room, she immediately pulled my pants down and started giving me head. It was a wild weekend because Amanda was a freak. We did it in every position from dusk till dawn. There was nothing this girl wasn't willing to do. By the end of the weekend, I was worn out.

A couple weeks later, Chara started visiting with me a lot. We would meet at the park or at restaurants and she just kept spending money on me. Then, we started sleeping together. I never thought Chara and I would get together because of the nasty looks she always gave me, but she was beautiful as well with caramel skin, and long, dark hair.

At this point, I found myself in three different relationships, outside of my wife. This went on for 3 ½ years! At this point, I realize that I can't keep doing this anymore. I'm getting older. I'm tired. My wife was fed up and I know that I need to start doing the right thing.

I pretended to get into another accident, hoping that I would be able to elude some of these girls, mentioning that I had some complications from the initial surgery.

Amanda decided to walk away. She'd really fallen in love with me and could not tolerate being in a love triangle anymore. She said it was hard to hear both of her friends talk about being with me. It was too much for her to take.

I decided to admit to both Brittney and Chara that I was seeing them both, but it did nothing but create animosity between them. But, what they didn't realize was that I wanted them both to leave me alone. I didn't need them fighting over me.

After my second attempt to break it off with Brittney after my elaborate accident scheme, she went to her brother's house with a bottle of liquor and a .38 under her pillow. Here we go again! Her parents were on their way to New York to see their other kids when they got the call from Chara that Brittney was threatening her life again.

Then Chara called me, trying to get me to talk to her again.

"She just wants attention," I said.

"No, you don't understand. She's really stupid. This chick will kill herself."

So, I called her father and told him that I really don't know what's going on. I told him once again that I'd done nothing wrong to his daughter but that she was planning on killing herself.

Her father got there 2 hours after I talked to him and there was a .38 under her pillow and she'd gone through a whole bottle of whiskey.

After that I stopped talking to her for a while, hoping to never hear from her again.

Meanwhile, Chara kept sending me gifts and buying me things and we continued having sex together.

Then, the time came for her to get married. In her culture, arranged marriages were a requirement when you reached a certain age. The way it worked was they had 7 different marriage ceremonies, but after the 3rd or 4th, it was considered official. Chara would receive a dowry from her parents once she completed that 4th ceremony. She received $250,00 just for graduating college. But, her dowry was a couple million.

She walked me through all of this one night when we were together.

"But, I love you. I don't love him, but I do have to go through with this. So, we're going to have to stop having sex."

Now, as much as I enjoyed sex, I was delighted to hear this because I wanted to leave this chick alone anyway.

"We're going to have to start having oral sex more often and you're going to have to start doing me in the butt."

I think my jaw dropped to the floor.

"Excuse me? Why?"

"Because I'm supposed to be a virgin when I get married."

"How do you know he's not going to want you like that? Aren't you supposed to be real submissive in your culture?"

"Yea, but I have the right to tell him if I want him in my butt or not."

"So, you want me there, but not your husband who's the same culture as you?"

I sighed, exasperated.

"Can you just do this for me?"

"Okay," I said hesitantly, "we'll try it. But, I'm not really into this. It's not one of my fantasies."

So, we did it, and she walked through hell the whole way through, but she wanted to go through with it. A couple of times, I saw her crying but she just told me to keep going. She said she just wanted to please me. I have to admit; she was a trooper.

A couple weeks later, she went and met the guy she was supposed to marry. She met him with her family and came back and told me that she'd be getting married next year on that exact date.

After she'd given me some money, about $750, to handle bills and groceries, she said that she needed to talk.

"I need you to do something for me," she asked.

"What's that?"

"I need you to kill my husband."

I almost fell out of the chair I was sitting in.

"You want me to what?"

"Well, you can at least permanently hurt him or kill him, just anything to keep him away from me," she said flippantly.

I was floored. Where was I finding these crazy chicks?

"Baby, I don't do that."

"But, you're from the streets," she said matter of factly, "you sold drugs, and guns and all that other stuff. You can do this."

"Let me tell you something. I have never in my life hurt anyone that didn't hurt me first, or hurt someone I love first. I've never been the one to start it. And, number 2, I've never told you that I've killed anybody. And, 3, why would you want to hurt someone when all they want to do is be with you? You don't do that. You get bad karma for that, and I don't believe in that. I pray to God for good things in my life. The reason why a lot of blessings don't come back is because I'm doing this stuff behind my wife's back. I'm not killing nobody."

"Then, just hurt him real bad so that he can't walk or something," she said, unfazed.

It was like I was talking to a brick wall.

"Are you crazy?!" What kind of TV show are you watching?"

She was very young and naïve to think that she could ask me to do some crazy crap like this without any consequences. Then again, maybe she was just trying to see where I'm at with us. She said that she wanted to do all of this because she loved me and wanted to spend her life with me. According to her, she only has to do the arranged marriage once, and if it doesn't work out, she can go on with her life as she pleases.

My mind was reeling because I couldn't believe this girl was asking me this.

"What if your family finds out what you're trying to do?"

"If my family finds out I'm not a virgin, in my culture, they believe in killing you for something like that."

I sat there for a minute trying to process all of this. As messed up as this situation was, I did feel for the girl a bit.

"If you don't want to be with somebody, say no. The worse that can happen is you don't get your money."

"Well, I need my money," she said, not budging.

"Well, I can't be a part of this."

"How much do you want?" she asked, thinking that she could bribe me into getting what she wanted.

"What part of this conversation did you not understand?"

"Forget you, then! Get the hell out!"

I looked at the door and then looked at her.

"Sweetheart, we are in a hotel room. We ain't home. I'll just go to my car."

I got up and started to leave.

"What good are you to me then?" she yelled.

"Ohh," I said turning around, "I see, now. So, you been buttering me up because you knew this day was coming."

"All the stuff that I do for you," she said burning with anger, tearing stinging her eyes, "and you can't do this one little thing for me?!"

"First of all, there is nothing simple about what you just asked me to do. Second, what do I ask you for other than to have sex with me? That's all I ask for. The rest, I can do without because I'm going to survive, regardless."

Then, I turned around to leave.

"Where do you think you're going?" she demanded, "you haven't handled your business yet!"

If that's what she really wanted, I was happy to oblige. So I handled my business – slow and hard and did everything under the sun to her from her ample breast to her round behind. She'd remember this last experience. Then, I walked out the door and never looked back.

Leaving Chara behind was one thing, but I still had the chore of dealing with Brittney. Every time I threatened to leave her, she tried to kill herself. It was becoming a vicious cycle and I was having a hard time figuring out how to quit her. She was becoming quite the nuisance.

I kept telling her to just live her life, but she would respond telling me that she did not want to go through life without me.

We were in a hotel room one evening while I was trying yet again to get this chick to let go. I knew I needed to be working on my marriage and wrestling with this girl was not helping my cause.

"There's no guarantee that you are going to spend your life with me, Brittney. You know that I'm married."

"Your wife ain't crap," she said, "I don't know what is wrong with you people."

I stopped short. Did she just say YOU PEOPLE?

"I've heard you say you people a few times now. What I need to know if you were referring to me and my wife or you niggas? What the hell are you talking about?"

"Well, you're half black," she said.

"Yea, and that is my better half because that is the half that raised me. I'm not prejudiced but will never denounce the black side of me. And, as messed up as my father and the Italian side of my family has been to me, I still love my Italian side as well. You people? Get in the room."

I shoved her in the room and started doing her real aggressive because I was pissed off. But the more aggressive I got, the more she liked it.

I started messing with her, injecting some X-rated pillow talk.

"Take this," I said, "Yea, you like it when this nigga is banging you, don't you?"

"Yea, I love this nigga banging me," she yelled out.

I can't believe it! She actually said it! She just called me a nigga!

After that night, I resolved to walk away from this girl completely, no matter what. That was just the last straw. I changed my phone number. She found a way to call me on every number I changed. She'd show up in places she knew I went to. I'd find her in my car, begging for us to get back together, crying.

This girl was impossible to get rid of. So, I tried another lie to get her to leave me alone.

I told her that I had some legal problems and that I may be going to jail for a while.

"Is that why you were trying to break up with me?" she said, "I'll wait for you."

"Baby, I'll be doing 10-20 years."

"I'll wait for you. I love you."

I was so sick of this crap. No matter what I tried, I couldn't shake this chick. I told my wife about the drama I was dealing with and it really only made matters worse between us. She was getting really fed up with my cheating. And, my wife has these set of girlfriends that only come around once or twice a year, but when they do, they fill her brain with negative things about me, wreaking havoc. So, she started venting to her friends, sharing her frustration about the trials in our marriage. She never said anything about our threesome or anything. That remained our little secret, but she did tell them that she thought I was stepping out on her.

So, they talked her into taking a girl's trip. She came to me one evening and told me that she was going to take a cruise with her girlfriends, mom, cousins and aunts. It would be a ladies trip and they were planning it for next year. They were going to fly to Florida and then take the cruise from there.

I was still dealing with Brittney at the time, so I was okay with this to start, but I always make a note to write everything down and pay attention. I never miss a beat.

A few months go by and my wife comes to me asking for a couple hundred dollars to put down on the trip.

"You're working," I said, "why don't you go ahead and take care of it?"

I wasn't working at the time because I'd had my appendix taken out and had been sick, leaving me out of work 6-8 months. My family was sending me money and I had saved some money so I was okay.

I gave my wife money to handle the bills, which left her the freedom to use her earned money for what she wanted. So, I put up a little fuss but ended up giving the money to her anyway.

After I gave her the money, she told me that they were going to take a flight to the islands with her friends and cousins.

In my mind, I thought, what happened to your mom and aunts? But, I didn't say anything. I just made a mental note. I also noticed that the date had changed from the original time she told me. But, again, I just paid attention and did not say anything.

Unfortunately, despite my desire to work things out with my wife, I could not ignore the distraction of other women, especially one like Michelle. I was working security at a nightclub one night when I met her. She'd just turned 21 so she was very young. I was 38 at the time, but something drew me to this girl. She was soft spoken, sweet and spiritually inclined, even though she was at the club partying every week. She reminded me of when I first met my wife but she didn't look anything like her. She had caramel skin, 5'4, shoulder length hair, with a big butt and a little waist. We started messing around. I told her about my wife, and she was okay with seeing me. We started seeing each other on a regular basis, like my wife was not even in the picture. My wife did meet her because I tried to have a threesome one time.

I had Michelle over to the house. We had movie on and had gotten rid of the kids for the weekend. I had the downstairs already set up with a blow up mattress. After dinner, we went downstairs and started dancing and then I started kissing my wife. Then, I turned around and started kissing Michelle. Michelle has on a skirt with no panties. Stephanie had on sweat pants but they were the ones that button up the side, so she was easy to access as well.

After a couple of glasses of wine and some dancing, the ladies started to loosen up, so I led them over to the bed. I pulled my wife's pants off and pulled her down on my face. Then, I positioned Michelle on top of me and we started to have sex.

Once we were into it, I glanced up at Michelle and noticed tears in her eyes. I stopped for a minute.

"Are you okay?"

"Yea, I'm fine. I can do this," she said, "I will do anything for you."

But, the next time I looked up, I noticed her wiping her eyes. This just didn't feel right, and I knew she didn't want to do this.

I stopped everything.

My wife sat up and looked at me and then at Michelle.

"Oh I see this is going to be a problem," she said.

She just went upstairs, angry before I had a chance to say anything to her.

That night, I had a long talk with Michelle and I told her that I loved her. She jumped into my arms.

"So, we don't have to do a threesome?" she asked.

I caressed her face.

"Baby, we don't have to do anything you don't want to do."

She smiled and then kissed me tenderly.

Then, she said good-bye and apologized to Stephanie who'd made it back down the stairs by now, and left.

Stephanie waited for the door to close.

"She is a problem," she said, "She has got to go. I want her out of your life – now!"

"No," I said bluntly.

"Why not?"

I looked at her matter-of-factly.

"Because you don't do anything for me anymore; we just cohabitate. You don't love me like you used to. You don't do nothing. But you want me to do everything. What have you done for me?"

I paused a moment while she stood there in silence before continuing.

"The problem is you're waiting on me to change and I'm waiting on you to change. But, we just keep bumping heads. Somebody has got to change."

"You never spend any time with me," she pouted.

I looked at her bug-eyed.

"I'm here most nights, but you just sit there and watch TV. You don't pay any attention to me when I'm here. Be clear on what you want."

"She has to go," she said.

"Well, she ain't going," I said, "Why do you think she is such a problem?"

"The other girls you've been with, you can care less. But, I see the way you kissed her. It was no different than how you kiss me. You never kissed any other woman like that. You kissed her with passion. You touched her with gentleness. I couldn't tell who you thought you were with, her or me just now. She can't stay. She's a threat. She has to go."

I got in her face.

"Then, you need to get yourself together then."

And I walked away. So, I pretended to get rid of Michelle. I wanted to test Stephanie to see if she was going to do what she said.

I just didn't let Michelle come to the house or anything, but we did continue to see each other. Months went by, and nothing changed. As a matter of fact, they got worse.

One year later...

I got a call from my buddy while I was chilling at the house.

"Yo Cody, what's up? You guys going on a trip or something?"

"I'm not going anywhere. What are you talking about?"

My buddy worked at the post office.

"Stephanie came in the post office today to take a picture for her passport."

"My wife isn't going anywhere where she needs a passport," I said.

"She's going to Jamaica," he said.

The plot thickens. I was quiet for a little while and then the night before she was scheduled to leave, I confronted her.

"You ain't going nowhere," I said.

"What are you talking about?" she said, "We already talked about this. You knew I was taking this trip."

"Yea, but the plans changed a lot from what you told me. You snuck out and got a passport. And, now you're going with your stank friends that only come around every couple of years to stir up trouble."

One of her friends was actually there when I confronted her and she tried to step to me to stick up for Stephanie.

"What you need to do is get out my house?"

She just stood there for a while like she was trying to think of something to say.

"Just go," Stephanie told her friend, "I'll talk to him."
She walked out the house.

"I don't know what you think you can say to change my mind."

"Cody, we've been through this," she said, "you knew about this trip."

"Okay Stephanie. Why isn't your family going with you like you said? When did that change? When did the venue change to Jamaica? Don't you think you owe me some kind of explanation?"

"I don't owe you nothing," she said calmly before walking out of the room.

I was pissed because I knew this trip was not going to be good for our relationship. I felt it in my soul.

The next thing I know, I get a call from Stephanie's mother.

"Cody, just let her go," she said.

"You don't understand. If she goes on this trip, something bad is going to happen. I just know it."

"Sweetie, you can't stop your wife from doing stuff."

"Yea, but the girls she's going with don't care nothing about her. Misery loves company. Those girls are crazy and they're not happy with their own life and want my wife to be like them jumping from man to man every 3-4 months. Your daughter knows these girls are ho's."

"That doesn't mean that she's one," her mother said calmly over the other line.

I took a deep breath.

"Right now, your daughter and are going through some stuff and she's fed up. If she goes on this trip, it's going to go wrong."

"You can't stop her, baby. You've got to let her go."

"Ok," I conceded, "but watch what I tell you."

So, I let her go on the trip against my best judgment. Stephanie was gone for a week. I got two calls from her – two!

Though I was good with my hands and had some experience over the years as a carpenter, I really wanted to be a cop. But, I had a felony on my record from my drug dealing.

A couple years ago, I was introduced to a guy who worked for the state troopers and always called himself Stephanie's brother. He asked me if I'd ever considered being a cop. I told him that I would love to be a cop but I had a felony charge from 10-15 years ago from selling drugs.

"Was it nonviolent?" he asked.

"Yes."

"Is that the only thing on your record?"

"Yes."

"I want to introduce you to some people."

He introduced me to some people that worked for the governor and they wanted me to file for my rights to restoration. I filed the paperwork. I received a letter telling me that I'd receive an answer in 8-12 months. Less than a year later, my rights were restored. Check one. That was nothing but God. I was on cloud 9. Now, I had to get my weapons rights. I was introduced to a lawyer who only charged me $600 to represent me, which was a blessing in itself. He got the case in court before a judge and I was granted my weapons rights. Next, I applied for my concealed weapons permit while I was still before the judge and he granted it to me.

Now, I started taking security classes. This was during the time that I was still dating the 3 college girls, so I used my relationship with them to pay for my courses. I got the necessary weapons training I needed. These girls shelled out about $6,000 for my classes. I wanted to be a police officer. But, despite all that I'd done to prepare for this, no one would hire me. My felony was still showing on my record. I was told to file for a pardon. I filed. I was denied.

Two years later, I tried again. In the meantime, I took a bail enforcement course to become a bounty hunter. I passed. My first assignment was a stripper that the bondman had been looking for over a year. I found her in a week. I knew the streets and I loved my new gig. I got an adrenaline rush, going in, kicking down doors.

To date, I've been a bounty hunter for almost 4 years. I just got turned down for my second pardon. But, I decided that I'm not giving up. I realized that things were not going right for me because I haven't been living right. I started going to church again. Things still were not improving at home. Stephanie and I argued all the time and our relationship continued to deteriorate but I still was not giving up on us.

Our anniversary was approaching. I decided to turn over a new leaf and really try to work on my marriage. I called up Michelle and told her that I needed to work on my marriage and that we needed to take some time off so that I could do that. She was so supportive which is why I love her. She asked me how much time I needed and I told her, 2 months. In that time, I should know whether or not what we have is still worth saving.

Michelle and I still talked, but it was as friends. She called and asked about the kids and Stephanie. We never talked about us. She didn't want to cloud my judgment during this period.

About a week before our anniversary, I decided I wanted to do some big things to really show Stephanie that I was serious about working on our marriage. I tried to put out of my mind the anxiety I had about her going on that trip with her friends. I just wanted us to get back to a good place again. So, I spent $4,000 on a nice diamond tennis bracelet for her. Our entire time together, we'd always rode around in old hoopties – by design. They were paid for, and I got them fixed up so they would run great and we didn't have to worry about a car payment. This system always worked great for me but Stephanie hated it. She always wanted something newer. So, I went out and bought her a Volvo C70. A buddy of mine worked at the car dealership and allowed me to put the car in

Stephanie's name. I couldn't put anything in my name because of child support. After I bought the car, I took it over to my buddy Nathan's house so that he could keep it until our anniversary.

chapter 14
payback is a mother

I sat there in the corner thinking about all of the things I'd done wrong in my life, the way I'd treated women I said I loved. All the way back to Camille. I really loved her, but my infidelity drove her away and I never got a chance to make it up to her. And now, I'd found the woman of my dreams in Stephanie, and my gallivanting with all of these women had led her to go out of the country and seek the attention of another man. I know technically she was not unfaithful to me, but it felt like she was. My heart was aching. I didn't know how to process the emotions going through my head right now. I needed to go outside and get some air. I couldn't breathe.

I went outside and put the diamond tennis bracelet in the glove compartment of the new car I'd just bought her and then called up my boy.

"Hey, I need you to come and get this car tomorrow."

"What's up?" he said, concerned.

I hung up the phone and turned it off. I wasn't in the state of mind to be answering any questions right now. What I needed was answers and they were not going to come from him.

I went back into the house and starting pacing the living room, trying to calm my nerves.

What made me such a bastard that I'd be with all of these different women and only marry this one girl after 600 women? What would make me such an idiot that I forgot how much I loved and cared for her? This must be karma coming back to me for all that I'd done.

I needed answers. I composed myself, then went back into our bedroom and woke my wife up.

"I love you," I told her.

"I love you too," she said.

I sat down on the bed.

"We're good now, right? Now, that I'm not doing anything wrong."

"What's wrong?" she asked, looking nervous.

"We're okay, right?"

"Cody, you're making me nervous. What's wrong?"

"In 9 years, have I ever put a hand on you?"

"No," she said, "you pulled my hair once because I was walking away. You never hit me."

"Have I ever abused you in any way?"

"No Cody, you're making me nervous," she said.

"If I've never done nothing wrong to you other than sleep with somebody else, why am I making you nervous?"

"You've got this look in your eyes," she said.

"Are we okay?"

"Yes."

"Would you cheat on me?"

"No."

"Now that I just want to be with you, would you be with another man?"

"No."

"In Jamaica, did you cheat on me?"

"No."

I got up from the bed.

"I don't care about anything that happened before tonight. Did you sleep with someone else?"

"No."

"Did you kiss anybody, touch anybody, suck anybody? You can tell me."

I made sure I covered everything.

"No."

"You can tell me," I said softly, "It's okay because we're going to work it out – start fresh."

"No, Cody. You're scaring me. Why are you asking all of these questions?"

Then, I held the phone up to her.

"What do you mean you'd never do this to me?"

And, for the first time in my life, I took an open hand swing at my wife. I missed her, thank God. I caught the tip of her chin with my fingertips.

She got out the bed and tried to run through me, naked, but I caught her and pushed her back down on the waterbed.

"You're not going nowhere. We're going to have this conversation right now."

"Didn't I tell you to stay away from your ho friends? Never stoop to this level. What is wrong with you?!"

She got up from the bed and started yelling.

"Kids! Kids!"

I closed the bedroom door and put a towel at the bottom of the door. Then, I put a finger in her face.

"Don't wake up my kids! You're not going to scare them."

"I want to leave," she said, running around the room frantically.

"You can leave. Get your clothes on," I said.

"Take me to my mother's."

"Get your clothes on."

She grabbed her purse and tried to walk out the room, naked.

She wasn't in her right mind.

I grabbed her arm and pulled her back in the room.

"Where are you going?"

"I want to leave."

"Don't you want to get dressed?" I asked looked at her standing in front of me naked with a purse on her shoulder.

"I want to leave. Wake the kids up. I want to go. I want to get out of here!"

"Stop screaming before you wake my kids and scare them half to death. This is the last time I am going to tell you," I was livid. "Put on your clothes now and I'll drop you off at your mother's."

But she just kept trying to leave. She was so distraught; she didn't realize what she was doing. She kept grabbing her purse and nothing else. So, I decided to give her some time to get herself together while I got the kids ready. I went into my son's room and told him to get his sister ready because they were going to the nanny's; it was an emergency. I saw a bit of panic in his eyes, thinking that maybe he heard some of the yelling coming from our room.

"Don't worry, little man. Nothing is wrong with mommy. Everything is going to be all right. Just get your stuff together."

I left him and went back in our room, thinking Stephanie would be ready to go. She was standing there wearing a scarf and shoes, and nothing else, but still holding on to her purse. And, she was still trying to leave.

"Put your clothes on now!" I yelled and just threw some things on the bed for her to put on.

She finally started to put her clothes on and the whole time she was shaking, and having a fit.

"What you shaking for? I didn't do nothing to you!"

About that time, my son hears me yelling and runs to try and protect his mom.

"Son, if you don't take you little butt in that room…"

"Don't hit mommy!"

"Have I ever hit mommy?"

He shook his head.

"No, but she keeps saying you gonna hit her."

"Go get your sister."

He listened to me and left the room to get his sister.

As we were going out of the house, I lined all of them up in front of me because I had all of the keys. Stephanie was the last one to leave before me, and as I was about to close the door, I snatched the purse from her and threw it in the house. There's something in that damn purse she's trying to hide.

"Get in the car!"

We got in the car and I drove them across town to my

mother-in-law's house.

"I'll bring you clothes tomorrow for work and school," I told them as they stepped out of the car.

Then, I peeled off. I had to know what was inside that purse. What was she trying to hide?

As soon as I got home, I emptied the contents of her purse, a YSL bag I'd gotten for her a while back. I found some cards with some guys' phone numbers on it. I didn't care about that crap. Something else was in this bag. After I'd dumped all of the contents of the bag, I noticed the bag was still heavy. I felt around inside and found another cell phone inside the lining of the bag.

I opened up the phone and after about 5 tries, I was able to crack the code. But, there were other things in the phone that were still locked. So, I called up my buddy who works for a cell phone store to see if he might be able to unlock the phone. I paced the floor all night, losing my mind. No sleep.

The next morning, I went to his store and he was able to unlock the apps in the phone. I started looking through it. Mostly all I found were just pictures of other guys. I started packing up some clothes for Stephanie and the kids and called her to let her know I would be dropping them off.

"Don't come to my parents' house," Stephanie said, "you know you and my father don't get along."

"Forget your father," I said, "I'm just dropping off clothes. I'll leave them in the driveway for you. And, I want to see my daughter. You always told me that if something happens between us, you gonna take my daughter and disappear. I want to see her."

When I got to her parents' house, two patrol cars were parked up front and the front door of the house was open. I didn't see my wife and kids anywhere.

Then, I see my father-in-law coming out of the house pointing but I can't hear what he's saying. The next thing I know, the 2 officers are running toward me, calling on their radio, putting their hands toward their guns.

I immediately pulled out my badge and put my hands toward my gun.

"Don't run up on me putting your hands on your gun like that," I said, "are you really this stupid?"

"Whoa," one of the officers said apologetically, "are you an officer?"

"Fugitive recovery agent," I replied, "don't run up on me like that."

"What are you doing here?"

I walked around to the rear of my vehicle, popped the trunk and pulled out the clothes.

"I'm bringing clothes for my wife and kids because we had a big fight last night."

"Did you beat your wife up?" one of the officers asked.

"No, I'd never beat my wife up. I dropped her off here. Why would I beat her up and then drop her off at her parents' house? Is that what my wife said?"

"Your wife hasn't opened her mouth the entire time we've been here," the officer said, "Just your father-in-law."

"What did he say?"

"That you beat your wife up and threatened to kill everybody."

I chuckled, sarcastically.

Then, my father-in-law came across the grass, starting to come up on me.

"Oh you want to come over here with your badge and your little gun," he said, "I got a gun in the house, too."

"I ain't afraid of that," I said, "Let me tell you something. In 9 years, you've never gotten this close to me. Don't think because these officers are here that you're tough, because you're a punk. You a coward. Unlike you, I don't abuse my wife. Don't ever run up on me and if you get within 3 feet of me, you gonna get knocked out because you invading my personal space."

My father-in-law looked at the officers standing there with me.

"Did you hear? He threatened me."

"No," one of the officers responded, "you approached him in a threatening manner. He has the right to tell you what he's going to do before he does it. You are within his personal boundaries. Now, you need to back up."

And, like the coward he was, he made some threatening statements to me while he ran back into the house. Once he was gone, the officers turned their attention back to me.

"You have a little position of power here," one of the officers said, "which is why you're not going to jail. Just pull off and leave. Obviously, you didn't beat your wife like they're saying."

So, I took the clothes, dropped them in the street and left.

I got a call from Stephanie later asking if I was going to be home. She wanted to come by the house to pick up some things for her and the kids. I told her that was fine. In the meantime, I needed the support of someone who loved me, so I called Michelle. She came over immediately.

"What can I do?" she asked, concerned.

"Nothing," I said, just hugging her. I just needed her loving support. We spent most of our time together in silence, just holding and comforting each other. Michelle said that she could assure Stephanie that nothing was going on between us when she arrived.

Later in the afternoon, close to 6:00, Stephanie came to the house, but she didn't come alone. She had an entourage of family and friends with her. Six cars pulled up in front of my house.

At that same time, an officer served me with an order of protection that said I threatened Stephanie and that she fears for her life and the life of her kids and doesn't feel safe. Are you kidding me?

As Stephanie and her crew were getting out of their cars, they noticed Michelle's car in the driveway and immediately start hurling threats and insults.

"I know he didn't bring that whore here!"

The officer was standing with me at the front door.

"This is still my house, officer. Am I right?"

"Yes it is."

"If any of them outside of my wife, steps one toe on my grass, I want them all locked up for trespassing."

"Yes sir."

The officer walked forward.

"Everybody here step off this property now. If you step on this grass, you are going to jail for trespassing. The only one allowed to step on the grass is Mrs. Jenkins."

They all stepped back and Stephanie came forward.

The officers had to escort her and follow her into each room because there were guns in the house.

One of her girlfriends pulled up about 5 minutes after she got there and asked if she could come into the house. I allowed her to come in because she was the less trifling than the other two friends she hung out with.

When she came into the house, I was in the bedroom while Stephanie was getting together her things. The officers, of course, followed.

"What's in the closet?" the officer asked.

"Shotgun and automatic rifle," I said.

"Give me that," he said.

I handed the guns to him and he put them in the far corner of the room. I was sitting on the laundry hamper while Stephanie was putting some things together.

"Come here baby," I said to her.

She walked over to me.

"Why would you do this to me?"

She just shook her head.

"It's getting out of control," she said.

"Then, why would you do it?" I asked.

"Give me some time," she said.

I sat there just shaking my head.

"You know this can mess me up. They'll take my weapons from me. Everything I've worked for, for almost 20 years. They'll take it all away. Why would you do this to me?"

"They told me at the magistrate's office, they wouldn't do that," she said.

"They lied," I said, "When they see a woman distraught and think she's been hurt, they'll tell her anything to get her to file papers and charges."

"The officers haven't taken anything from you," she said.

The officer in the room stepped in.

"But, unfortunately, he is going to get a summons in the mail telling him that he has to relinquish his concealed weapons permit and will not be able to carry a gun until further notice and this case is over."

"They didn't tell me that," she said.

She walked closer to me and stood between my legs and just started kissing me, long and hard.

As she was kissing me, I kept one eye open and noticed the officer signaling to me by pointing to his eyes to say, 'I see everything.'

After that, my son came inside to get some things for him and his sister in his room.

We went down to the laundry room where Michelle was.

"What's that whore doing in my house?" Stephanie questioned, referred to Michelle.

"She's here to tell you something," I said.

"What?"

"She's here to tell you that we stopped seeing each other a long time ago."

"I don't believe this crap. Get her the hell out of my house!"

Michelle walked toward the door and I followed her out.

My wife followed me.

"You just going to walk her outside?"

"With your crazy family out there? Yes!"

"That's the problem! Her!"

"But I left her alone and you still went out and did stupid crap."

I asked one of the officers to escort Michelle to her car. Before she left, she said her peace.

"I see how this is going to go," she said, "Cody, I love you and I'm not going anywhere. If she wants to do this – if she wants to lie on you, I'm with you for life."

"I'm with you for life, too," I said. I hugged her and sent her with the officer to her car, while the other officer stayed with us in the house.

When I went back in the house, Stephanie's girlfriend was talking to her.

"Why would you do this to him?" she said, "You know everything he's worked for."

"Right," I said, chiming in.

"Shut up," she said, "because if you weren't cheating and making my girlfriend do all kinds of stuff, it would not have gotten this far."

"Ok," I said because I knew she was right.

Before leaving, Stephanie kissed me again and told me she loved me.

"Remember you are grown, "I reminded her, all the chicks in your family are miserable and lonely. Remember who you are."

I told my son to be good and told him I loved him and they left.

As she was walking to the car, her stupid aunts started yelling to me that he wasn't my son, that he was my stepson.

"That's why you are bitter," I yelled back, "That's why you 50 and still living with your mama and can't keep a man. Get the hell off my property!" They left. The next day I showed up at Stephanie's job with the paperwork for the order of protection.

"Let's go to court and get this dismissed now. You don't have to tell your family. I'll stay away from you and give you time. But, we've got to get this fixed."

We went to court and she told the officials that she made a rash mistake, and that her family put her up to it. She told them that I never hit or abused her and that she loved me. They dropped the order of protection.

We talked every day afterward. I told her that I loved her and that I was sorry for doing wrong. Three days later, another order of protection was served from the county of Henrico. The first had been served by the City of Richmond. I didn't even know there was an order until I was talking to one of her friends on the phone. She was checking on me to see if I was okay.

"I told her that I was about to go see Stephanie and the kids and give them some money and make sure everything was okay with them."

"You can't go see them," she said.

"Why not?"

"You've got an order of protection against you."

"No, she dropped that," I said.

"And now she has a new one," she said, "Her father told her to get an order of protection or she couldn't stay with him."

Her father has always been a problem. So, I started making calls to different police precincts and by the time I got to the third one, I found it.

"Yep, we were just about to come down to serve you," the Henrico officer said.

The next day, Stephanie drops the second order of protection.

We decided to meet for lunch.

But, beforehand, I decide to humble myself and go meet her father at his house, admit I was wrong, and try to make peace.

I left my weapons at home, but phoned the county sheriffs department in his area beforehand to let them know what I was doing. They documented my call.

I went to his house and knocked on the door.

I stepped off his property and waited on the grass until he came to the door.

He opened the door and peered at me behind the glass for a moment.

"Wait a minute," he said before disappearing for a couple minutes.

He came back and walked across the lawn, pulling a gun from his waist and cocking it.

"If you step one toenail onto my property, I'll blow your head off! You better not come near me or my family again or you're a dead man."

I pulled my shirt up to show him that I had no weapons on me.

"Chill out," I said.

A scared nigga will kill you and he was as scared as they come.

"You better get out of here before I kill you right now!" he said, hands shaking on the gun.

"Ok," I said, walking away, "You know you're a coward right?"

"I'll kill you!" he yelled.

"You better be glad I'm a changed man because where I come from, they kill you for crap like this."

I pulled around the corner and called the Hanover Sheriff immediately and told them exactly what had just happened.

"Anytime you want to take a warrant out on him, we'll pick him up," they said.

Then, I got a call from my wife.

"Why would you go there and threaten my father's life and pull a gun out on him?" she asked.

"What?!"

"My mother just called me and told me that you kicked in the door, pulled a gun out and threatened my father!"

"Are you crazy?! I don't even have a gun on me. I called the police department before I went over there. I was trying to make amends."

"That's not what he said."

By this time, I was at the police station.

"The police are here right now."

I handed the phone to the officer and he gave her a rundown of what happened.

Then, I drove to see her.

"If you lock my father up, you'll never see me and those kids again," she threatened.

Furious, I drove off. I picked up Michelle and she kept telling me to pray and have faith. We went to her church. He was a young pastor and I liked him. I kept praying and trying to get my life right. I never told anyone at the church that I was married. I'd been contemplating divorce for a while now. No one knew that I had been trying to get a divorce for a couple of years, but every time I would bring it up Stephanie would tell me to get out of her face.

"Aren't you happy with that young chick you got?" she would scream at me, "I'm not gonna let the world know I can't keep my husband."

Also I had to consider my daughter and stepson. I wanted them to be old enough to handle it and I didn't want my stepson to think that I didn't want him in my life. I just didn't think it would ever come to this in this way.

A few days later, I received a call from Hanover County Sheriff. Another order of protection! This time taken out by Stephanie and her father! I was done with this crap!

"Michelle, I want you to take my kids, get on a plane and go to my mother. I'm going to give you all of the money out of my pocket. I'm not going out like this! They getting ready to take everything from me."

We were riding in my truck and I was ready to do some things.

"Pray and have faith," Michelle said, "It's going to be fine."

"I'm going to air these people out!"

"You can't just go kill people!"

"This man just ruined my life in a matter of hours. I'm not ever going to get my life back. They'll bury me in jail!"

"It's going to be okay," Michelle kept saying, trying to ease my rage by rubbing my back.

"I'm going to air her brother and her father out! That way I'll be looking out for my mother-in-law. She can finally be happy and my wife can move on with her life."

Michelle was scared because I was going over the edge.

She called my mother and put her on speaker. I told my mother to shut up for the first time in my life. My mind was made up.

270

Then, Michelle tried my stepfather.

He tried screaming at me and yelling at me to calm down and think.

Michelle started praying in tongues loudly.

I couldn't think straight. Before I knew it, I had pulled over to a gas station and just started crying in Michelle's lap.

I had my rifle in the back seat and my handgun in my lap. I folded the seat down on the rifle, put my handgun under the front seat and pulled myself together. I started praying with Michelle and asking God to please forgive me over and over. I have never in my life had thoughts like I had that night.

"Let's go to the sheriff's office to see what they want."

We prayed again and then Michelle said a prayer over me, asking me to heal my heart and spirit.

I felt a calm come over me and we went to the sheriff's office. I told them I was there for the papers I'd been served. The officer started looking through my history.

"I saw you were served twice before and it was dismissed," he said, "Just so you know, your wife did not want to take out the order of protection. Her father said that if she didn't do it, her and the kids had to get the hell out of his house. I just thought you should know because I was here to do the paperwork when they came."

Michelle nudged my arm.

"Can't you still take out that warrant?"

Oh yeah!

"Yes, I'd like to take out a warrant on her father," I said.

The officer checked the computer.

"Okay," he said smiling.

They picked him up at 1:00 in the morning and arrested him.

Michelle stayed with me in the hotel I was forced to live in for the next 3 weeks and I hired a lawyer. We had a meeting to go over the case. I had the 3 cases for the order of protection but the fact remained that he pulled a gun on a law enforcement official.

I went over my case with my lawyer. He tried to make a case for his age. "I don't care if he's in his 50s and has health problems," I said, "He's going to jail, or he can drop all charges and I'll drop all charges."

Then he retorted by saying that I threatened to kill him.

"What did you say?" his lawyer asked.

My lawyer told me that I didn't have to say anything, but I told him I was fine.

"No, I said where I'm from, you get killed for stuff like this and it's true, you do. But, I never said I wanted to kill him."

He dropped all charges.

I dropped my charges.

Now, I had to go to court with my wife.

In the mediation room, I told her lawyer that I didn't put my hands on her or abuse her.

The deputy sheriff also said that he watched her father make her get an order of protection against me.

"So, what are we going to do? Drop it or go to court?"

She decided to take it to court.

The court date was set and in between, I filed for custody of my daughter and my stepson.

I started receiving a series of angry texts from Stephanie.

"Ah, you don't like this game? Where I come from, we don't call the police. You wanted to play the legal game, so I'll play with you."

She ran out of money to keep a lawyer so now I had a lawyer and she didn't.

When we were in court, she was the one asking questions.

She started making up things but it only made her look worse.

"Didn't on this day, you drag me by my hair?" she asked while I was on the stand.

"No, I've never put my hands on you," I said calmly.

"Have you ever hit, smacked or punched me in the face?"

"No."

Then, she starts to make up this ludicrous story about me dragging her in the room and smacking her because she didn't cook dinner.

"Are you kidding me?" I said and started laughing.

The judge admonished me and told me to stop laughing on the stand. I complied.

272

"My mother would kill me if I ever slapped a woman, especially my wife, in front of her. I never put my hands on any woman. I don't do that."

They put her on the stand next.

My lawyer ripped her a new one.

"Did you tell Mr. Jenkins that he could work in construction?"

"Yes," she said, "he's an excellent carpenter."

"He can work in construction, in Wal-Mart, or anywhere else, but he can't be in law enforcement?"

She started fidgeting on the stand.

"I just don't think he should carry a weapon."

"Why? You just said he was amazing. When he was doing fugitive recovery, how good was he?"

"The best," she said, "he gets people they can't find in years in days."

"But you don't think he can do this now? You're saying this because you're bitter and angry, right?"

"No.." she said, fumbling and struggling for words to stay.

The rest of her cross-examination was shaky like this.

The judge stated that he had heard enough and went into his chambers to deliberate.

She sat there with her aunts, looking nervous.

I had my lawyer, friends and co-workers supporting me.

"Don't worry, we're gonna hurry up so you can get a divorce," one of her aunts yelled over to me.

My wife got out of her chair and admonished her aunt.

"Don't play with him like that. He's half Italian and they don't believe in divorce."

"Stop being scared of him," her aunt said.

"I'm not scared of him, but certain things send him to the wrong place. Just don't - because he hasn't done anything to me."

I stuck my tongue out at her aunt.

Bitter trick!

"Divorce me tomorrow. I'll sign the paper work right now, she wont get nothing!" I said.

Little did they know, it had already been explained to me that she couldn't get anything from a divorce anyway, because she had committed an abandonment of marriage.

"So that means, for you illiterate dumbies, is that you cannot leave your spouse destitute and take the children from an able and willing parent without notice." I said to her aunts with a smile.

Just then, the judge emerged from his chambers, ready to give his verdict.

Paty ✓
Dulce
Yoana
Hilda abarca
oscar
Naty
Paty
Antonio M.
Mirna L.
Marlene
Prina
Jing
Migda

CPSIA information can be obtained
at www.ICGtesting.com
Printed in the USA
LVHW02s2123260718
584965LV00001B/6/P

9 780979 624148